The POLITICS of IDENTITY

WHO COUNTS AS ABORIGINAL TODAY?

Bronwyn Carlson

Aboriginal Studies Press

First published in 2016
by Aboriginal Studies Press

Reprinted in 2017, 2019.

© Bronwyn Carlson 2016

All rights reserved. No part of this book may be reproduced or transmitted in any form or by any means, electronic or mechanical, including photocopying, recording or by any information storage and retrieval system, without prior permission in writing from the publisher. The Australian *Copyright Act 1968* (the Act) allows a maximum of one chapter or 10 per cent of this book, whichever is the greater, to be photocopied by any educational institution for its education purposes provided that the educational institution (or body that administers it) has given a remuneration notice to Copyright Agency Limited (CAL) under the Act.

Aboriginal Studies Press
is the publishing arm of the
Australian Institute of Aboriginal
and Torres Strait Islander Studies.
GPO Box 553, Canberra, ACT 2601
Phone: (61 2) 6246 1183
Fax: (61 2) 6261 4288
Email: asp@aiatsis.gov.au
Web: www.aiatsis.gov.au/aboriginal-studies-press

National Library of Australia
Cataloguing-In-Publication data:

National Library of Australia Cataloguing-in-Publication entry

Creator: Carlson, Bronwyn, author.

Title: The politics of identity : who counts as Aboriginal today? / Bronwyn Carlson.

ISBN: 9781925302134 (pb)
        9781922059970 (ebook: pdf)
        9781922059987 (ebook: ePub)
        9781922059994 (ebook: kindle)

Subjects: Identity politics — Australia. Aboriginal Australians — Identity. Indigenous peoples — Ethnic identity.

Dewey Number: 305.89915

Printed in Australia by SOS Print

CONTENTS

Acknowledgments vi
Introduction 1

PART ONE

Chapter 1 – Constructing the Aborigine 17
Chapter 2 – Positioning 'part-Aboriginal' people 29
Chapter 3 – Challenging the colonial Aborigine 37
Chapter 4 – Quantifying Aboriginality by acculturation,
    adaptation and allegiance 53
Chapter 5 – The changing meaning of Aboriginal identity 69
Chapter 6 – Shifts in the social and political context 85
Chapter 7 – Discovering and reconstructing Aboriginal identity . . . 98
Chapter 8 – Beyond the discourse 116

PART TWO

Chapter 9 – Confirmation of Aboriginality 131
Chapter 10 – Conflict, community and the regulation
    of Aboriginal identity 144
Chapter 11 – Community discourse on the Confirmation of
    Aboriginality and Aboriginal identity: a case study . . 153
Chapter 12 – Researching the politics of identity 163
Chapter 13 – Identity journeys: when Aboriginal heritage
    was always known 183
Chapter 14 – Identity journeys: discovering Aboriginal heritage . . 196
Chapter 15 – The continuing contest over the definition of
    Aboriginal identity 206
Chapter 16 – Learning and performing an Aboriginal identity . . . 226
Chapter 17 – Tensions at the cultural interface 239
Chapter 18 – Aboriginal identity, community and social media . . 251

Concluding remarks 263
References 274
Index 288

ACKNOWLEDGMENTS

This book is a result of extensive research undertaken as part of my doctoral degree. It is concerned with contemporary struggles relating to Aboriginal identity in Australia: the 'who' and 'what' of Aboriginality, the processes of identification and confirmation. As well as being a research endeavour, the book is a personal project, one that considers the many layers of cultural identity that have affected me, my family, my extended networks and a vast number of Aboriginal people, including the interviewees who generously gave their time, thought and labour to participate in the study. I thank you all for your efforts, your insight and thoughtful responses.

I have four children — Anastasia, Jason, Rebecca and Connor — and a growing number of grandchildren Scarlet, Jack, Aurora and two more on the way. They are all part of the reason I wanted to undertake this study. It is because of them that I persevered and it is my pride in them that gives me hope that they will always know they can do anything they set their minds to. I was lucky enough to have a wonderful nana who inspired me to always want to know more. Nana Evelyn always believed in me. My nana on my dad's side was Nana Joyce, and even though she had very little she left me $270. I used it to pay for the books I needed to start at university. I acknowledge the love and inspiration of both my nanas.

I also thank my PhD supervisors, Professor Martin Nakata and Dr Colleen McGloin, and my mentor Ms Victoria Nakata. Academia is an inspiring place when people like you are part of it. Thank you eternally for your wholehearted assistance, steadfast support and intellectual generosity over the years. I am grateful for your friendship and for the encouragement you all gave towards the publication of my research.

I also acknowledge with gratitude the Australian Institute of Aboriginal and Torres Strait Islander Studies for selecting my thesis for the Stanner Award and to Aboriginal Studies Press for their assistance in transforming the thesis into this book.

Last, but by no means least, I thank my husband, Mike, who will no doubt never read beyond this page (because this book has no pictures!). It is because of your unrelenting belief in me that this was possible.

INTRODUCTION

EARLY DAYS

For as long as I can remember, my parents never missed an opportunity to accuse each other's family of being the one who had been 'touched by the tar brush'.[1] My father would pass comments like, 'it's your mother's side that are the Abos'. My mother would in turn accuse my father of being the 'guilty' one. I learned a number of things from these everyday expressions of domestic tension. One was that 'being Aboriginal' must not be a good thing. Another was that any reference to being Aboriginal was an insult. But I also learnt at an early age that the colour of a person's skin carried meaning — it signified something. For me, knowing we were 'touched by the tar brush' meant we were not white. But in that era, not being recognisably black also meant I was not Aboriginal. This was an early source of anxiety about who I was and how I was to represent myself.

I remember as a young girl being asked if I was Aboriginal and replying that my maternal grandmother was. My answer was based on my lived understanding of Aboriginality as somehow signified by skin colour or 'look'. Nana was 'dark' and therefore could be called Aboriginal. But could I? All I knew was that our family were 'part-Aboriginal'. It was not until I was much older that I was able to establish with certainty the facts of my

---

1 'Touched by the tar brush' is a racial epithet, which is used to describe someone of 'mixed descent'. For example, in an online discussion about Barack Obama, the then United States Senator from Illinois and a candidate for the Democratic Party's nomination in the 2008 U.S. presidential election the question, was posed '…why does everyone label him "black"? If someone is half "white" and half "black", is he still "black"?' A reply posted on the page informed: 'I believe that the technical term is "touched by the tar brush", see <http://jakchat/com/forums/ubbthreads.php/ubb/showflat/Number/69985>. The term, and others like 'those with a bit of the splash', is also outlined by Ian Anderson in 'I, the "Hybrid" Aborigine: Film and Representation' (1997) as derogatory terms used in Australia to describe mixed descent Aboriginal people.

mother's ancestry from a long line of Aboriginal women who originate from South Australia. In the interim years, the way our Aboriginality was *not* discussed at home had as much effect on the anxiety I felt about my ambiguous status, as the way it was used as a tool of insult.

But it was not just domestic tensions at home around the meaning of skin colour that produced confusion about what it meant for me to be 'part-Aboriginal'. My childhood, growing up in the 1960s and 1970s, was overlaid by a range of commentaries about what being Aboriginal signified out in the world beyond our home, infiltrating my self-awareness. I cannot recall any positive message about being Aboriginal. For example, through schools, the media and everyday interactions I was faced with frequent assertions that 'Aboriginal people' were a passive lot who just wanted to look after the land. I learnt that 'they' lived in the bush and were dirty. I remember the images we were bombarded with of semi-naked children with fly-infested noses. For the most part, I was positioned to see Aboriginal people as wanting and in need of help.

In my childhood mind, one exception to this negativity was the TV show *Boney*[2] where so-called 'full-blood' Aboriginal people were portrayed as mystical 'beings' and were to be feared as sorcerers. Little did I know at this time that the main Aboriginal character of the show was a white person covered in black paint. Nevertheless, some of these representations connected with my own experiences and reflected some things that I already knew. 'Pointing the bone' was a common saying in my childhood, as was a fear of the 'Kadachi Man'.[3] He wore feather boots, and no one ever heard or saw him coming. If we were ever naughty, it was common for our parents to caution my brother, sisters and I that if we didn't behave the Kadachi Man would get us.

Throughout my childhood, my family moved regularly from town to town, and from state to state. I attended schools in Geelong, Victoria; Oodnadatta, South Australia; Katherine, Northern Territory; and still others throughout the Illawarra in New South Wales. Later, I came to

---

2   For information about the television series *Boney* see, <http://www.tv.com/boney/show/4027/summary.html>.

3   The Kadachi Man is often portrayed as myth by non-Aboriginal people. However, we understood the Kadachi Man to be real and a significant threat if you were bad. To demonstrate the significance of the threat, in a heinous case of sexual assault on two Aboriginal boys in 2003 the Kadachi Man was used to threaten the young Aboriginal victims to remain silenced. See <www.theage.com.au/articles/2003/10/10/1065676145635.html>.

understand that our regular moves, which my mother called 'moonlight flits', were more about having outstayed our welcome. In the middle of the night we would pack our possessions into an old Falcon car, and depart on another 'journey'. As a young child, over time this developed into an unsettling feeling of not belonging or being welcome anywhere.

When I was seven years old my father took us to New Zealand, which in terms of our regular moves was the mother of all moonlight flits. All I knew about New Zealand was what I had learned at school — that Māori people were scary natives who ate people and, like savages, would kill without cause. Needless to say, my sisters[4] and I were petrified by the time the plane landed in New Zealand, and really concerned as to whether we would be safe living in grass huts. Although in time I came to understand how and why Indigenous people are portrayed as primitive savages, at the age of seven it was a terrifying experience, such was the power of those unmediated images on my young mind.

Life in New Zealand mirrored our lives in Australia. There were lots of 'relocations'. Drunken parties were commonplace, as were fights and arguments. We were no strangers to poverty. But as young children we did not understand that we were poor or that we had nothing; that was just the way it was. I do remember my mother making the most out of what we had, which was a lot of empty wooden beer crates. In our lounge room we had beer crates covered in old blankets for seats. In our bedrooms we had mattresses on beer crates, and to store our clothes we had more beer crates. My sisters and I used to entertain ourselves with beer bottle tops, building toy houses, and making up all sorts of games.

After two years of living in New Zealand, my father returned to Australia. I was almost ten. If we thought we had nothing until then, we were mistaken. He left us with no money, no possessions, and soon we were served an eviction notice. As Australians, we were not entitled to government assistance in New Zealand. We lived on handouts from church groups and other organisations, and learned over time that it was good to avoid those to whom we owed money. As we struggled from day to day, I realised that not everyone lived as poorly as we did, and I began to resent that fact. My younger sister and I began rebelling and soon ran into trouble with the police. We eventually earned a reputation for being 'uncontrollable'. I spent some time in Bollard Girls Home in New

---

4   I am the middle daughter, and have an older and younger sister.

Zealand, and at the age of fifteen, I was deported to Australia with my younger sister in tow. As part of our punishment the court ordered us to live in Australia with our father and not return to New Zealand for a period of twelve months.

My sister and I were both sent to live in Katherine in the Northern Territory with my father and his new family. I felt we were neither welcomed nor wanted, which inevitably resulted in further rebellious behaviour. I remember getting into trouble just for hanging out too much with the 'blacks'. Katherine in the 1980s was a racist town. I recall once overhearing a conversation between some men on the street who were commenting that if you ran over a black, you should then reverse over them to ensure they were dead as it would mean less paper work. That way, they also contended, the death could more easily be contributed to the victim being drunk. In those days most people also kept shotguns with salt pellets to shoot at the blacks if they came onto their property. At night, it was common for the local white teenagers to drive their Mini-Moke vehicles through the blacks' camp yelling abuse, just for a laugh.

It was not long before I was sent to Wollongong to live with my Aunty. I loved Wollongong because my Nana also lived there. But by now I had many issues and had become a very angry person. Still, I loved being near my Nana and I cherished those times with her. Nana's house was the only place I recognised as a home. She was the only stable element in my life growing up. I returned to live with my mother in New Zealand after I'd turned sixteen. Nana died not long after that.

Through my schooling in New Zealand I learnt about Māori people and their culture in a similar way to how I was taught about Aboriginal people in Australia. In all my Social Studies classes, both Māori and Aboriginal were people who had lived in the past. I learned that Māori were warriors and that their warrior status was the difference between them and Aboriginal people in Australia — Māori fought for their land, Aboriginal Australians did not. I was also taught that Māori were defeated.

Social Studies also began to uncover some of the mystery of my own ambiguous status. I learned about blood quantum as a measure of differences between 'full-blood', 'half-caste', 'part-Māori' and so forth. In New Zealand, 'half-caste' people were positioned both outside of being Māori and outside of being white, just as we were in Australia. Those of us who were 'touched by the tar brush' seemed to be quarantined, perceived as not being of any place or any group. These ideas filled my head. I came to believe that as a 'half-caste' or less, a person was not entitled to be considered Māori, or in my case, Aboriginal in Australia. I recall watching a television show which showed Māori protesting, and someone commented that 'they' (Māori) were as white as 'us', 'they cannot be Indigenous'.

COMING HOME

I returned to Australia again in my early thirties, now with a family of my own. It was 1998, and Pauline Hanson was gaining ascendency with her provocative views on the 'privileges' of being Aboriginal in contemporary Australian society. Aboriginal protesters were prominent in the media and I remember the same types of remarks being made about Aboriginal protesters as those made about Māori protesters. Many comments made reference to the lightness of most Aboriginal people's skin colour. I recall some commentators' use of wedge politics to emphasise the differences between remote and urban Aboriginal people. The suggestion was that 'the real Aboriginal people' were the ones still on the land and these urban 'white' Aboriginal people were somehow fraudulently passing as 'Aboriginal' to receive benefits denied to other Australians.

Although I had grown up in changing times for Aboriginal people, I had been consistently schooled in entrenched colonial (although evolving) media images and representations of what it meant to be an Aboriginal or Indigenous person. Throughout my younger years, my mind was kept busy, returning me to the issue of 'colour' and 'looks' as the markers of Aboriginal identity. My lack of such distinct physical markers was fundamental to my ambiguous status. Now, as an adult, I became interested in exploring the firmly planted, but rarely discussed, family assertion of being 'touched by the tar brush'. I spoke with my relatives, including an old great-aunt, my Nana's sister, who has since passed away. I was told stories of Nana's mother, who was commonly referred to as Kit. Another aunt confirmed that indeed Nana Kit was Aboriginal but added that such things were not really spoken of in the family.

So, despite open confirmation of this knowledge, not all the family accepted that they were of Aboriginal descent. Even today, there are members of our extended family who still see Aboriginality as singularly a factor of colour or looks, and therefore don't see themselves as being Aboriginal, or don't feel confident with publicly identifying as Aboriginal. My cousin commented I was lucky that my hair and eyes are dark because that made it easier for me to identify as Aboriginal. I understand this as I was also conditioned to think that Aboriginality was something that was only afforded to those who were dark-skinned or 'looked' Aboriginal. I also understand that in many ways my generation had it far easier than my Nana's or aunties' difficult circumstances, when it came to identifying, accepting and acknowledging our Aboriginal lineage. Historical circumstances had conditioned previous generations of our family to avoid the attention of the authorities.

I recognised that my search for information needed to extend past the family level. I needed to understand how and why I was understood as not being Aboriginal enough. I wanted to know how and why historical legacies continued to assign such weighted meaning to black/white lines in the everyday, given the history of dispossession and the subsequent administration of Aboriginal lives in Australia. I wanted to know why so many of us were suspended in the land of not belonging.

ACCESS TO KNOWLEDGE

In my frequently dislocated youth, my education had been somewhat limited, so the opportunity to study at university in the 1990s was a time of great excitement for me. But I lacked confidence about my abilities. What I did not realise at the time was that I came to university studies with a wealth of knowledge and experience that seemed to fit directly into the historical as well as the theoretical knowledge of the social science disciplines. I soon enrolled, as a mature age student, in a Bachelor of Arts degree with majors in Sociology and Aboriginal Studies. I went on to complete the degree with Distinction, and followed it with first-class Honours.

University opened up a new world for me. I now understood what being 'touched by the tar brush' meant. I now knew that 'being' Aboriginal was more than just the colour of one's skin. I was fortunate enough to learn about Australia's history in a time and in a way that was inclusive of many voices, including Aboriginal ones. I met other Aboriginal people who, like me, had spent most of their lives living outside of both worlds — not quite white, not quite black — but who also did not know why. For the first time in my life I didn't feel alone; instead, I felt reassured of my place. I soon developed enough confidence to combine my experiential knowledge with the knowledge of the social sciences in the academy to contest many of the ideas I had been given. It was a highly liberating experience for me to peel back the layers of knowledge.

INTRODUCTION

I soon came to realise that understanding the social production of Aboriginal identities through the social sciences is quite different from understanding and resolving one's personal Aboriginal identity in the everyday world. But I found the personal empowerment that came from engaging with the way that Western systems of thought and their institutional apparatuses have organised thinking and practices around who counted as Aboriginal and who did not, was soon to be severely tested.

THE POLITICS OF IDENTITY AND THE OFFICIAL CRITERIA

Early in my studies I thought it would be the right thing to do to present myself to the local Aboriginal organisations and make some contacts throughout the Aboriginal community. Like many people who learn of — or confirm — their Aboriginal heritage later in life, and whose family connections are located elsewhere, I wanted to connect and contribute to what I imagined was my 'local community' or 'the Aboriginal community' where I was born and now lived in the Illawarra. However, I quickly learned that this was not going to be a straightforward process. Identifying as Aboriginal involves far more than knowing or claiming to be a descendant of Aboriginal families. It demands much more than an understanding of how the imposed identity categories of the past have been overturned to allow Aboriginal people to determine what it means to be Aboriginal. After what I had been through, I did not expect to be questioned about my family, and where we hailed from, in order to validate my claim to Aboriginality. It was little surprise to discover the numerous non-Aboriginal mechanisms of questioning the legitimacy of a person's claimed Aboriginal status. But in my excitement to at last be free (albeit self-consciously) to express my suppressed Aboriginal identity, I had not contemplated the existence of an Aboriginal apparatus to arbitrate the legitimacy of my claim.

I soon learned of the official criteria that must be met for an individual to be accepted as Aboriginal in Australia. The public authentication of Aboriginality requires fulfilment of a three-part assessment which has been widely accepted by governments since the 1970s (Boladeras 2002). A person can be accepted if the candidate in question is 'a person of Aboriginal or Torres Strait Islander descent and who identifies as an Aboriginal or Torres Strait Islander, and is accepted as such by the community in which he (she) lives or has lived' (Gardiner-Garden 2002–03, p. 4). Proof of the last requirement requires a supporting letter from an Aboriginal council or organisation. Formal Confirmation of Aboriginality is important to have in order to work in identified positions[5] and to access services designed specifically for Aboriginal people within and beyond Aboriginal organisations. It is not a trivial or sentimental certificate; it is a quasi-legal document. I discuss the Confirmation of Aboriginality in more detail in Chapter 9.

I discovered that compliance with the three-pronged definition does not always fit the multitude of experiences, relocations and policy prescriptions that we as Aboriginal people have had to face under colonial conditions. While most who seek a formal Confirmation of Aboriginality document already identify, and already know or have traced their family lineages, the issue of being recognised and accepted 'by the community in which he (she) lives' can provide a stumbling block. In some cases, establishing community acceptance can be fraught for those without kin connections, a history of residence in a local area, the visible physical markers of Aboriginality or a particular colonial experience. This is especially so if those who oversee verification of the processes and documents either do not know an applicant or for whatever reason are not kindly disposed towards them.

However, the issue of community acceptance is not just fraught in the Confirmation of Aboriginality process. It can introduce tensions that are difficult to resolve, even when a Confirmation of Aboriginality has been formally obtained. I have two separate Confirmation of Aboriginality documents, for instance, yet I am not exempt from accusations of being a fraud. I have been telephoned and emailed and accused directly of not being Aboriginal because of a disagreement: 'Listen to you with your fuckin' Māori accent. You are not Aboriginal!' yelled one accuser over the phone. I have also been summoned to present myself and my complete genealogy, once again, to 'the community' to provide further proof of my Aboriginality.

These tensions are very complex and historically embedded, and are difficult to publicly discuss in a rational manner due to their emotive nature. They resist easy or unsubstantiated description and invite more serious analysis. Nevertheless, in local settings, some who have cultural or historical claims to 'the place' or who have a shared historical experience

---

5   An identified position is one in which Aboriginality is deemed by the prospective employer as a necessary attribute to fulfil the duties involved. Often the position requires an intimate knowledge of Aboriginal and/or Torres Strait Islander peoples, cultures and history at the local level.

of Aboriginal community life, wherever that may have been, often resent the presence of outsiders or 'newcomers', especially those who for a range of reasons lived outside of Aboriginal communities in previous generations. As a result, I have observed that identification with a geographical place and/or a particular colonial experience counts towards local acceptance, while the inter-generational experience of 'non-belonging' and ambiguous identity counts against it.

Today, Aboriginal organisations are tasked with both requiring and confirming Aboriginal identity for work, for any committee membership, and for access to a range of services and support. Aboriginal organisations are also usually locally embedded, invested and oriented, even while also configured in sets of relations with the wider pan-Aboriginal collective community and its relations with non-Aboriginal Australia. Theoretically, the Confirmation of Aboriginality process is a nationally instituted mechanism and should allow individuals or families from a cultural group originating anywhere across Australia to be recognised as Aboriginal wherever they live, as long as the veracity of lineage, connections, histories and recognition can be satisfied in the confirmation process. In practice, interpretation of what is meant by 'community' recognition of an individual is subject to varied and variable interpretation at the local level, over time, and with little regard for any official process.

My story is not an uncommon one. Although I was born in Wollongong, my Aboriginal ancestry is from South Australia; I mostly grew up elsewhere and only returned to Wollongong as an adult. For me, the criteria 'accepted as such by the community in which he (she) lives' is open to question on the grounds that 'I am not from here'. Some official interpretations of community recognition accommodate proof of lineage and historical circumstances as criteria for acceptance back into the fold of what is now understood to be a pan-Aboriginal Australian community. Others interpret community recognition more literally as meaning that a local community consensus confers acceptance by more subjective and local assessment criteria. In this case, community acceptance is not just a matter of family history and the desire to identify and reconnect. It also comes to be about insider/outsider tensions, about personal perceptions, about how the 'newcomer' thinks and behaves, and about the degree to which an individual or family accepts and conforms to local values and practices.

For those who insist on these local criteria, it is easier to question an 'outsider' Aboriginal person who is not from 'their' community and who has not been socialised via the local community historical experience or is not a member of local kin networks. So even with a Confirmation of Aboriginality I can continually be called into question; I can be abused, slandered and libelled, albeit on the basis of my accent rather than colour. My colour now seems sufficient to confirm Māori heritage, even though I have none. It is important to underline that this questioning is not confined to the local context or local matters. Questions of my identity ripple out into other communities far afield, as networks of gossip are sent to 'out' me, putting my professional status, career and livelihood at risk. On the personal level, my history of dislocation and un-belonging continues to impact as I am made to pay yet again for my family history — a family history wrought in the difficult circumstances of colonial encounters. Under this regime, my identity status is still able to be suspended. And I have not yet even begun to deal with the attitudes of non-Aboriginal people towards the accepted signifiers of Aboriginality.

A NOT SO UNCOMMON STORY

As I became aware of how 'my story' is repeated in many places across Australia, I began to wonder about the cost to the wider Aboriginal community. My experience sensitised and attuned me to both the processes and practices around the Confirmation of Aboriginality, and to the public regulation of Aboriginal identity by Aboriginal people 'in the community'. I observed these in a myriad of enactments by some people in relation to others, as I participated in community organisations and workplaces over time. I came to understand that the practice of questioning Aboriginal identity was not confined to the Confirmation of Aboriginality process. No one was immune — not people who have spent their entire lives in an Aboriginal community, or those who have been working in identified positions for years. The 'community acceptance' criteria seemed to provide licence for any individual to challenge — and be challenged — at any moment in time, for any reason.

Over time, I wondered if there would be fewer grounds for challenges if the 'community' held more confidence in the Confirmation of Aboriginality process — a process which appears to lack consistency. For example, I worked for a while in an organisation where Aboriginal people would routinely come to seek a Confirmation of Aboriginality document. One client's attempt was met with a particular kind of refusal: 'She has lived white all her life so she may as well continue.' Another's was dismissed because the approver did not know the applicant whilst growing up. It was a huge shock to me when I first witnessed the basis for such decisions — decisions that impact on lives in both emotional and material ways. But I soon learned that not only was this common but also an accepted practice in other organisations as well. I recall attending a local meeting of another major organisation where someone's application to become a member was discussed. The coordinator held up a photo and announced that you could tell the person in the picture was definitely Koori[6] by the way they looked. As a result of 'looking' Aboriginal, the person was accepted as a member. Not expecting this to be part of an official process, or the extent of the process, I was reminded of my cousin's comment about my dark eyes and hair.

Amidst the many manifestations of identity questioning that I had witnessed, I was drawn back to the way various physical markers of Aboriginality are still highly significant in deciding who counts as Aboriginal and who can be subject to ongoing challenges. But I noticed as well that language and behaviour are also significant. For example, an Aboriginal CEO, also a university graduate, was accused of not 'sounding like a Koori', a comment that questioned his identity and by inference his legitimacy in the role. Others are accused of not behaving or thinking Aboriginal, even if they look Aboriginal. The term 'coconut' — brown on the outside and white on the inside — is a standard accusation against an Aboriginal person, used derogatively in attempts to surveil behaviour and thinking and to regulate what being Aboriginal means.

And so over time I observed how the question of an individual's identity was not always about concern for the veracity of identity claims per se. In the context of community organisations, people who have long been accepted as Aboriginal can suddenly be placed under a cloud of suspicion by disgruntled community members. This has become a well-practised manipulative strategy for those with a grievance. It creates doubt about someone's authenticity as an Aboriginal Australian and questions their legitimacy to serve the community in a particular role or claim a perceived benefit.

These examples demonstrate the arbitrariness of subjective assessments for being granted a Confirmation of Aboriginality. Inconsistent

---

6   Koori is a term used by many to refer to Aboriginal people from either New South Wales or Victoria.

practices around confirming who counts as Aboriginal make it easy for some and difficult for others to reclaim identities, which are their inherent right. They also lay the grounds for challenges, many of which use identity questions to express personal or factional grievances with various aspects of decision-making within Aboriginal organisations. The community practices enacted beyond the official Confirmation of Aboriginality process leave few Aboriginal identities secure and many devalued. Questions of identity are shamefully manipulated at great personal cost to many.

I could argue that these practices deny some of the particular personal histories of being an Aboriginal Australian. But I would also have to concede that they can be understood as an assertion of Aboriginal identity that has always been grounded in place and particular kin networks and relations. They can also be understood as an assertion of Aboriginal identity that is grounded in the assumed shared colonial/historical experience from which the political collective has mounted resistance. However, the diversity of this shared experience is not always fully comprehended at local and regional levels, and this ignorance leads to assumptions, speculation and ultimately gossip about individuals' claims to Aboriginal identity.

Sadly, in the process, new lines of inclusion and exclusion operate and arbitrate 'who counts' and 'who does not count' as Aboriginal. Aboriginal Australians whose lives were shaped by the arbitrariness of colonial categories to serve policies of protection and assimilation still in many cases cannot return from their exile. The formerly colonised now enact on their own what has historically been enacted on them by their colonisers. Who determines 'who counts' today affects each subsequent generation of Aboriginal descendants, as it has done in the past. The 'community' as the final arbitrators of identity wield great influence on the status of Aboriginal individuals and their families — and in some places this influence does not appear to be mediated by consistent, transparent or accountable processes.

THIS BOOK

Increasingly, Aboriginal people are speaking openly about their experiences of being confronted by accusations, dismissals and abuse from their own people when trying to formally confirm their Aboriginality or carry out their roles. Speaking publicly carries risk of attack and further trauma and exclusion. Also entering these discussions are questions around what constitutes valid expressions of Aboriginal identity in contemporary times, given what we now know of colonial history, the politics of self-determination and the extent of urban experience. Not to mention what the reach of social communication technologies into Aboriginal communities means for identity issues.

It is the emergence of these discussions that intersects with my own experiences, those of others, and my intellectual interests that have led to this book. Armed with a range of perceptions of what it means to be Aboriginal, and in the face of Aboriginal community sensibilities, community judgments, and the ever-present risk of public censure, individuals find and express their Aboriginal identities in a wide range of ways. For example, I pursued my family history and I studied Indigenous academic subjects, history and the sociology disciplines to understand the 'what and how' of colonial and historical practices. I then went to work for the Aboriginal community with a commitment to contribute to improved services. While I now know what being 'Aboriginal' means to me and for me, I cannot know what it means for everyone and nor do I claim to.

Over time, I became particularly interested in the ways people publicly signal to others that they are indeed Aboriginal, when their physical appearance or experience does not make this obvious. I observed that the expressions of Aboriginal identity are multifarious, but also noticed what appeared to be patterns and pathways for people who are in the process of discovering or reconnecting to their heritage. I am now drawn to explore what motivates and rationalises the desire to signal Aboriginality as opposed to just 'knowing' one is Aboriginal or to just 'being' Aboriginal. This focus emerges from a lifetime of confronting the significance of looking like, sounding like, behaving like or thinking like an Aboriginal person as criteria for recognition or non-recognition as an Aboriginal person.

This book is born from my interest to explore in more detail reversions and conversions to the accepted and acceptable markers and behaviours that enable people to 'sign themselves in' and be 'recognisable' as Aboriginal community members today. My interest in these issues led me to commence and successfully complete a Doctor of Philosophy. This book is one of the outcomes of my doctoral research. My interest in this journey of contemporary Indigenous life experience was not so much concerned with what might emerge to demonstrate, or be recognised as, or count as a sign of a legitimate Aboriginal contemporary identity. Rather, my interest was to explore how the primary and now pan-Aboriginal collective will to survive as a distinct people also carries secondary, often negative, effects for many Aboriginal individuals.

These more recently reconfigured Aboriginal modes of inclusion/exclusion — purportedly to protect, preserve and strengthen what it means to be Aboriginal in Australia today — are an important site for deeper investigation and analysis. I contend that both the processes and patterns of behaviours associated with identifying and being accepted as Aboriginal are as much a problem as they purport to be a solution to re-assert a collective and self-defined Aboriginal identity today. Questions of Aboriginal identity are serious ones in the wake of the colonial era and interesting ones in the global era. Therefore, the point of my exploration was not to solve the 'problem' but to understand the basis of our current thinking and how it shapes the practices around identity.

My aim has been to sketch the historical contingencies on which current Aboriginal identity discourses are conditioned, so as to have a better understanding of some of the assumptions in which current 'everyday' arguments and counter-arguments are rooted. I had little idea when I started this process, just how deeply these historical contingencies are implicated in the current struggle over questions of 'who is' and 'what counts' as Aboriginal. Indeed, my appreciation of both the meaning of the diversity of Aboriginal experience and my knowledge of the history of Aboriginal experience has grown immeasurably in the process. This enables me to better appreciate the varying investments in questions of Aboriginal identity at different sites and in different contexts.

My own personal struggles around identity, my frustrations and 'impatience' have all been mediated through this process, enabling me to put a 'critical' measure of distance between my own experiences and my role as a researcher whose textual production will eventually form part of the discursive matrix. The continuing goal — for me and for you, the reader — is to contribute to the ongoing conversation about identity in Aboriginal Australia and beyond.

INTRODUCTION

THIS BOOK HAS TWO PARTS

Part One begins by looking at the colonial construction of Aboriginality and provides a context for the way much research undertaken in the early twentieth century attempted to construct Aboriginal identity by positioning 'part-Aboriginal' within the constraints of assimilation policies and practices. Part One also explores a significant period of transition that occurred through the 1960s until the Australian bicentennial of 'settlement' in 1988 then shifts to focuses on the changing meanings of Aboriginal identity by exploring the literature from the 1970s through to current times. The second half of Part One highlights the growing body of academic identity studies undertaken by Aboriginal scholars and focuses on the ways that Aboriginal identities have been and continue to be discursively produced and conditioned by Aboriginal people, and considers the possibilities for a counter discourse on Aboriginal identities.

Part Two deals with the contemporary contests of Aboriginality with a focus on the Confirmation of Aboriginality process. Part Two also discusses the Aboriginal community processes and discourses that now regulate who is and what counts as Aboriginal today. Additionally this section draws on the data collected from interviews I conducted with Aboriginal people, as part of my studies, exploring the negotiation, construction and expression of contemporary Aboriginal identities.

The concluding remarks provide a reflection of the research and its potential contribution to a scholarly understanding of urban Aboriginal identities in their contemporary formations. In my concluding comments, I consider the discursive changes surrounding discourses of Aboriginality. In addition, I reflect on how this research might generate positive changes through a more comprehensive understanding of the historical and contemporary aspects that have and continue to constitute 'who counts'.

PART ONE

CHAPTER 1
CONSTRUCTING THE ABORIGINE

> The census categories of Aboriginal and half-caste could not be so well-defined as to offer precise information — another indication that the part-Aboriginal has been regarded by governments as a phenomenon of transition rather than as an end in himself. The 'solution' of the Aboriginal problem would come when he disappeared altogether into a 'white' community without 'coloured' enclaves.
>
> (Rowley 1971, p. 3)

Contemporary struggles around Aboriginal identity have emerged in the shadow of colonialism and occur primarily around questions of 'who' is Aboriginal and 'what' are the characteristics that support and confirm any legitimate claim to 'be' an Aboriginal person. As the anthropologist Myrna Tonkinson reminded us, these questions 'have been posed in a variety of ways and have evoked a variety of responses over Australia's two-hundred year history' (1990, p. 191). Debates around Aboriginal identity also draw on contemporary and generalised understandings of traditional forms of identification (Tonkinson 1990).

Any investigation of the struggles around Aboriginal identity, identity recovery or confirmation processes cannot overlook, then, the historical context from which these questions have emerged, the legacy of which still impacts on Aboriginal individuals, families and communities today. This history is vast and varies across the country and across time periods encompassing Aboriginal experience from pre-colonial, to colonial and subsequent periods. It is represented in both the oral or recorded memories of Aboriginal people as well as official and scholarly sources. In relation to contemporary identity struggles, this history is not past or done with. It is present and evident in how we think and what we do today.

When selecting material for my doctoral research into Aboriginal identity, I considered Tonkinson's assertion that questions of 'who' and 'what' Aboriginal people are have been posed in different ways since Europeans arrived. To find an analytical lens through which to approach my research I began with my own experiences of Aboriginality. I then posed a further set of questions to enable me to draw the historical through to my present concerns and interests that form the heart of this book. For me, these key questions were:

- What has given shape to the currently accepted arguments for, claims to, judgments of and expressions of Aboriginal identity?
- What has enabled the filtering out of other possible experiences, expressions or criteria for claiming, acknowledging and recognising Aboriginality?
- What evidence of this history is brought to bear in arguments, claims and practices around what it means to be Aboriginal today?

This sort of questioning enabled me to concentrate on explicating the various ways of and rationales for talking about who and what Aboriginal people are and how these have changed over time, in order to better understand what has given shape to the contemporary discussions and meanings of Aboriginal identity. Such an approach invokes at the outset the work of French philosopher Michel Foucault who argued that we become subjects through what he calls the 'materiality of discursive practices' (quoted in D'Cruz 2001). In other words we identify as cultured people according to the lived experiences, ideas and practices of the dominant culture. Foucault's analysis of how we become cultural subjects allowed me to consider how changing conditions for Aboriginal people can affect and transform the ways Aboriginal people were and are able to be talked about and acted upon, as well as any possibilities for self-transformation. This approach also includes, for example, the inter-connected web of practices shaped by the colonial imagination, social theories of comparative cultures, government policy, law and legislation, and administrative regulations. These considerations have a particular material effect on those Aboriginal people who are thus imagined, theorised, legislated and regulated, and who also self-regulate accordingly. Historically, such conditions positioned white Australians as ideal, normative, superior and progressive explorers, settlers, nation-builders and citizens.

The Aboriginal position has been constituted in an ongoing and largely unresolved tension with the nation-state, which recognises Aboriginal Australians as the descendants of the original inhabitants — equal citizens but culturally distinct from other Australians. Under United Nations instruments ratified by the Australian government, Aboriginal Australians (and Torres Strait Islanders) have a range of enshrined rights to determine the development and maintenance of their Indigenous social, economic, legal and political forms of organisation and practice, alongside the right to participate fully in Australian society as we so choose. Contemporary Aboriginal discourses and practices — developed in the intersections of older traditions, Aboriginal colonial experiences, political resistance to colonial practices, and ongoing contests with the continuing broader frameworks and requirements of the omnipresent nation-state — now also condition the space in which Aboriginal identities are produced.

When I commenced this research, I wanted to ensure that my approach would allow the focus to be maintained on the debates as well as the real lives in which various claims about Aboriginal identity are produced and continue to be produced. This was because such focus avoids the urge to endlessly confirm or dispute the verity of changing truth claims about 'who' and 'what' constitutes Aboriginal identity that have been made over time.

To this end, my intent here is to provide only enough historical context so we can understand who and what can be counted as the evidence of 'being' an Aboriginal person. Further, while an aim is to understand the evolving context of these discussions in broad terms, my interest in this book is also centred on a specific group of Aboriginal people — those with Aboriginal heritage who, for a range of reasons, have been inter-generationally dislocated from larger communities of Aboriginal people and who now want to identify as and be recognised as Aboriginal. These are people who are re-discovering and reconnecting with lost or disrupted Aboriginal heritage.

THE EARLY HISTORICAL CONTEXT: COLONIAL CONSTRUCTIONS OF ABORIGINALITY

Despite the existence of hundreds of self-identifying and named autonomous groups across the continent, the original inhabitants of Australia have always been understood and named by Europeans as a singular group — the Aborigines (Bourke et al. 2006). This identifier is a European word and concept, not an Aboriginal one. The identification of 'the Aborigine' was historically constructed in European thought and imagination as the primitive native and understood in terms of distance from the 'civilised' European male who stood at the top of a global human racial and cultural hierarchy. This hierarchy was predicated on the concept of European cultural progress as the indicator of superior intelligence — and as measured via the meanings constructed during the Enlightenment in Europe throughout the seventeenth and eighteenth centuries (Gascoigne 1994). This strand of European thought theorised a hierarchy of the progress of different human cultures in direct relation to biological and racial determinants. In this schema, 'full-blood' Aboriginal people of Australia were 'seen as archaic survivors from the dawn of man's existence' (Attwood & Markus 1997, p. 1). 'Full-blood' Aboriginal people were assumed to be a 'dying race' with 'the wandering savage…doomed to extinction by the progress of that type of humanity with which it was impossible to assimilate him' (Turner 1904 quoted in Attwood & Markus 1997, p. 1). The position of 'part-Aboriginal' people with an admixture of European blood was an increasing source for official concern, however, especially with the growth of this population in the 'contact zones' where Aboriginal and non-Aboriginal people lived in proximity during and following frontier expansion, violence and dispossession (Bleakley 1961). The presence of European blood indicated a genetic inheritance that embodied the capacity to progress culturally.

Historically, various shifting policies in relation to Aboriginal people across Australia had rolled out since colonisation and more stridently as colonial governments become more established in the nineteenth century in response to the growth and consolidation of the white population across the continent. Policies aimed at Aboriginal people were initially in the form of Imperial instructions and plans for the separate colonies. These emphasised humane treatment and encouraged protection from labour exploitation and alcohol, as well as access to education and equal justice (Reynolds 1972). These intentions failed abysmally in their implementation as the frontier relentlessly and violently appropriated Aboriginal lands and women. According to legal historian John McCorquodale,

> [t]he proliferation of children having 'white blood' in their veins, and the decline of the 'full-blood' population, prompted a legislative response to redeem the former and protect the latter. (1997, p. 26)

Various 'protection' policies began to be developed from the mid-1800s when Responsible Government began to be granted to the Australian colonies. From the late nineteenth through to the early twentieth centuries, these protection policies saw the establishment of the reserve and mission systems as a way of managing the so-called 'remnant' Aboriginal populations while facilitating the occupation of Aboriginal lands (Reynolds 1972).

While there were differences between the states' practices, governments generally mobilised racial thinking to differentiate and manage Aboriginal people, and to determine who came within the bounds of legislation designed for 'protection' or segregation, and who could be exempted from such regulation. To this end, Aboriginal individuals were defined by the various states according to the quantum of Aboriginal and/or European blood and 'preponderance of blood' tests became the framework for determining who was Aboriginal (McCorquodale 1997). The application of this thinking continued to be an administrative convenience for governments across Australia long after racial theorising was discredited in the intellectual domain in the early to mid-twentieth century (Tonkinson 1990; Gardiner-Garden 2002–03).

In his legislative history of defining Aboriginal people in Australia, McCorquodale (1986, 1997) identified 67 definitions that classified Aboriginal people in 700 pieces of legislation. Historically, all states defined Aboriginal status through blood quantum, starting with the introduction of 'half-caste' in New South Wales legislation in 1839 and extending across all colonies, states and territories, as they came into existence. More finely graded categories of blood admixtures were introduced over time and jurisdictions 'to include, exclude or distinguish between the classifications provided' (McCorquodale 1997, p. 29). Definitions and categories varied across all governments and across a wide range of legislation within states 'in a way which extended bureaucratic discretion over a wider range of subjects and minimised external or individual "interference" [in the administration of Aboriginal people's lives]' (McCorquodale 1997, p. 26). Common denominations were 'full-blood' and 'half-caste', with quarter (quadroon), eighth (octoroon) (McCorquodale 1997) and even three-, five- and seven-eighths (see Reay 1951) emerging in some places. As McCorquodale's analysis reveals, '[a] new species of legal creature was created and sustained as a separate class, subject to separate laws and separately administered' (1997, p. 29).

THE 'PROBLEM' OF THE GROWING 'PART-ABORIGINAL' PRESENCE

The effects and confusion wrought by the application of myriad and often contradictory definitions of Aboriginality determined within and imposed through a range of legislation, policy and regulations across Australia by the mid-1930s has been captured by historian Peter Read in a well-cited assemblage. Its last sentences also hint at the ongoing legacy for younger generations in the later political era of Aboriginal self-determination:

> In 1935 a fair-skinned Australian of part-indigenous descent was ejected from a hotel for being an Aboriginal. He returned to his home on the mission station to find himself refused entry because he was not an Aboriginal. He tried to remove his children but was told he could not because they were Aboriginal. He walked to the next town where he was arrested for being an Aboriginal vagrant and placed on the local reserve. During World War II he tried to enlist but was told he could not because he was Aboriginal. He went interstate and joined up as a non-Aboriginal person. After the war he could not acquire a passport without permission because he was Aboriginal. He received exemption from the Aborigines Protection Act — and was told that he could no longer visit his relations on the reserve because he was not an Aboriginal. He was denied permission to enter the Returned Servicemen's Club because he was. In the 1980s his daughter went to university on an Aboriginal study grant. On the first day a student demanded to know, 'What gives you the right to call yourself Aboriginal?' (1998, p. 169)

According to Read (1998), the regulation of Aboriginal identity rationalised and continually intensified a 'practice of [Aboriginal] extinction by legislation' (1998, p. 170) or 'of redefining the other out of existence' (1998, p. 173). Further, Read contends that the contradictions in definitions based on blood quantum which accumulated across the range of legislation up till the mid-1960s, were not the result of legislative or bureaucratic bungling or incompetent implementation, as the absurdity could suggest, but an intentional program designed

> to puzzle, divide, and ultimately cause to vanish, the indigenous people who continued to pose a problem by their unwillingness to disappear. These seemingly mutually excluding definitions, at first sight idiotic, were no accident. Likewise, the divisions in the minds of Aboriginal people as to what exactly they were supposed to be was [sic] no coincidence. (1998, p. 170)

A 1928 investigation of the position of northern and central Australian Aboriginal and 'part-Aboriginal' people recommended proposals for 'absorbing those with a preponderance of white blood into the white population' (Bleakley 1929, p. 29). By isolating 'full-blood' Aboriginal people on reserves, it was reasoned that further mixing of the 'full-blood' Aboriginal and white populations could not occur and eventually all 'part-Aboriginal' people could be absorbed into the general population.

In 1937, these ideas informed a national shift to official policies of assimilation (as opposed to long-time unofficial ones, such as Christianisation, mission and reserve life, rudimentary education, and encouragement or coercion to labour) at the Initial Conference of Commonwealth and State Aboriginal Authorities (Reynolds 1972). Significantly, this policy only applied to people of mixed descent:

> [T]his conference believes that the destiny of the natives of aboriginal origin, but not of the full blood, lies in their ultimate absorption by the people of the Commonwealth, and it therefore recommends that all efforts be directed to that end. (quoted in Reynolds 1972, p. 172)

Although all Aboriginal people suffered degrading treatment and deprivations, it was 'part-Aboriginal' people who felt the full force of assimilation policy (and the forerunners to it) as they were subjected to the 'plethora of legislation giving effect to government policy…[which was] accompanied by provisions less than clear and precise, not only in their meaning but in their intended application' (McCorquodale 1997, p. 32). This imprecision opened the space for clarification of the meanings in discrete legislative instruments, as well as discretionary interpretation of the regulations at all levels of administrative authority (McCorquodale 1997). The deliberations of legal and administrative opinion were applied to questions of 'who' is to be recognised as Aboriginal or 'part-Aboriginal' or not Aboriginal under the particular terms of any particular Act or for the purposes of any particular administrative goals and decision-making over particular Aboriginal and/or 'part-Aboriginal' people.

This was not always just about controlling where Aboriginal people, including children, could live or their degree of participation in white society. Definitions and determinations across different Acts of legislation could be as capricious in intent as controlling government expenditure on Aboriginal people. By excluding 'part-Aboriginal' people for the purpose of an Act, expenses for maintaining Aboriginal people on missions or reserves could be controlled. 'Half-caste' minors were often deemed Aboriginal within legislation, but then excluded on reaching adulthood. Likewise, those 'part-Aboriginal' people who did not live with or associate with 'Aborigines' could be excluded from entitlements from the public purse on this basis but be given other freedoms instead on this same basis. 'Part-Aboriginal' people were grossly, expediently and often cruelly manipulated in these ways (McCorquodale 1997).

An example of this is the Victorian practice of classifying 'half-caste', 'quadroon' and 'octoroon' children as Aboriginal for the purposes of residing on reserves with their parents but to evict them at the age of eighteen. In these ways, Aboriginal families were effectively fractured on the basis of blood preponderance, which denied and severed kin affiliations. According to historian Charles Rowley, from 1916 until 1957, not only could these individuals be forced to leave, but

> [o]nly brief visits to the station were subsequently possible, and this at the discretion of the manager; that even such a visit was limited to a maximum of ten days. (1971, p. 45)

Rowley also described the widespread application in administrative practice of the so-called 'averment principle', where the reference to someone as being Aboriginal was 'sufficient evidence' of the truth of their status for any particular purposes under consideration. This was often a charge or complaint in relation to regulations in which decisions to move or convict an individual were made. Furthermore, it was accepted practice 'to decide on sight whether a person was Aboriginal' and to accept this decision until it could be disproved (1971, pp. 45–6). Rowley reported how under this regime anthropologist Diane Barwick was able to 'establish actual cases in the records where the same person was described at different times, as "full-blood", "half-caste", and "three-quarter" caste' (1971, p. 44).

Across the web-like legislative terrain and under restrictive administrative regimes, the admixture of Aboriginal and European ancestry, the colour of skin, and associated Aboriginal cultural behaviours were used into the first part of the twentieth century as very real measures to differentiate, divide, re-organise and manage Aboriginal people on an individual and collective basis. These superficial and artificial measures, often assumed to also be measures of Aboriginal cognitive and social capacity, determined the course of Aboriginal lives and the futures of subsequent generations. In the interpretation and implementation of legislation and policy, quite arbitrary and subjective judgments by individual officials about an Aboriginal individual's physical characteristics (and the assumed derivative cognitive capacity and cultural behaviours) exercised a range of inclusions and exclusions to various relative benefits and freedoms or negative sanctions. These inclusions and exclusions impacted on place of residence, control of finances, control over children, rights to privacy, permission to marry, access to schools and hospitals, the use of liquor and freedom of movement, among others (Rowley 1971). Any relative benefits and freedoms were conditional, rendering any Aboriginal (i.e. 'part-Aboriginal') beneficiaries vulnerable to the vagaries, perceptions and whims of white officials, white community opinion and shifting interpretations of policy. As McCorquodale stated,

> [f]or Aborigines, therefore, the vacuity or bankruptcy of policy in some states was matched only by the ingenuity of others in extending the reach of legislative control. Those who escaped [control] through having a lesser amount of 'black' blood suddenly found themselves made subject to law; those who obtained exemption could lose it. 'Half-castes' might be placed on the same footing with 'full-bloods' for some purposes (testimony, liquor), but not others (reserves, guardianship of children). (McCorquodale 1997, pp. 29–30)

Among Aboriginal people, the effect of this regime of identification was to produce varied Aboriginal and 'part-Aboriginal' experiences. Many 'part-Aboriginal' people were not free to leave missions and reserves, and over generations these groups invested older traditional identities with an additional layer of identification forged in the common experience of belonging to these communities and reserves (Peters-Little 2000). Many others did not, could not, and/or would not reside on missions and reserves and had less investment in such reconstructed communal identities (Rowley 1971). The effect was the alteration of relations within, between and across Aboriginal families and groups, all of whom had traditionally named and defined identity and social relations among themselves on a quite different basis. This history bears heavily on the ongoing efforts of diversely constituted Aboriginal people to forge a consensus on the questions of 'who' is and 'what it means' to be a member of the contemporary Aboriginal collective.

It needs to be emphasised that this fragmentation and division of Aboriginal families and groups was undertaken in a sanctioned way as it unfolded across the entire continent in order to variously protect, segregate, absorb and/or assimilate the entire Aboriginal population. These regimes were not necessarily exclusive of each other either. From the protection through to the assimilation eras of late nineteenth and mid-twentieth centuries, mixed-descent Aboriginal people were often at once and continuously both the subject of segregation practices and the focus of practices designed to absorb and assimilate them (Anderson 1994). 'Part-Aboriginal' children were particularly vulnerable subjects for absorption. The statement of Robert Donaldson, later Chief Inspector of the New South Wales Aborigines Protection Board, to the Australian Catholic Congress in 1909 (and footnoted by Read) gives a good illustration as to how early this thinking and practice emerged:

> If the removed children are prevented returning to the camps, then soon 'the old people will have passed away, and their progeny will be absorbed into the industrial classes of the colony'. (Donaldson quoted in Read 1998, p. 176)

Thus, wherever and whenever 'part-Aboriginal' people lived, they were the objects of white authority, and subject to racialised thinking and regulatory practices. While missions and reserves promoted segregation from white society, they were still sites for erasure of traditional identities. On the basis of colour or judgments of neglect or of a child's 'best interests', thousands of mixed-descent children were systematically taken to institutions, fostered or adopted into white families and separated permanently from family and kin (Wilson 1997).

A FOCUS ON ASSIMILATION POST-1937

In the context of the practice of the times, especially in the period post-1937, there was arguably little room to freely 'choose' to 'be' or freely determine 'how to be' Aboriginal. Nor was there much scope for a 'part-Aboriginal' individual to fully understand the long-term consequences of any 'choice' or pragmatic decision taken when presented with an opportunity or option. In the light of Read's assembled example and McCorquodale's analysis of legal definitions, the reference to division in the *minds* of Aboriginal people is not without warrant. As Read noted:

> Separated Aboriginal children who identified themselves later in life as 'white' were intended to do so. The families who moved off reserves to live in towns (if they were allowed), or hundreds of kilometres from other Aboriginal people (if they were not), were meant to leave these sites of Aboriginal community. (1998, p. 171)

However, nor can it be assumed that these administrative regimes achieved their goals of rendering 'part-Aboriginal' people completely discontinuous with their own understandings of self, and their relation to the material and spiritual worlds and each other. The passage of time confirms continuity of, or reversion to, Aboriginal practices in changing circumstances, despite the destruction of the conditions in which Aboriginal social practices were traditionally anchored (see, for example, Langton 1981). Continuities and discontinuities in the face of change can both be understood in terms of the imperative to survive and continue on, and can also be measured against the shifting social realities over generations that set in motion different ways and degrees of being Aboriginal or relating to Aboriginal kin or communities. The horror of individual and family experiences of removal of 'part-Aboriginal' children has been investigated and some instances documented (see, for example, Wilson 1997). But the stories of the other impositions, pressures, attractions, directives and 'choices' that were presented to many 'part-Aboriginal' individuals and their families, or of the fragmented families whose individual members were subjected to different conditions on the basis of racial and cultural judgments, are still being told — and indeed are irretrievable in many cases, especially in the longer-colonised parts of south-eastern Australia.

In understanding this history, it is important to remember that the State administrative instrumentalities of close surveillance meant that 'part-Aboriginal' people who were light-skinned or who did not 'look' Aboriginal or exhibit Aboriginal social 'characteristics' and/or who were exempted from State control, were nevertheless not white. They were 'conditionally' designated not Aboriginal but still 'known' to be Aboriginal unless they were able to 'pass' into the wider society beyond the purview of officials. Rowley noted in reference to the situation in New South Wales that 'the growing part-Aboriginal population seems to have remained…part of the changing Aboriginal society. European descent was not really relevant, except for those who could "pass"' (1971, p. 12). 'Passing' did require invisibility within the general population and it cannot be denied that some of these 'part-Aboriginal' people over time lost the connections to their Aboriginal heritage. Darlene Johnston, for example, suggested that '[t]he experience of 'passing' can be understood as a refusal to adopt either a hybrid identity or a strict dichotomy between a white identity or an Aboriginal one' (1993, p. 21). The question of whether in the initial instance this denotes resistance to the practices of colonial administration, acquiescence to white authority, or betrayal of Aboriginal kin and/or identity is impossible to answer, though judgments are arguably made categorically according to the latter two more often than not.

This said, segregation, protection, absorption and assimilation policies were all designed with the intent to erase the existence and/or visibility of Aboriginal and 'part-Aboriginal' people and associated cultural practices. However, assimilation proved a difficult and unachievable policy goal. Even though an unrecorded number of 'part-Aboriginal' people were effectively assimilated into the general Australian population over generations, many who chose or were coerced in that direction found little acceptance in the white community. Most continued to be ambiguously and ambivalently situated as not Aboriginal but not white either (Anderson 1994). In Australia, then, the contemporary identity struggles of Aboriginal people, and the research that relates to them, cannot be understood without some understanding of this historical policy and regulatory context that governed Aboriginal people before the political era of Aboriginal self-determination in the 1970s.

CHAPTER 2
POSITIONING 'PART-ABORIGINAL' PEOPLE

> These 'true' Aborigines are not going to become 'white' in the foreseeable future, though they can and will become worthy Australian citizens.
>
> (Elkin 1964, p. 379)

Until the early 1960s, whether consciously resistant to assimilatory practices or not, 'part-Aboriginal' people continued to be viewed as an increasing social problem for white society in Australia. As a result, research interest in the urban or rural dislocated and generally mixed-descent Aboriginal people gained sustained currency in the post-1937 assimilation era for the first time.

It is useful at this point to consider the different periods and foci of research interest in Australian Aboriginal societies. Anthropologist Nicolas Peterson (1990) noted the early unsystematic documentation of 'Aborigines' that occurred from 1606 when European explorers started visiting Australian shores. Following decades of white settlement, from 1870, more systematic research of an ethnographic nature was produced by natural scientists and administrators whose work brought them into close and prolonged proximity with particular groups of Aboriginal people (e.g. Fison & Howitt 1880; Roth 1897; Spencer & Gillen 1899, 1904; Howitt 1904; Spencer 1914).

In 1926 the first department of Anthropology was established at the University of Sydney. It undertook research in Aboriginal Australia as well as in New Guinea and the Pacific. But there was an interesting difference in rationales for these two areas of interest. Anthropology in New Guinea and the Pacific was considered useful to colonial administration whereas it was perceived to be of no practical value to administration in Aboriginal

Australia. Rather, in Australia, anthropology was interested in gathering data on the primordial nature of man before it vanished:

> Spencer and Gillen saved from oblivion a vast amount of material which demonstrated the value of the Australian evidence in its bearing upon the early history of society and culture. Even now much further study is needed for which the data still exist, especially among the remoter and less known tribes. A few years more and it will be too late; the evidence will have vanished forever. (*Nature*, 1930, quoted in Peterson 1990, p. 13)

So, this 'rescue' or 'salvage' anthropology until the 1960s essentially sought to document the social, political and economic organisation and beliefs of a dying people, and focused on more remote groups whose traditions still organised daily life (Goldsworthy 1988). Due to the encroachment of Western influences, after the Second World War 'there was a widespread academic view, both within and beyond Australia, that Aboriginal societies and cultures could no longer provide a special insight' (Peterson 1990, p. 14) to the study of the early nature of man. According to Peterson (1990), Aboriginal anthropology entered 'lean' times as funding sources dried up.

Not mentioned in Peterson's history, which is concerned with the developments that led to the establishment of the Institute of Aboriginal Studies in Canberra in 1961, is the production of research on 'part-Aboriginal' people with a much longer history of life on missions or government reserves, on the fringes of towns, or living in white communities. In contrast to the interest in remote traditional Aboriginal societies, 'part-Aboriginal' people became a subject of research interest for very different and very practical reasons, namely, for the purposes of a more positive administrative approach to achieving assimilation goals (Elkin 1964).

ASSOCIATING COLOUR WITH CLASS

In 1933, Anglican clergyman and Professor of Anthropology Adolphus Peter Elkin, whose ideas on the perceived benefits of assimilation for Aboriginal people became very influential in the Australian public domain, become the head of Anthropology at the University of Sydney. Four years later, the official assimilation policy era commenced in earnest. While the anthropology of this era is much more commonly associated with rescue anthropology, significant numbers of studies of 'part-Aboriginal' people were also being conducted; Elkin emerges as influential in the direction of this research inquiry, at least in New South Wales. Indeed, Elkin, along with others, viewed assimilation as a positive outcome for Aboriginal administration that recognised 'that there was a future for the Aborigines', but still needed 'to convince public opinion and authority' (1964, p. 369).

Between the 1940s and the end of the 1960s a body of such studies was completed (see, for example, the work of anthropologists, Reay 1944/1945; Reay & Sitlington 1948; Reay 1951; Bell 1955/56; Fink 1957/58; Beckett 1958; Fink 1960). These warrant some attention for what they contribute towards what the Aboriginal scholar Marcia Langton referred to two decades later as 'the insidious ideology of tribal and de-tribalized Aborigines' (1981, p. 16). Langton laid responsibility for this dichotomy at the feet of anthropologists, while criticising the 'assimilationist assumptions' of the frameworks used in these early studies of urbanizing 'part-Aborigines' (1981, p. 17). Anthropologists' ethnological descriptions of traditionally functioning Aboriginal groups positioned 'urbanising' Aboriginal groups as having lost the basis for any legitimate claims to be Aboriginal. Early studies of 'part-Aboriginal' people are, for all intents and purposes, studies of their position along a linear continuum towards complete assimilation into a non-Aboriginal world.

These early studies of 'part-Aboriginal' people living in close proximity to centres of white population in urban or rural areas reflect administrative and research interest in the adjustment of 'part-Aboriginal' or mixed-descent people, with an emphasis on the impediments of Aboriginal social behaviours for assimilation. These impediments were measured consistently in relation to economic participation and social subscription to the European ethos and interpreted consistently in relation to colour, which was understood and measured through degrees of European blood. The theoretical frames of 'assimilationist assumptions' are evident and discernible in the themes that were consistently drawn through these studies.

The Aborigines Welfare Board, for example, funded the 1944 research study by Marie Reay, *A half-caste Aboriginal community in North-Western New South Wales*, under the direction of Elkin. Under discussion were class and the isolation of 'part-Aboriginal' people from middle-class mores. Socialisation was occurring with lower-class whites to the detriment of the social progress of 'part-Aboriginal' people. Reay also commented on race relations, noting that marriage to Aboriginal women was considered akin to racial treason by whites and that white town folk did not like dark half-castes. This way of thinking anchors a strand in the popular discourse that shaped the practical interpretation of policy for decades. The commonsense remedy for overcoming racial intolerance in the white community was logically understood to require Aboriginal people to behave like Europeans and live the European way, or be justifiably excluded from socialising in white society.

These themes featured again in Marie Reay and Grace Sitlington's (1948) study of *Class and status in a mixed-blood community (Moree, NSW)*. This study described those of 'part-Aboriginal' descent living in and around Moree by dividing and relating them in four 'class zones' (1948, p. 180), all of which sat below the white class system. Personal and social characteristics of 'part-Aboriginal' people in prescribed upper and lower classes were then described. Positive characteristics valued as virtues in white society were ascribed to the upper Aboriginal class, including self-reliance and independence from welfare and government. Negative characteristics were ascribed to the lower class, including sexual promiscuity, habitual drinking, lack of financial knowledge and inadequate approaches to child development. The latter signals a stereotypical view that continues to be perpetuated in much mainstream media today.

These researchers also asserted a common theme in this research era — that upper class 'Aborigines' preferred not to associate with those in the lower class, and participated actively to maintain the division between them. No reference is made to the possibility that research participants associated white researchers with the authority of the Aborigines Welfare Board, and that this might influence participant statements, or that punitive sanctions might apply if 'part-Aboriginal' people did move easily across these groups. However, the report also noted that while 'part-Aboriginal' women were more likely to uphold European standards, many had developed scales of behaviour in relation to public and private spheres, acting 'whiter' in public than in private. It is possible to suggest perhaps a degree of ambivalence or a fluid negotiation of European values, rather than a categorical conversion to them that entailed leaving Aboriginal values behind. But at the time, the research inference was one of slippage back towards Aboriginal ways as evidence of weakness of the 'part-Aboriginal' character and the challenges for achieving assimilation.

In 1945 to 1946, again under the direction of Elkin, Reay (1951) conducted a further study, *Mixed-blood marriage in North-Western New South Wales: A survey of the marital conditions of 264 Aboriginal and mixed-blood women*. The study is illuminating for its reference to blood quantum and the associated identification of different groups of mixed-blood women. The sample population is described as '12 full-blood, 26 are three-quarter caste, 129 are half-caste, 77 quadroon and 20 octoroon or lighter' and these different categories are all defined (1951, p. 116). Reay noted that excluded from the sample are three-eighth, five-eighth and seven-eighth castes of women. In her statistics on marriages, Reay consistently differentiated between Aboriginal and mixed-blood people. The study concluded that half-castes and Aboriginal women tended to 'merge' with lighter castes, 'thus making the mixed-blood population progressively lighter' (1951, p. 122). It asserted that Aboriginal women who were lighter preferred to have lighter partners in the hope that in the future their children could pass easily into the general community. There was concern that some lighter people still had at times a dark child. According to Reay, marriage of mixed-blood women to white men was limited as it resulted in diminished status for the white man and/or made them potentially liable for prosecution for consorting with 'an Aborigine'.

ASSOCIATING COLOUR WITH NEGATIVE ABORIGINAL CULTURAL BEHAVIOURS

Thematic analysis that relates class, colour, intermarriage and behaviour to positive and negative cultural characteristics that assist or impede assimilation continued through the 1950s. In reporting a 1954–55 study looking at the economic life of 'mixed-blood' Aboriginal people from the South Coast of New South Wales, James Bell (1955/56) also made reference to the relation of colour to cultural behaviour and of cultural behaviour to class hierarchy. Colour, cultural behaviour and class level were viewed as interconnected and related to economic participation and changing Aboriginal social relations. Familiar strands of the discourse on 'part-Aboriginal' characteristics were in evidence.

However, Bell's study concluded that the lack of successful economic assimilation into the white community was due to lack of education, training and the racial prejudice of whites, with the effect that the Aboriginal population's subsequent 'dependency upon the white community takes the form of intelligent parasitism on the part of the Aborigines' (1955/56, p. 199). Bell mentioned that excluded from the study are

'Aborigines of very light caste who are lost in the general population and numbered with it' (1955/56, p. 182). The report also stated that those who do find work and remain in work were generally those who wanted to dissociate themselves from the general Aboriginal community as part of a class hierarchy. In his discussion of white prejudice, Bell noted that the darker the children, the more they suffered racism and discrimination, adding that 'the dark children in general do not aspire to advance above the unskilled level' (1955/1956, p. 191).

During the 1950s, the obstacles to assimilation and a close association of these obstacles to Aboriginal 'class', now named as a problem of 'ethnic caste', were examined by Ruth Fink (1957/1958, 1960), once again under the guidance of Elkin. Fink's field research of 1954 led to her nominating three categories of Aboriginal 'classes': upper — for those who were striving to assimilate; middle — for those who were in transition towards assimilation; and lower — for those who remained on missions and reserves and did not make any effort to assimilate. In an era of an increasing half-caste population, concern about how to assist upward social mobility was the focus. Fink's research related levels of colour to levels of status along the black-low/white–high caste continuum, and noted white Australian attitudes against assimilation and for segregation of Aboriginal people.

It is notable that Fink argued 'out-marriage' as a solution for those 'part-Aboriginal' people disposed to participation in white society, 'for it is only by ridding themselves of their aboriginal [sic] features that they can escape the stigma of the caste barrier' (1957/1958, p. 101). Further, Aboriginal people who wanted to change their status from lower caste must demonstrate that they did not belong to the 'coloured group' (1957/1958, p. 101). Significantly, Fink's observations identified Aboriginal people who resisted assimilation as viewing their low status as a form of recognition of their Aboriginal status. Fink argued that those who chose to stay on reserves and missions were only 'aboriginal in its self image' (1957/1958, p. 103), that is to say they perpetuated the negative stereotype of Aboriginal by living it. Her study provides early evidence of Aboriginal resistance to assimilation and Aboriginal inversion of the signifiers of colonial classifications.

By the beginning of the 1960s, then, understanding of 'part-Aboriginal' identities reflects the presence and persistence of colonial thinking that associates colour with negative Aboriginal cultural behaviours. Discussion of who and what counts as being Aboriginal occurs within the context of attempts to understand impediments to assimilation or economic participation in the wider society. This is measured along a colour/culture continuum, based on degrees of blood admixture and degrees of distance from white society. Understandings of Aboriginal people are firmly co-opted into European social theories of class via established analytical research frameworks. Concepts of class — concepts entirely alien to Aboriginal societies — are introduced in relation to behaviour to differentiate, relate and understand Aboriginal sub-groups along 'diluting' colour lines. These studies reflect and also support the thinking that overcoming the disadvantages and negative aspects of being Aboriginal requires leaving the Aboriginal ethos behind, and that this is easier to do as colour lightens.

No account is taken of Aboriginal experience of these administrative regimes for Aboriginal identity or social relations. No consideration is given to 'part-Aboriginal' people as valuing continuity with Aboriginal social relations and values. Little account is taken of the colonial history that has conditioned the living reality of 'part-Aboriginal' people. As Langton (1981) pointed out, there was no attempt to access Aboriginal responses or to see both the 'positive' and 'negative' behaviours as constructed through the imperative to adjust and adapt to the reality of the situation in order to survive. 'Part-Aboriginal' experience can only be understood in its relations to European social classifications. During this period the focus of research about Aboriginal people and culture closely shadowed government administrative interests so that in addition to the bias of culture-bound researchers, the research is arguably politically bound where researchers have a concern to safeguard their future research interests.

As the long-term objects of social policy, 'part-Aboriginal' people were meant to disappear into the general Australian population, subsumed and invisible within the white lower working class. For a range of reasons, not the least of which was white racism and exclusion, this did not occur. Nor did 'the full-bloods' die out as had been predicted. In the post-Second World War era, in response to the Holocaust, human rights emerged as a focus of the United Nations. Colonised populations across the globe began to mobilise towards the goal of independence. Australia's treatment of its Aboriginal population, including the policy of assimilation, became increasingly difficult to defend in the international context, both on a human rights level, and in the context of global decolonisation. While sections of Australian society and Aboriginal people themselves were questioning policy and practice, governments were slow to shift their position (Attwood & Markus 2007; Clark 2008).

At the close of the 1950s, the Federal Minister of External Affairs, Paul Hasluck, made the following comments in a presentation to the Australian and New Zealand Association for the Advancement of Science (ANZAAS):

> [T]he problem is not one of finding ways in which two… societies can live side by side…but of finding the way in which the remnants of the aboriginal race can best become members of a single Australian society…The more it crumbles, the more readily may its fragments be mingled with the rest of the people living in Australia. (quoted in Clark 2008, p. 43)

But far from crumbling and mingling, the fragmented 'part-Aboriginal' population was already mingling and organising — actively resisting policy restrictions and garnering growing support for their cause from within the white Australian community (Clark 2008).

In contrast to Hasluck's stance, anthropologist William Edward Hanley (W E H) Stanner represented the changing thinking about Aboriginal affairs and futures. Addressing the concept of continuity and change in Aboriginal identity, he posed in 1958 that,

> [a]ssimilation means that the Aborigines must lose their identity, cease to be themselves, become as we are. Let us leave aside the question that they may not want to, and the possibility — would myself put it far higher than a possibility — that very determined forces of opposition will appear. Suppose they do not know how to cease being themselves? (Stanner 1979, p. 50)

The winds of change were stirring and Aboriginal people were at the forefront. The logic of assimilation was already a matter of contest in some quarters and the colonial definitions of 'who' and 'what' were Aboriginal people were now being challenged from the Aboriginal side.

CHAPTER 3
CHALLENGING THE COLONIAL ABORIGINE

> The Aboriginal people of Australia today — full-blood and part-blood — do not want the sympathy of white people... We have had enough of this in the past...All our lives Aboriginals have lived in a secondary position to the white Australian. I no longer wish for this situation. Therefore I, and approximately 250,000 others like me, claim our ancestry. We are Aboriginal Australians — proud of our country and our race.
>
> (Charles Perkins, *The Australian*, 8 April 1968, p. 8)

In the second half of the twentieth century the colonial rationales for defining, regulating, and researching 'part-Aboriginal' people came under challenge in a changing social context. Deeper understandings of both traditional Aboriginal worldviews and Aboriginal views of 'white' administration, society and the Aboriginal place within it, unsettled the policy goals of assimilation. The entry of the Commonwealth government into national Aboriginal affairs from 1967 followed the landmark 1967 Referendum to remove discriminatory references to Aboriginal people in the Australian Constitution. During this time of considerable Aboriginal activism, the influence of Aboriginal leaders who pursued the political quest of self-determination produced a new discursive relation between Aboriginal people and governments with changing material effects.

Within this period, research on Aboriginal identity slowly began to reflect the wider shifts on those formerly understood as 'part-Aboriginal' people. While Aboriginal people, including emerging Aboriginal scholars, wrested for control over the meanings surrounding Aboriginality and the processes for participating in the Australian state, anthropologists and social science researchers confronted the limits of their own parameters for understanding who and what Aboriginal people were or could be.

At the beginning of the 1960s, while researching in remote Arnhem Land, the anthropologist Catherine Berndt signalled a challenge for the discipline of anthropology by reporting an emergent Aboriginal perspective. In a derivative paper (1961), she discussed the ways Aboriginal people name themselves amidst changing family and community social relations. She expressed the view that it is 'unfashionable these days to suggest that Aborigines need to turn their backs on all that is 'Aboriginal' before they can enjoy the same material benefits as their fellow Australians' (1961, p. 30). Noting southern calls for northern Aboriginal people to be able to retain their Aboriginal identity, she stated:

> [s]ome [calls] come from people of part-Aboriginal descent who themselves have no firsthand knowledge of Aboriginal traditions, but whose own search for identity takes the form of a second or third generation 'reversion' to a broader, non-'tribal' Aboriginal identification — and thus impels them to present themselves as spokesmen for less fortunate, or less articulate.

She went on to say:

> Perhaps it is only in such circumstances — among people who have largely lost touch with this social and cultural heritage — that the word 'Aboriginal' comes to assume an overall, Australia-wide, meaning as a label for self-definition. (1961, p. 30)

Here Berndt identified the appropriation of the colonially imposed nomination of Aboriginal by those who have lost their tribal connections as an inclusive label that reconnects them to all other Aboriginal people, whether still traditional or not. For 'salvage' or 'rescue' anthropologists preoccupied with understanding traditional cultures of discrete groups, the 'part-Aboriginal' population had been of little ethnological interest. Berndt's acknowledgement of their presence and sphere of influence appears as early evidence of the representation of the Aboriginal political voice in academic research and the heralding of the decline of assimilation policies as Aboriginal people pushed an agenda initially of equal citizenship and, later, of political self-determination.

The states' policies and administration practices clearly lagged behind or chose to ignore this Aboriginal view. At the 1961 Conference of Commonwealth and State Aboriginal Authorities 'full-blood' Aboriginal people were drawn into the scope of administrative policies of assimilation for the first time:

> The policy of assimilation means that all Aborigines and part-Aborigines are expected to attain the same manner of living as other Australians, and to live as members of a single Australian community enjoying the same rights and privileges, accepting the same customs and influenced by the same beliefs, as other Australians. (quoted in Reynolds 1972, p. 175)

At the 1965 Conference, the language of policy changed again, signalling an easing of administrative restrictions but without repudiating assimilation as the goal:

> The policy of assimilation seeks that all persons of aboriginal descent will choose to attain a similar manner of living to that of other Australians and live as members of a single community. (quoted in Reynolds 1972, p. 175)

By 1964, however, the Aboriginal view was clearly known. Elkin had acknowledged in print that Aboriginal people of mixed descent

> regard themselves as a separate group in the community… they think of themselves as Aborigines and are not ashamed of the fact. Indeed, it is from amongst them, including those consciously seeking assimilation, that individuals and groups have been arising for nearly three decades to become vocal on behalf of the Aborigines as a whole. They form associations…They talk of their rights. They proclaim against injustices…And they protest against the treatment of the Aborigines up north…

He added:

> their action is a sign that they are realising their existence, and indeed their solidarity as a group. The Aborigines, wherever they are, and of whatever noticeable degree of caste, are one. (Elkin 1964, p. 377)

Elkin drew attention to a noteworthy area of misattribution and omission in popular understanding of the rise of Aboriginal activism in this period — the history of Aboriginal activism that reflected a practised resistance and a long-articulated analysis of oppressive government control within and across Aboriginal communities (see, for example, Attwood & Markus 2004; Horner 2004; Taffe 2005; Maynard 2007; Clark 2008). Aboriginal activism of the 1960s and 1970s attracted non-Aboriginal support and media attention, and employed tactics and language that mirrored the African-American Civil Rights and other social movements of the time. But these sources of strategy were not the source of inspiration for Aboriginal objection to policy. As Elkin stated, this had a much longer history and it would seem that those involved in Aboriginal administration and anthropology were keenly aware of the history of Aboriginal objections.

Elkin also conceded that 'part-Aboriginal' people had worked out that they were 'an out-group…regarded as a caste lower in status than the "white" citizen' and that they lacked 'full community life in the context in which they find themselves' (1964, p. 378). Using the various earlier studies on mixed-descent Aboriginal people and intermarriage, he noted that 'the part-Aboriginal population is apparently reaching at least a temporary, stationary position as regards colour and caste around the quadroon–three-eighth "degrees"' and conceded that

> facts of marriage and survival make more obvious the existence of a distinct Aboriginal people in Australia. The shade of colour and features become the symbol of distinction and of 'belonging'. (1964, p. 379)

Elkin also signalled an emphasis on integration through citizenship as the goal for all Aboriginal people, including 'full-bloods':

> These 'true' Aborigines are not going to become 'white' in the foreseeable future, though they can and will become worthy Australian citizens. To become the latter does not imply that they must turn their backs on their own history and culture…For in the process of change they will need this heritage as a source of moral strength and courage, and as firm ground for further advance. (1964, p. 379)

This did not render the concept of assimilation redundant. The process of assimilation was now seen to be fundamental to the achievement of full citizenship:

> The future of the Aborigines, whether full-blood or other, lies within the general framework and current of Australian economic, political, social and religious life. The old order is passing, and a new order is being entered through the process of assimilation; but the rate varies according to the types of Aborigines and their geographical position. (1964, p. 375)

Interestingly, Elkin asserted that in 1964 more New South Wales Aboriginal people were living outside of reserves and missions than on them because 'they prefer to do so rather than be subject to even a mild degree of specific supervision, such as prevails on settlements' (1964, p. 373). So although he insisted that assimilation occurred in sequence via participation in economic, political, social and finally religious spheres of Australian life, he had to acknowledge the trends:

> [A]n ambivalent attitude is rising towards assimilation. Although the Aborigines more and more want to be a part of Australian life in their own right, they want to reach this goal as Aborigines…giving rise to a group-consciousness with an emphasis on Aboriginal tradition and solidarity. (1964, p. 380)

EMERGING ABORIGINAL VOICES

The Aboriginal view, then, was not so easily suppressed. It became increasingly vocal and visible and was articulated with increasing momentum by anthropologists and other supporters in the academic, government and bureaucratic intersections where policy for Aboriginal people was formulated (see Coombs 1976; Stanner 1979). Denominations based on blood quantum gradually lost credence in the more informed intersections of academic and government discourse, and 'part-Aboriginal' people came to be nominally accepted as Aboriginal. Thus different understandings of who Aboriginal people were, or could be, began to enter the political discourse and the rhetoric of Aboriginal policy.

Formal policy transition in Aboriginal Affairs began to occur following the 1967 Referendum, though the substance of it took longer. The Referendum supported changes to the Australian Constitution in relation to Aboriginal people and in effect gave the Commonwealth government powers to legislate on matters of Aboriginal affairs for the whole of Australia (Attwood & Markus 1997). For the first time, the states and territories were required to consider the implications of Commonwealth legislation for their own activities. The Commonwealth government quickly established a Council for Aboriginal Affairs and then an Office of Aboriginal Affairs to identify and study problems faced by Aboriginal people, and develop appropriate policies and administrative mechanisms. An early element was 'to establish communication with Aboriginal communities and groups and to ensure their wishes and views were effectively presented to the government and its advisors' (Coombs 1976, p. 2).

In these early communications, Chairman of the Council for Aboriginal Affairs (1967–1976) Herbert Coombs and others quickly recognised not only 'the fundamental rejection of assimilation into white society' by Aboriginal people in isolated, rural and urban settings but also what gave rise to this rejection in these different contexts (1976, p. 3). However, it was also established that '[o]n the other hand, the content of what would in their eyes be an acceptable alternative was obscure' (1976, p. 4). According to Coombs,

> [u]rban Aborigines aspired to a separate identity within Australian society but at the same time they wanted roles within its economy which were difficult to reconcile with separateness and independence. (1976, p. 4)

The political shift away from policies of assimilation to self-determination followed a slow path from 1965 to 1975. While the Whitlam Labor government enacted changes that demonstrated a commitment to Aboriginal self-determination, it did not repudiate assimilation. According to Coombs' (1976) reflections of these developments, 1975 was the first time that no reference was made to assimilation in the detail of proposed policies and programs. In the Coalition's federal election campaign in December of that year it was stated that '[w]e recognise the fundamental right of Aborigines to retain their racial identity and traditional life style or where desired to adopt a partially or wholly European life style' (1976, p. 6).

Another major development that emerged in this transition period from policies of assimilation to those of self-determination was the presence of Aboriginal organisations as part of the network of 'institutional' or bureaucratic regimes. The Whitlam Labor government, in its effort to support Aboriginal people's 'right to independent and distinctively Aboriginal development', had provided a 'legal basis for the incorporation of Aboriginal communities and their organisations' (Coombs 1976, p. 6). These emerging organisations, and those Aboriginal people who worked to bring them into being, became a critical interface between Aboriginal people's political goals of self-determination and the continuing practical need to be engaged with the systems and resources of white government.

The emergence of these organisations is relevant here to the changing conditions in which Aboriginal identities could now be produced. In urban areas, Aboriginal-controlled organisations — such as the Aboriginal Legal Service and the Aboriginal Medical Service — 'were intended to be as much about autonomy and self-determination as they were about service provision' (Maddison 2009, p. 33) and have been cornerstones in urban, regional and remote Aboriginal community life through to the present. These organisations include land councils, community councils, alternative Aboriginal education and training organisations, such as Tranby College and the National Aboriginal and Islander Skills Development Association (NAISDA), co-operatives such as Boomali arts cooperative, and community media organisations such as Koori Radio, to give some New South Wales examples.

Some organisations were and are discrete and local entities; others are networked on a state or national basis. The National Aboriginal Association of Community Health Organisations (NAACHO), for example, is now a national network of community health organisations, while the NSW Aboriginal Education Consultative Group Inc (AECG) is a state-wide network of community-driven education advisory groups, with counterparts in all other states. These organisations became the local institutional faces of the Aboriginal community and, among other functions, formally confirm community recognition of Aboriginal individuals' identity status by issuing Confirmation of Aboriginality certificates stamped with the organisation's Common Seal.

CHANGING IDENTITY CATEGORIES AND DEFINITIONS OF ABORIGINALITY

The early transitions in the political context initially had little effect on the definitional classifications and judicial interpretations of who and what were to be accepted as evidence of Aboriginality. As in the bureaucracy, the legislation continued to lag. As McCorquodale (1997) reported, in Queensland *The Aborigines and Torres Strait Islanders' Affairs Act 1965* which came into being in 1965 as controls were being eased was a veritable 'serological nightmare' (1997, p. 27) with categories for 'Aborigine', 'part-Aborigine', assisted 'Aborigine', Islander and assisted Islander. These were all further defined and differentiated through five categories which made reference to 'full-bloods', those with a preponderance of the blood of a 'full-blood', 'part-Aborigines' who live as spouses of 'full-bloods' or live with those with a preponderance of Aboriginal blood, residents of reserves (unless they have no Aboriginal blood), and even outlining when an Islander may be considered Aboriginal. In addition to this were further definitions for the children of these categories to cover those who may have one parent who has no Aboriginal blood or to cover those of parents 'to have a strain of such blood so that the person defined himself had at least a 25 percent strain but not a preponderance of such blood' (1997, p. 27).

However, during the 1980s and 1990s there was a political shift towards the acceptance of Aboriginal self-definition by descent from the original inhabitants and recognition by other Aboriginal people at a community level, though it is difficult to find any focused analysis of how this came into being or practice. Scholar John Gardiner-Garden noted that the Commonwealth did not formally table a new definition until 1981:

> An Aboriginal or Torres Strait Islander is a person of Aboriginal or Torres Strait Islander descent who identifies as an Aboriginal or Torres Strait Islander and is accepted as such by the community in which he (she) lives. (2002–03, p. 4)

However, McCorquodale's analysis (1997) revealed that in the interim period of transition across the 1960s and 1970s, the informal adoption of descent identification by local community acceptance appears to be uneven across states and the different Acts within states, as does the disappearance of the blood-descent criterion. South Australia, for example, had used 'descent from the original inhabitants' as early as 1939, and blood-descent criterion appeared in some legislation through to 1979 though in much simpler terms than Queensland. The South Australian criteria included 'a person of Aboriginal blood' or 'wholly or partly descended from those who inhabited Australia prior to European colonisation' (1997, p. 28).

The Commonwealth had never defined Aboriginal people in legislation but made reference to them, using the dominant expression of 'aboriginal native of Australia' first used in 1902 and last used in 1973 and also used the term 'the Aboriginal race' (McCorquodale 1997, p. 25). During the 1960s and 1970s, determinations of Aboriginality by the Commonwealth were made in the context of administering regulations and legislation, as they always had been across Australian states and territories. The following three cases presented by McCorquodale illustrate the continuing state of flux. In a 1961 legal opinion, in the context of Aboriginal voting rights, it was determined that the expression in the Constitution,

> 'people of…the aboriginal race' applied only to persons of Aboriginal descent and to persons in whom 'aboriginal blood preponderates'. On that view, a person 'of the half blood, or a person in whom European or other non-Aboriginal 'blood' preponderated, could not be considered as belonging to 'the Aboriginal race'. Indeed a person of the 'half-blood' would not belong to any race at all. (1997, p. 33)

A decade later in 1971, in the Court of Petty Sessions in Western Australia, consideration of the meaning of 'aboriginal native of Australia' under the terms of the National Service Regulations (Commonwealth) was given in a case where an Aboriginal person was claiming exemption from national service on these grounds. The Court held that a person with an admixture of blood did not meet the definition of Aboriginal.

> To claim exemption he had to establish on the balance of probabilities that he had lived as 'an aboriginal native' or among Aborigines…A person could not be held to be living 'as an aboriginal native' when it was shown by evidence that he was living in a house situated amongst those occupied by white citizens of Australia, was generally in regular employment and had been so during the previous five years, owned his own car, travelled to Perth three times a year to visit friends and relatives, conducted himself in a manner acceptable to responsible white citizens of his area, dressed well, and was able satisfactorily to speak the English language. (quoted in McCorquodale 1997, p.30)

The Court even based its determination on the individual's personal relationships.

> His 'marriage' to a *de facto* wife of even lesser 'Aboriginal blood' and their residing with their children in an ordinary white community was a stronger factor negativing his falling within the purview of the legislative exemption. (quoted in McCorquodale 1997, p. 30)

In the absence of definitions in Commonwealth legislation, the case appeared to uphold definitions within Western Australian legislation. The racist reasoning demonstrates the continuing convenient judgments underpinning such determinations.

In 1978, administrative discretion in determining Aboriginal status under Commonwealth law was on display in a Senate debate of 12 September.

Firstly, for the purposes of Legal Aid it had been determined in consultation with the government:

> An 'Aboriginal' was a member or descendant of the Aboriginal race, including Torres Strait Islands, and where it is in the interests of justice in the circumstances of a particular case, a person living in a domestic relationship with Aboriginal. Any degree of Aboriginality sufficed. (McCorquodale 1997, p. 33)

Secondly, for the purposes of Commonwealth law:

> 'Aboriginality' was not exclusively a status conferred or withdrawn by legislation; it might also be the result of administrative decision, based on application, investigation, consideration or other form of review, decision and certification then required in respect of housing loans, enterprise loans, and grants from the Aboriginal Benefit Trust Account. (1997, p. 33, citing Australian Senate Debates, 12 September 1978, p. 503)

And thirdly:

> [t]he criteria employed by third parties or organisations enjoying recognition as bodies authorised to issue certificates which would be recognised for approved government purposes were neither stated nor known. Further, even in the absence of such certification, the particular government or instrumentality…might 'pursue those of differing Aboriginal

organisations, proceeded according to their own methods of determination'. (1997, pp. 33–4)

As in the past, the new Commonwealth three-pronged definition allowed determination of eligibility for services and benefits and, as Gardiner-Garden (2002–03) outlined, wound its way into other legislation as well. In 1983, in the High Court, Justice Deane accepted this definition 'as giving meaning to the expression "Aboriginal race" with s.51 (xvi) of the Constitution' (quoted in Gardiner-Garden 2002–03, p. 4).

However, not all were happy in the court of public opinion. A long-standing logic about who and what 'Aborigines' are persisted. This logic recruited common and popular perceptions in the wider community, that a 'real' Aboriginal person is someone who still looks and lives like the traditional, remote Aborigines of colonial imagination. The more a claimant bore the markers and trappings of European heritage and lifestyle, the more illegitimate the claim of Aboriginality was considered to be. Nonetheless, even looking 'unmistakably' Aboriginal was not enough evidence for some in their quest to undermine Aboriginal individuals' legitimacy to represent the interests of Aboriginal people. Political theorist Colin Tatz (1979) recorded a 1978 exchange in a Queensland Parliamentary Debate (QPD691) between Mr Russell James (Russ) Hinze (Local Government Minister) and the Liberal member for Townsville Dr Norman Scott-Young about the federal Aboriginal Senator, Neville Bonner:

> Mr. Hinze: Would you say that Senator Bonner is an Aborigine?
>
> Dr. Scott-Young: No. Senator Bonner claims to be an Aborigine.
>
> Mr. Hinze: Do you think he might be an Indian or an Afghan?
>
> Dr. Scott-Young: I do not know. He claims to be an Aborigine.

Likewise Peter Read noted that '[i]n the 1960s Charles Perkins was told more than once that he could not be Aboriginal because he was a university graduate' (1998, p. 169). To be educated and successful was to disqualify one from being Aboriginal. Gardiner-Garden also captured the essential elements of the continuing popular debate, citing the well-known Victorian state president of the Returned Services League (RSL), Bruce Ruxton, who asked the government 'to amend the definition of Aborigine to eliminate the part-whites who are making a racket out of being so-called

Aborigines at enormous cost to the taxpayers' (2002–03, p. 5). The national RSL president, Alf Garland, in his attempts to explain Ruxton's position, reverted to the suggestion of assessing blood quantum, provoking the following observation by a *Sydney Morning Herald* journalist in 1988:

> When any of their numerous and varied kind put a foot wrong — and even when they don't — white Australians will have no difficulty at all in identifying them as Aborigines and ascribing their short-comings to their Aboriginality. But when there is some benefit flowing the Aborigines' way, such whites will raise silly questions. As Mr Ruxton did. (quoted in Gardiner-Garden 2002–03, p. 5)

These examples illustrate the possibilities for establishing 'self-determined' Aboriginal identities that could be produced in the future. While freedoms were being fought for and won by Aboriginal people, the legislative and regulatory framework remained intact to continue the arbitrary and capricious judgments on questions of who and what Aboriginal people are. As McCorquodale surmised,

> [s]uch ill-defined — or, in the absence of any, unknown — criteria promote the prospects of individual abuse, refusal or neglect of any application dependent upon a demonstration, to administrative satisfaction, of a sufficient degree of Aboriginality. (1997, p. 34)

CHANGING CONCEPTS OF ABORIGINAL IDENTITY IN RESEARCH

During the 1960s research studies reflected changing perceptions about who and what was to count as 'Aboriginal', as the category of 'part-Aboriginal' and the goals of assimilation were politically rejected by 'non-traditional' Aboriginal people in the longer-settled areas of eastern Australia. Nevertheless, an enduring rationale for numerous studies of 'part-Aboriginal' people in regional and metropolitan centres continued to centre on a need to understand what these particular 'Aboriginal' people were becoming and their processes of adaptation. Robert McKeich (1977) noted retrospectively that studies of 'part-Aboriginal' people fell into two categories: ethnographies and 'problem areas'. For McKeich,

> Ethnographic descriptions tend to be couched in structural-functionalist terms; they demonstrate unique features of Aboriginal and/or part-Aboriginal cultures, or else they highlight cultural differences by making cross-cultural comparisons.

On the other hand,

> Problem areas usually focus upon difficulties encountered by people of Aboriginal descent in adjusting to European-Australian contact. Special interest is paid to the major institutions of 'white' society (e.g. health, education, employment, housing, crime and the like), and these so-called under-privileged people are seen to have problems or they are problems, because 'their ways' are different from 'our ways'. (1977, p. 252)

The research undertaken in this transition period does tend to reflect McKeich's analysis. As well, changes in focus in the research conducted proceeded unevenly and assimilationist assumptions persisted throughout the 1960s and into the 1970s with, however, increasing recognition of the significance of capturing Aboriginal views.

In the 1960s, amidst the continuing preoccupation with 'part-Aboriginal' people's identity and social orientation as the perceived choice between Aboriginal and/or European ethos, anthropologists and other social scientists began to consider Aboriginal patterns of social change in 'urbanised' or 'detribalised' settings, still with an interest in understanding processes of adjustment for the goal of assimilation. In these studies (see for example, Barwick 1962; Gale 1964, 1972; Beckett 1965; Biddle 1969) old themes persist but new perceptions emerge. In 1962, for example, the anthropologist Diane Barwick, in a social study on the assimilation of 'part-Aboriginal' people in Melbourne, once again drew on associations between class, cultural behaviour and participation in the broader society. Significantly, early references to factionalism in the Aboriginal community appear. Although she reported that all restrictions on Aboriginal people were repealed in 1957 in Victoria and there was no need for 'part-Aboriginal' people to 'pass' as not Aboriginal, she provided evidence that the goal of assimilation persisted as the way forward for 'part-Aboriginal' people and was still used in the 1959 Report of the Victorian Aborigines Welfare Board.

> Some of the people now regarded as Aborigines could 'pass' as whites and become assimilated if they broke away from their old mode of living, associates, surroundings and behaviour. (1962, p. 22)

Thus Barwick noted the persistent assumptions of assimilationist frameworks even as official policy was being reconsidered. However, even in the interpretations of the research, 'part-Aboriginal' people's disinclination to 'pass' as and be acknowledged as white, now that assimilation policies could not determine or sanction the imposed distinctions between Aboriginal people, was not altogether interpreted as a positive inclination towards re-establishing severed kin relationships. Rather, another persistent analysis was added to the negative stereotypical mix. Barwick noted that with the repeal of restrictions, the *advantages* of 'passing' as white decreased and acknowledgement of Aboriginality now encouraged *access* to charitable assistance. This analysis (see Bell 1955/56; also see Elkin 1964, p. 364, for a description of early 'intelligent parasitism' on the frontier as a form of Aboriginal adaptation), which infers that Aboriginal people follow the identity path that brings the most material rewards, persists to the present. Barwick also discussed Aboriginal recognition of each other, identifying an early manifestation of tension within the Aboriginal community, which has evolved in form and substance over time through to the present. She noted that

> [t]he materially successful person who 'passes' and denies his ancestry threatens the self esteem of others; the person who 'mixes' and who is 'isn't ashamed of being black' is forgiven other faults. (1962, p. 22)

The use of the term 'factionalism' began to be used to describe such tensions within Aboriginal communities. Barwick noted that government policy, government administration and white-run welfare organisations helped with the continuing factionalism of three groups in her study, but noted that despite factionalism '[b]oth dark and fair are concerned about the status of Aborigines and are equally involved in these separatist activities' (1962, p. 18).

Despite persisting assimilationist assumptions, Barwick's observations and approach differentiates her work from earlier work in the field. It included analysis of Aboriginal practices, including tendencies to factionalism, as responses produced by adaptation to changing circumstances. There is attention to observations of the internal negotiations occurring within the Aboriginal community. Barwick also discussed how the Australian Aborigines League was concerned about the physical and cultural extinction of Aboriginal people and suggested 'importing fresh black blood' (1962, p. 19) and encouraging Victorian 'part-Aborigines' to marry 'full-bloods' from other states (see also Broome 2015). Her work is evidence of the increasing volume of diverse Aboriginal voices in research in the 1960s.

Also in this period, the anthropologist Jeremy Beckett (1965) looked at kinship, mobility and community among 'part-Aboriginal' people in the far west region of New South Wales. He outlined the demographics of the Aboriginal population over a period of time, including where they lived and moved to, factors of economic disadvantage such as exclusion from work and white attitudes towards them. Although he discussed colour and looks, he gave recognition to 'those who are physically indistinguishable [from whites] but retain Aboriginal identity because of known kinship with darker people or their adherence to Aboriginal ways' (1965, p. 2). He pointed out that while traditional ways were no longer practised, people still identified as Aboriginal and most fell short of living to white standards. In conclusion the study noted that

> Aborigines are deemed to have a common culture in which open-handedness, particularly towards kin, is valued, and any form of exclusiveness or superiority disapproved as an attempt to ape white people. (1965, p. 22)

Thus, in an era of official policy change and of rising public concern about the Aboriginal situation, it appears to be anthropologists who were expanding the Aboriginal identity discourse to include more positive and broader, shared and continuing Aboriginal cultural characteristics in the 'part-Aboriginal' population. Various findings of research conducted at this time began to support the notion that Aboriginal people do not have to give up being Aboriginal to participate in white society. However, Aboriginal rejection of those who 'ape' white people is noted and this reflects a strong persistent theme in contemporary Aboriginal identity politics. Even so, at this point in time, Beckett also posed that findings from his study indicated that Aboriginal people were focussed on their own community and kinship networks at the local level and as yet were not focused on goals of political unity. Nevertheless, Beckett's identification of this theme signalled an emerging condition of Aboriginal identity as requiring the rejection of white ways, at least as signs of superiority over other Aboriginal people. European class measures of social hierarchy were excluded and Aboriginal social relations, including changing ones, began to be articulated as a basis of a recognisable and continuing Aboriginal identity.

CHAPTER 4
QUANTIFYING ABORIGINALITY BY ACCULTURATION, ADAPTATION AND ALLEGIANCE

> These positions seem to be a convenient way for white writers to 'fit' Aborigines into certain phases of what is essentially white Australian history.
>
> (Langton 1981, p. 20).

While the 1960s in Australia saw a shift in how anthropological research positioned Aboriginality, not all those involved in researching Aboriginal peoples were trained in anthropology. In 1963, the Social Science Research Council of Australia commissioned a major project titled *Aborigines in Australian Society*, the purpose of which was to

> [elucidate] the problems arising from contacts between Aborigines and non-Aborigines and formulating policy from these; drawing together existing knowledge in various parts of Australia and undertaking such further original research as can be carried out over a period of three years. (Gale 1972, p. vi)

Social scientist Ellen Biddle (1969) and geographer Fay Gale (1972) were two researchers who conducted social surveys as part of this project on Aboriginal people who were migrating to the metropolitan areas of Queensland and South Australia respectively.

Ellen Biddle had previously conducted a social survey of Aboriginal people as part of her doctoral research. Her dissertation, 'The assimilation of Aborigines in Brisbane, Australia 1965', examined Aboriginal participation in white society in relation to living standards, education levels and employment types. Biddle's social survey found that Aboriginal people were not assimilated to any great degree; and that among the population studied, education was very low and the type of employment gained was in 'low ranking job categories', with 87 per cent of workers in the three lowest-ranking job categories (1969, p. 1). The Queensland reserve system, which had contained Aboriginal people separate and apart from non-Aboriginal society unless they met the Protector's criteria for exemption to live outside it, was assessed as part of the reason for slow assimilation:

> The charitable and responsible establishment of the reserve and settlement system can be seen in retrospect as an understandable historical policy but one which only succeeded in holding back the assimilation of many aborigines. (1969, p. 58)

However, according to Biddle's findings the younger Aboriginal people were 'doing better' (1969, p. 1), having more education and skills and greater engagement in aspects of non-Aboriginal society. On this basis Biddle asserted that 'amalgamation' was taking place and drew attention to a significant percentage of Aboriginal people with non-Aboriginal spouses to support her point.

An interesting aspect of the study was the difficulty Biddle expressed in determining and identifying who counts as Aboriginal. In a changing policy context, Biddle's study recruited participants on the basis of self-identification or identification by other Aboriginal people who recognised them as Aboriginal. This referral system, however, was found to be problematic and revealed the field of confusion around who and what counted as being Aboriginal. For example, Biddle explained, 'one woman…termed herself as Polynesian…even though she thought there were some aborigines in her family background' (1969, p. 93). In some instances, those referred to as being Aboriginal did not openly and publicly identify as Aboriginal. As for the self-identifying participants, some were confused as to their legal status as Aboriginal under the *Queensland Act* (1939). In other instances, a referred person was found to be not Aboriginal at all. As Biddle explained:

> Many did not know their status…many misunderstood their status; and some, 6.9 percent of adults, did not consider themselves as aborigines at all…Instead, they termed themselves Polynesians, South Sea Islanders, Maori, Singalese, and the like. (1969, p. 94)

Biddle reported that the respondents saw themselves as being Aboriginal in an 'undefined and unexplored' (1969, p. 94) sense but when given the legal definition, rejected their status as Aboriginal. There was, according to Biddle, good reason why people were cautious about identifying as Aboriginal under the Queensland government's definition. Firstly, many did not have a clear and definite knowledge of their descent as there were few records; and by the time of her surveys there were many generations of intermarriage. Secondly, the restriction on their movements, (such as being free to leave the mission or move freely to seek employment outside of the State), which would apply if they met the criteria under the *Queensland Act* (1939), was something to avoid (1969, p. 95). The study did reveal nevertheless that although some did not identify as and/or meet the definition of Aboriginal in legal terms, they did have Aboriginal heritage that was privately acknowledged (1969, p. 96).

Biddle's study also discussed the concept of 'passing as non-Aboriginal', but unlike the situation in Victoria reported by Barwick (1962), she suggested that it was an understandable response given the restrictive nature of Aboriginal legislation (Biddle 1969, p. 215). Biddle referred to Brereton's (1962) work on assimilation rates in NSW and cited his measures for 'passing' as non-Aboriginal. These included: the distancing of oneself from other mixed-descent peoples; engaging and socialising with non-Aboriginal people; living in homes which were to the standard of non-Aboriginal people; and for the Commonwealth Census purposes, considering themselves non-Aboriginal. Criteria for 'passing' entailed avoiding any Aboriginal cultural and social behaviours which were seen as being negative, revealing once again the constraints and pressures of either identity choice of 'part-Aboriginal' people. The internally negotiated ties to Aboriginal heritage and sensibilities, despite measures taken to remain free of regulating authorities, were not considered.

Despite the increasing numbers of Aboriginal people living and working in the greater Brisbane metropolitan area in 1965, despite confusion about who was Aboriginal in the legal sense as opposed to self-identification and identification by others, and despite reports of 'passing', Biddle concluded that the Aboriginal people she surveyed were 'more acculturated to the dominant white society than they are assimilated' (1969, p. 236).

Fay Gale (1972) also conducted urban research in the last half of the 1960s, as part of the *Aborigines in Australian Society* project sponsored by the Social Science Council of Australia. Her focus was the extent of social change in the Aboriginal population migrating from isolated rural towns, missions or reserves into Adelaide. Gale's questions were concerned with the reasons for this movement, their situation and their adjustment to the changes. She drew attention to the diversity within this migratory population and identified six groups that exhibited 'widely differing adaptations to European society' (1972, p. 2). These were: those who lived and thought as a traditionally-oriented group (generally 'full-blood'); those who no longer lived as Aboriginal but were not living as Europeans (both 'full-blood' and 'mixed-blood' and generally from reserves or missions); those who had long lived on reserves or missions and were long-adapted to European ways and who in isolated circumstances had 'developed a sub-culture which blends traits of traditional and western culture' (1972, p. 3); fringe-dwellers who were the first to migrate to the city; those who had integrated through living and working among Europeans independent of government assistance; and those who had 'become absorbed into the general population and seldom think of themselves as Aborigines' (1972, p. 3). These now unrecognisably Aboriginal light-skinned people were distinguished from other light-skinned 'absorbed' people who were still recognised by their relatives as Aboriginal. Of course, Gale could not identify those who had 'passed over' (her term) into the white community but she asserted that '[t]here must be many such people' (1972, p. 3).

THE POLITICS OF REASSERTION AND SELF-DETERMINATION OF THE MEANING OF ABORIGINALITY

By the early 1970s then, amidst the changing social conditions which reflected the easing of assimilation policies and pre-empted a policy era of self-determination, the idea that a person of mixed descent could acculturate to white social values, without forsaking an understanding of self as also Aboriginal, began to receive a measure of consideration. Nevertheless, older lines of thought associated with government administration and assimilation policy discourse persisted in the focus of research or evolved to maintain a focus on Aboriginal behaviour as a problem. Emerging analysis introduced new strands into discussion, namely factionalism as an Aboriginal community problem rather than a legacy of colonial policies. Also entering analysis was the idea that some 'part-Aboriginal' people, who formerly 'chose' to pass as white, switched their allegiances to identify and emphasise their Aboriginal inheritance and connections on a pragmatic and/or material basis. However, from the Aboriginal perspective this reversal of identity choices for 'part-Aboriginal' people signalled the emergence of the politics of re-assertion and self-determination of the meaning of Aboriginality.

Research related to Aboriginal identity in the 1970s begins to reflect the shift in governments' Aboriginal policy-making amidst changing Aboriginal and non-Aboriginal relations. Significantly, some research studies and conversations about Aboriginal identity evidence the birth of a different language for speaking about the social or cultural behaviours of Aboriginal people and their relation to the rest of Australian society. The language of acculturation and adaptation replaces that of assimilation.

However, perceived Aboriginal 'problems' associated with identification or with cultural practices in the acculturation process became a topic for psychology and medicine, including mental health (e.g. Dawson 1969; Berry 1970; Bianchi, Cawte & Kiloh 1970; Cawte 1973). Some of these pathologise the effects of generations of colonisation as individual 'instability and frank mental illness' (e.g. Cawte 1973, p. 365). As Aboriginal academic Marcia Langton noted, '[t]hese "mental disorders" might be regarded by other observers as justifiable resistance to brutal racism, exploitation and enforced relegation to subhuman conditions' (1981, p. 18). Her comments reflect increasingly visible and audible Aboriginal political activism, which produced over the coming decades some retrospective analysis of both the focus and the theorising in studies of 'part-Aboriginal' experience in previous decades.

These studies evidence what the then anthropology student Anne-Katrin Eckermann (1973, 1977a) was to note as the preoccupation of researchers with understanding and comparing Aboriginal people's culture change in terms of value conflict and along a continuum from Aboriginal to European:

> When urban/rural Aboriginal groups have been described, researchers have frequently explained differences between Aboriginal people and Europeans by reference to the unique value system prevalent in the minority group. Aboriginal values have generally been imputed on the basis of observed behaviour in the research situation. Similarly, researchers have postulated problems associated with the adoption of European values and practices; in fact they have definitely

> implied the existence of conflicting values in the contact situation. Further, there has been a tendency to see different communities at different stages along a continuum from a traditional way of life to a European way of life. (1973, p. 4)

A methodological shift emerges in studies by Frith, Hausfeld and Moodie (1974) and Hausfeld (1977), which allowed some illumination of the significance of historical and local specificities in shaping the contemporary health conditions and responses of these communities to change and adaptation. In one community in New South Wales, despite the absence of 'tradition', 'language' and 'knowledge of the local country', 'kinship bonds remain strong and functional in the organisation of support and sharing systems in the community' (Hausfeld 1977, p. 267). However the researcher commented:

> My impression is that I have studied Coasttown at a time when the traditional is finally departing. This is perhaps why so many of those interviewed seemed troubled with identity problems, finding it difficult to express their Aboriginality. 'Blood', even a tiny proportion of Aboriginal ancestry, was the major claim to Aboriginality. Being an Aboriginal seemed to be important to almost all — it provided an identity and I suspect, an excuse. (1977, p. 268)

In contrast, Forestville, a community at the other end of the state, was understood to be much less acculturated while facing rapid changes, and was found to be suffering higher levels of emotional disturbance and stress than Coasttown.

Anne-Katrin Eckermann continued Frith, Hausfeld and Moodie's (1974) approach and her two ethnographical studies (1973, 1977a) are useful in drawing attention to the challenges of past methodological approaches to the study of 'part-Aboriginal' people. She used her studies to examine the 'adequacy of the assimilation/culture-contact/culture-continuum framework' (1977a, p. 1). Eckermann questioned the premises and conclusions of much of the research that stressed the differences in value systems as the root cause of the Aboriginal 'problems'.

> Inferences have been made about Aboriginal problems caused by contact with European culture which is assumed to be based on a system of values different from that operant

in the Aboriginal culture. Further, the concepts of culture conflict and the idea of a continuum from the traditional to the European are strongly evidenced in the literature.

Eckermann insisted that

> The following questions need clarification. Are Aboriginal values remnants of the past or a response to European exclusion and poverty? Are the features of Aboriginal values elements of a separate belief-system which is in conflict with the so called European culture, or are they expressions of identity? Are these 'values' in fact particularly 'Aboriginal' or are they shared by other groups in the society? Does a strong identification as 'Aboriginal' and its concomitant membership of a close knit group preclude 'striving' and 'getting ahead' — values which are thought to be particularly European? (1973, p. 11)

Eckermann (1973, 1977b) was able to demonstrate that Aboriginal people in an urban situation could maintain an internal Aboriginal identity while distant from traditional life and land, and while meeting the demands of 'industrial' society. She found that while the Aboriginal people she studied could be considered 'assimilated', 'integrated' or 'acculturated',

> a strong and positive sense of being Aboriginal persists and is perpetuated. I believe this identification to be due to a number of factors, most importantly those associated with child-rearing practices, common historical experiences and a rich and flourishing system of folklore. (1977b, p. 288)

The interrelation between child-rearing practices and 'folk-beliefs' were considered integral to group and individual identity:

> Through socialisation the urban minority perpetuates the values and beliefs which distinguish it; through socialisation, it ensures its members are not lost to the majority and that its children, while being 'acceptable' to the majority, will also 'fit into' their own group. (1977b, p. 298)

She interpreted the 'folk-belief' as a critical aspect of urbanising Aboriginal identification:

> Such an adherence lends a distinguishing consciousness to this group of urban Aborigines, which believes it to be peculiar to themselves, and to provide real or imaginary links with a common past about which so little is remembered. Certainly, continual reference to such folk-beliefs within the family circle plays an important part in instilling in the child an awareness of his Aboriginality. None of these elements, however, has any bearing on the life of the community as such; that is, they do not influence the individual's economic or social activities within the wider European society. (1977b, p. 301)

Eckermann's conclusions in both studies support the shift away from earlier studies, which associated Aboriginality with intrinsic and negative cultural characteristics that were in conflict with European ones. In the 1977 urban study, historical, social and economic specificities allowed a space for the production of positive Aboriginal identities:

> [U]rban Aborigines will never become 'just' poor black whites. Further, the whole nexus of folk-lore, in-group identity and emphasis on 'Aboriginality' provides the individual with a screen through which he can identify himself positively as 'coloured', possessing qualities no white man has. (1977b, p. 318)

One participant, however, reflected on 'in-group' racial jokes:

> Do you think we really mean it, I mean when we call each other 'black boongs'; and 'dirty abos' you think we really mean it? Always thought it was just joking, Aboriginal humour you know, but sometimes I wonder, really. (1977b, p. 301)

In her 1977 doctoral study, entitled, 'Half-caste, out-caste: An ethnographic analysis of the process underlying adaptation among Aboriginal people in Rural Town, South-West Queensland' Eckermann established similar findings in relation to Aboriginal adjustment in a rural setting by further developing an 'adaptive theoretical framework' which allowed an interpretation of 'cumulative causation'. Her findings once again implicate the significance of historical, social and economic specificities for shaping the possibilities to regenerate positive identities. She affirmed that in the rural situation she studied,

> [t]he factors underlying this inability to cope or adapt successfully are not related to any misunderstanding of European values or to existence in a culture-contact/culture-vacuum situation. Rather they are a product of chronic poverty and Aboriginal people's frustrations in trying to establish their worth and equality in a white society from which they have been excluded since first European settlement in South West Queensland. (1977a, p. ii)

Eckermann (1977a) also noted and attempted to explain an emerging tension within the re-asserted Aboriginal position. She cited Chicka Dixon, a leading Aboriginal political figure from the 1960s until his death in 2009, who expressed strong feelings about people who 'pass' as non-Aboriginal or deny their Aboriginal heritage: 'Now I spit on these people' (Dixon quoted in Eckermann 1977a, p. 21). However, in both of Eckermann's studies, Aboriginal condemnation of Aboriginal behaviour was understood through explanations within 'minority' psychology:

> In Rural Town the results of segregation and isolation have shaped an Aboriginal minority which is torn by self-hatred, 'colour' consciousness, tensions and insecurity; a group weakened by internal factions, and by self-criticism. Not withstanding these destructive pressures Aboriginal identity in Rural Town is also associated with a number of positive components. (1977b, pp. 195–6)

Thus tensions across the differences within this emerging pan-Aboriginal identification were again identified (see for example, Barwick 1962) but these tensions were understood as a psychological effect of colonialism and framed within a theory of cumulative causation.

ABORIGINAL ETHNICITY AND THE EMERGENCE OF THE PAN-ABORIGINAL COMMUNITY

Analysis of Aboriginality as an ethnicity also emerges in other research conducted in this period. James Pierson's research, conducted in the early 1970s, examined adaptation, ethnic identity and general ways of life of people who identify as Aboriginal in Adelaide. Aboriginal 'ethnicity' was viewed as a contemporary adaptation, which provided urban Aboriginal people with advantages, understood in terms of relationships and resources. Aboriginality was termed as an ethnic category formed around 'self-identification as an Aborigine, differentiation by others on biological and/or cultural criteria and acceptance or rejection by whites or Aborigines for being Aboriginal' (1977, p. 315). Further, Aboriginality was described as:

> not necessarily hav[ing] anything to do with so called tribalism or adherence to traditional cultural practices. It includes pride in cultural traits of traditional societies, however, even when the person has had no firsthand experience with them. (p. 315)

The anthropologists Berndt and Berndt's assertion that Aboriginality 'means no more than a common identification in physical terms, the accident of Aboriginal descent' (1964, p. 445) was used as an important reference point against which to draw this analysis of Aboriginality. So Pierson also included Aboriginal perspectives from his research findings on the general criteria used by Adelaide Aboriginal people:

> judging a person to be an Aborigine are biological (either visual or knowledge of genealogical background). And associational (i.e. one's current associates and one's childhood background). A recognized Aboriginal identity, a wide range of contacts in the city, and pride in being Aboriginal can all provide some security for a person and all are a part of Aboriginality. (Pierson 1977, p. 316)

Pierson's research begins to provide more perceptive detail about the purposefulness of urban Aboriginal social organisation around the idea of a pan-Aboriginal community. He commented on Aboriginal-specific groups formed to provide social support for Aboriginal people and the role these groups played in re-establishing pride within historically demoralised people. Pierson also noted how Aboriginal social groups connected with, and knew the details and interrelations between, members of the Aboriginal population across Adelaide. In the urban context, where Aboriginal people were often isolated from white society and came from various locations around the country, the collective concept of Aboriginality enabled people to coalesce on an inclusive, common basis of identification. He pre-empted, in his scholarly analysis, a claim that Langton would soon assert in her contest with social scientists about the persistence of

Aboriginal social principles in urban contexts where the observable conditions of traditional social organisation were no longer in evidence.

A few years later in the 1980s, historian Heather Goodall (1982) provided an example of how concerns about how 'part-Aborigines'/ 'Aborigines' were understood through colonial and anthropological assumptions began to infiltrate and be taken up in other areas of scholarly study. Goodall aligned her approach to historical study with the emerging Aboriginal position. She asserted that the existing research on the history of Aboriginal people and identity in New South Wales and the south-eastern corner of Australia, when it was considered, was more administrative than theoretical and confined to the history of the practical implementation of government policy. So, when reflecting on historical work done by Bobby Hardy (1976), *Lament for Barkindji: The vanished tribes of the Darling River Region*, Goodall contended that she 'has simply reflected the perpetuation of the same stereotypes which imbued Elkin's writing' (Goodall 1982, p. 6). Similarly, with work done as part of a Masters degree at Sydney University Susan Johnston (1970), 'The New South Wales Government policy towards Aborigines, 1880 to 1909', Goodall asserted that the '[t]he weight of Elkin's work was such, however, that Johnston, despite her own empirical data, reached conclusions in conformity with Elkin's "historical" theory' (Goodall 1982, p. 5).

Goodall suggested that fundamental misconceptions have carried through in later works. In particular, she challenged the idea that there was ever a homogenous Aboriginal society, '[t]he concept of a uniformed 'aboriginal' society was borne out of European preconceptions and ignorance at the time of invasion' (1982, p. 14). Goodall highlighted that the pervasiveness of anthropological understanding of Aboriginal people which frames perceptions of who Aboriginal people are and Aboriginal identity in particular ways flows over and shapes the production of historical accounts. As she contended, '[s]tereotypes have continued to substitute for reality' (1982, p. 14).

Questions of Aboriginal identity and concepts of Aboriginality also begin to appear in studies of the position of Aboriginal people in relation to wider Australian institutional contexts. In the context of an emerging pan-Aboriginal concept of identity, the educationalist Deirdre Jordan (1983, p. xxx) in 'Identity as a problem in the sociology of knowledge: The social construction of Aboriginal identity with special reference to the 'world' of education', 'attempts to map Aboriginal "worlds" in order to establish the components of a viable individual and group identity for Aboriginal people' (1983, p. xxx). She sorted communities of Aboriginal people into categories of traditional, rural and urban regions. Although her attempt was to signal difference among Aboriginal peoples in terms of geographical location, and to reject the idea that Aboriginal people make up a monolithic group, her objective was to explore 'the possibility of structuring a specifically Aboriginal identity' (1983, p. 1) to accommodate these different contemporary realities. Jordan's work suggests the possible assemblage of a legitimate Aboriginal identity, which originates from the traditional and recruits newer meanings along a linear path of dilution from rural to urban contexts. Jordan identified Aboriginal ideals within traditional communities and made comparisons between traditional and urban communities. For example, the tradition-oriented community at remote Strelley in the Pilbara region of Western Australia

> exercised autonomy in all areas. The continuity of the group was provided for by the indoctrination of the group into a common ideology, and by establishing processes for continual adaptation within the ideological base, and continuity of leadership. (1983, p. xxxii)

In comparison, Jordan referred to the urban community of metropolitan Adelaide in terms of lack:

> In the metropolitan urban situation, among Aboriginal people, there was seen to be a lack of cohesion, a lack of clearly articulated ideology, a lack of an economic base for autonomy, a lack of acknowledged leadership. (1983, p. xxxii)

When discussing urban Aboriginal identity, Jordan stated urban Aboriginal people were, 'taking up the challenge of determining their own future offered them in the seventies by Government policy, and cannot see what an identity that is specifically Aboriginal looks like' (1983, p. 1). In brief, Jordan's analysis was that 'urban Aborigines' were more 'orientated towards white society' which results in a lack of orientation to Aboriginal society (1983, p. 461). Observing that urban Aboriginal people 'elect not to be socialised into the law' (1983, p. 461) she regarded this as precluding urban Aboriginal people from making decisions for 'traditional-orientated' people. For Jordan, relations between urban-oriented and traditional-oriented Aboriginal people were skewed in favour of urban Aboriginal people because they were more likely to hold government jobs and be in a position to speak for traditional people. This position fails to regard the historical or contemporary factors that have produced the 'lack' in traditional cultural knowledges and laws and the relocation of many Aboriginal groups to urban settings.

In the conclusion to her research Jordan suggested there should be a possibility for urban Aboriginal people to identify as Aboriginal Australian, to be 'proud to be an Aborigine' yet have an identity that is not 'distinguished by cultural differences' (1983, p. 463). She drew a comparison with 'Italian-Australian or Greek-Australian' (1983, p. 462) and asserted that it would seem 'oppressive to argue that all part-Aborigines/part-Europeans should opt for a part-Aboriginal identity rather than a part-European identity' (1983, p. 463).

On the surface level, Jordan (1983) raised legitimate points about the status of 'part-Aboriginal' people and assumptions made about identity choices. Plurality of identity in what was an era of emerging multicultural policy in Australia was a possibility. In the context of education, the differences between urban and traditional-oriented people were starkly evident and relevant to informing practice. However, dig a little deeper, and you find Jordan's adherence to the idea of the 'real Aborigine' as a cultural entity found in particular geographical locations, and the tribal/detribalised dichotomy, which Langton (1981) so vehemently objects to. Jordan's work followed and developed a strand of thinking about who counts and who does not count as Aboriginal that interrogated the meanings of the emerging pan-Aboriginal identity, which sought to be inclusive of urban and dislocated experiences, by once again dividing and relating the differences within this broader collective. Jordan's theoretical approach to understanding emerging identity formations does not deny the agency of urban Aboriginal people to acculturate without conceding their Aboriginal heritage. But arguably Jordan's division along the urban–traditional continuum contributes to a strand in the ongoing discourse that delegitimises Aboriginal attempts to reconstruct Aboriginal ways of relating in the wake of diverse colonial experiences. Her contribution to the discourse of questions around who can speak for whom in relation to Aboriginal affairs is significant to the evolving discussions of Aboriginal identity and indeed permeates public discourse in Aboriginal affairs through to the present.

THE INFLUENCE OF IDENTITY ON COMMUNITY DEVELOPMENT

In the policy arena, David Pollard's 1985 dissertation *Welfare policy and Aborigines: Towards an understanding of recent developments in New South Wales government policy in Aboriginal welfare* examined the Aboriginal Affairs policies in New South Wales in the 1980s which, he claimed, were led by a 'legacy of guilt' (Pollard 1985, p. ii). While focused on the direction of policy and such things as community development and problems of factionalism in community organisations, Pollard did comment on identity–policy relations, which he saw as implicated in the factionalism and perceived failures of policy. Pollard focused considerably on the idea of a unified community (1985, pp. 48–51) and contended that if Aboriginal people could work more productively together, community development may be more effective. Like others before him, Pollard neglected the historical conditions that have given rise to the community situations that he highlighted in his analysis. Rather, the internal differences and conflicts in Aboriginal communities and organisations were seen to be located in the failures of Aboriginal people or Aboriginal analysis of their reality.

Pollard also bought into the concept of an authentic Aboriginal identity attached to the notion of geographical places of belonging, which renders the quest for a reconstructed identity more difficult in urban locations.

> A number of institutions help to weld the community together, especially in areas of significant Aboriginal population, like Redfern. Moreover, the group clearly has to desire to maintain an identity, to identify with the past, which, in some respects is lost and irretrievable, but in another is a social construct exercising a powerful influence on what people do.

Pollard continued,

> In some respects the quest for identity may be more difficult in New South Wales…The search for Aboriginal identity in New South Wales is carried on without that final place of belonging for many people, that final geographical locus where one indisputably belongs or which constitutes the foundation of one's identity. (1985, p. 65)

He expressed concerns that while people continued to identify as Aboriginal, that Aboriginal identity may have been in the 'early stages of profound change' (1985, p. 378). Continuing an earlier line of thought, Pollard argued this change could be a result of 'the more obvious advantages which society can make available' (1985, p. 378). Pollard's thesis was that policy for Aboriginal people should be from a perspective of their shared aspirations with the rest of Australia as opposed to the perspective of their differences from other Australians (1985, p. 378).

Pollard was, however, careful not to suggest the term assimilation, acknowledging it has a 'heavy burden of historical association' (1985, p. 377). He contended that Aboriginal people's desire for 'a steady job, a good house, a decent education' expresses 'a corresponding desire to conform to the sets of value associated with them' (1985, p. 377). Although Aboriginal people were not 'losing their sense of identity', he suggested that 'because of their participation in the life of the mainstream of society, [they] end up essentially indistinguishable in outward form from the rest, while enacting from time to time some signs of a separateness otherwise quite latent' (1985, p. 377). For Pollard, any participation with what he termed 'mainstream of society' confirmed that Aboriginal people were under the influence of the 'renewed pull of assimilation' which he viewed as replacing the 'push of the government' (1985, p. 378).

In this way, Pollard continued understandings of Aboriginal identity along a continuum between authentic (real) Aboriginal identities attached to a geographical place of true belonging as opposed to the indistinguishable acculturated Aboriginal, living in the mainstream of society. His inference was that there would be less internal conflict within Aboriginal community organisations and the community development sphere if the latter recognised their location and their associated loyalties to those values. But also evident is the influence of Eckermann's (1977a) theorising that linked Aboriginality to social and economic disadvantage. Living successfully the 'mainstream' way began to call into question Aboriginal distinctiveness from the rest of the population. This thinking is part of a strand of everyday discourse that posits middle class values as antithetical to Aboriginal values and a contra-indicator for the claim of being Aboriginal. The more successful Aboriginal individuals are, the more they must defend their Aboriginal status by exhibiting other recognisable signs of Aboriginal characteristics.

All these studies bear out McKeich's (1977) assertions. In sum, research in the transition period of the 1960s to the 1980s evidenced the scholarly struggle over theoretical frameworks for understanding the problems of 'assimilating', 'acculturating' and 'adapting' Aboriginal people and their ways or expressions of Aboriginal identity. Historical theories and previously popular held notions and schools of thought weaved their way through analysis and arguments, persisting as bases of understanding Aboriginal people and affairs, even as the framing of questions around Aboriginal identity shifted. The distinction between 'real Aborigines' and those dislocated, 'part-Aboriginal' people who 'lack' traditional connections or the markers of disadvantage was held open in this period. The 'problem' of changing Aboriginal identities as these manifest in practical contexts such as policy, internal community factionalism, education, history and research method emerged as an area of research interest. As Langton (1981) noted, despite its shifting focus, research continued to overwhelmingly investigate the position of Aboriginal people in relation to white society, and '[t]hese positions seem to be a convenient way for white writers to 'fit' Aborigines into certain phases of what is essentially white Australian history' (1981, p. 20).

However, during this period, research shifted from a pre-occupation with the barriers to assimilation to include recognition that the Aboriginal view of experience provides different theoretical insights. It has included analytical assertions that Aboriginality shares characteristics with ethnic minority positions and introduced notions of the constructed nature of 'urbanising' Aboriginal identities.

CHAPTER 5
THE CHANGING MEANING OF ABORIGINAL IDENTITY

> 'Are Aborigines today so destitute a human category that their culture can be given no credit beyond a highly romanticised past and a limited number of material artefacts?' (Chase 1981, p. 24)

Between the 1970s and 1990s, more complex conversations developed between social scientists and in the inter-locutions between public, government and Indigenous people and communities. Both within research and the broader public sphere, Aboriginal perspectives on identity were emerging and gaining recognition. The concept of a pan-Aboriginal identity also began to be discussed within Aboriginal communities as Aboriginal political activity developed a unified basis for action *vis-à-vis* the nation-state. Within this more complex conversation emerged some rumblings of contest around who and what were to count as 'real Aborigines', and the problems for those formerly 'part-Aboriginal' people who were seeking to re-define themselves on their own terms. Debates over the legitimacy of the concept of Aboriginality and the definitional criteria of the concept engaged social scientists and became a subject of scholarly debate. Both these strands about who and what Aboriginal people were and could become extended through the 1980s and into the 1990s, and indeed still continue today, not just in the social sciences but in the Aboriginal community and among the wider public.

As these complex conversations develop, the differences in meaning around the terminology of Aboriginal identity and Aboriginality are rarely defined and often used inter-changeably. It is useful to highlight that Aboriginal identity is more closely associated now with how Aboriginal people name and express themselves from within their spheres of reference. Aboriginality, on the other hand, is more closely associated with the condition of being Aboriginal, and discussions of the concept are generally contextualised beyond the personal and within relations to the nation-state and the political framework of self-determination, which asserts the right to control what it means to be Aboriginal. In this sense the criteria of Aboriginality are often assumed to be the same reference points from which many Aboriginal people construct their own personal identities, even though these are not always reflected in individual subscriptions and expressions of identity (see, for example, Dillon 2011). The scholarly conversations therefore reflect various investments in the politics of both self-determination and identity, as well as allegiance to various forms of social inquiry and analysis. The aim here is not to sort these strands out so much as to acknowledge their presence and the dense network of knowledge–power relations in the spaces where Aboriginal people attempt to 'make our way' on our own terms.

PAN-ABORIGINALITY AND RECONSTRUCTING ABORIGINAL IDENTITIES

In 1971, the anthropologist Ronald Berndt, speaking of 'part-Aboriginal' and/or non-traditionally oriented Aboriginal people, stated,

> [p]eople of Aboriginal descent, especially in the southern areas, are much more articulate than they were a couple of decades ago. While the majority of those represented in this category are for all practical purposes Australian-Europeans, their knowledge of the traditional Aboriginal heritage is not at first hand and indeed for most of them it is far removed. Yet they seek a common social identity in that Aboriginal past — in the idea of it, because anything closer to traditional actuality, would find them completely at sea. (1971, p. 41)

In 1973, anthropologist John Von Sturmer more categorically asserted that, '"Aboriginality" is a fiction which takes on meaning only in terms of white ethnocentrism' (1973, p. 16). These comments reflected the anthropological view of traditional identity forms and functions, and a concomitant view that urban Aboriginal people's quest towards a politically motivated pan-Aboriginality that acknowledged what was shared and common across all Aboriginal groups, including traditional ones, was a problematic identity claim. The matter was discussed by people in various disciplines including by Berndt (1977), who continued to develop his thoughts on the matter via his understandings of traditional identity forms and practices:

> The 'reality' of traditional Aboriginal life, then, has to do with first-hand experience within it, and with particular kinds of identification. It was and is a unique situation, which cannot be merely assumed by someone outside the system. Nevertheless, it is possible to have a particular perspective based on what is assumed to be an Aboriginal way of life — that is, to have an idea or vision of it. Whether we think of this as a 'mirage' or not is really beside the point. Certainly it is a mirage in relation to traditional Aboriginal life as it existed in the past...But as a viable view, believed in by those who wish to believe in it, it has a reality of its own. (1977, p. 5)

Berndt, while acknowledging the diverse experiences of (part) Aboriginal people who survived contact and colonial regimes, saw non-traditional Aboriginal identity as 'an "Aboriginalisation" of certain aspects of the wider Australian society and culture, moulded to fit their own frames of reference' (1977, p. 7), and an adaptive response to external pressures and trauma that produced internal insecurity, in contrast to the continuing secure identities of traditionally oriented groups.

In this schema, the concept of a pan-Aboriginality that forges a common Aboriginal identity across the diverse experiences, forms and practices of identity is considered contrived in that it seeks to differentiate all those of Aboriginal descent from non-Aboriginal people by emphasising the 'common' heritage and experience. However, Berndt argued this is more than political; it also sought the demarcation of identity boundaries for the purposes of emotional security.

What continued to concern Berndt was that, in working from the idea of the traditional elements of Aboriginal society, the recovered identity conflated into

> a kind of digest or telescoping of the many traditional societies and cultures into a generalised and abstract frame, focused on specific elements in contrast to others. (1977, p. 9)

This resulted in an openness and crossing of social boundaries that was not found in traditional identity forms that had worked against wider political organisation across groups, while encouraging interdependence between smaller, localised social entities. The quest for pan-Aboriginal identity works against the traditional inward orientation of social identity forms that promoted co-operation in the interest of survival. On the other hand, Berndt conceded that pan-Aboriginality engages the common experience of colonialism that is now also part of the Aboriginal heritage.

Erich Kolig (1973), on the basis of research in the Kimberley region of Western Australia, while in general agreement with this view, took issue with the idea of pan-Aboriginality as 'fiction' or 'mirage':

> Certainly, pan-Aboriginality is a 'white product' — it would be foolish to deny this...European pressure did force upon Aborigines the acceptance of pan-Aboriginality as a fact of life in the modern Australian society; but it has not succeeded in prescribing how Aborigines have to define, and conceive of, their Aboriginality. Their Aboriginality is neither a 'white' mirage, nor a fiction, nor a jest of the fate that has favoured the 'white man'...Aborigines do not just float helplessly on the tide of change, but, in their own terms, they meaningfully and significantly adjust...They identify; they are not just identified. (1973, p. 36)

However, Kolig did note the shifting trends of Kimberley Aboriginal people at this time, especially the young, to define themselves in comparison to white Australians through 'oppositional feelings, from the awareness of deprivation, discrimination and suppression' (1973, p. 49). He noted also, the differences between this emerging Aboriginality and those of urban Aboriginal people, likening it to two factions who coalesce around a common quest but from different roots.

From a political action and non-anthropological position, Colin Tatz defended the development of an Aboriginality founded not just on distinction from all other Australians but on Aboriginal rejection of the white society that had rejected them. He articulated the logic of the black consciousness movement:

> The basic precept is that blacks want to know, and must know, more about who they were and who they are if they are seriously concerned about whom they intend to become...A basic tenet is that the black man must reject all

value systems that seek to make him a foreigner in his own country and which reduce his human dignity. He must build up his own value systems, and see himself as self-defined and not defined by others...

Tatz went on to say:

Group cohesion and solidarity therefore become much more important than ever before. Thus in order to join the open society on anything like equal terms, black people should first close their ranks: not as evidence of anti-whitism, but as an exclusion of whites for the time it will take to realise their immediate aspirations of black consciousness. (1977, p. 387)

Tatz (1979) later added to this argument by drawing attention to the arguments of Aboriginal people for reconstructing Aboriginal identities. He quoted the following statements by activists Michael Anderson, Paul Coe and Grandfather Koori respectively:

The answer for my people is to teach them how to be themselves.

We are hoping for, and pushing for, the revitalisation of Aboriginal culture: It is the only possible means of counteracting the present government policy of assimilation.

You say you want your Aboriginality back? That means having some rules, don't it? And the first two orders of those rules is share and care...You build Aboriginality, boy, or you got nothing. There's no other choice to it. It'll be easier, now, with bits of land handed back to us, here'n there... (Tatz 1979, p. 87)

'REAL ABORIGINES' AND REVIVALISTS

While the case for reintroducing cultural specificities as elements of reconstructed identity is strongly made, and two persisting elements of Aboriginality begin to be described in terms of connection to land and the ethos of sharing and caring, others criticise the dichotomy being constructed along urban–traditional lines between 'real Aborigines' and revivalists. For example, in 1981, historian Athol Chase drew attention to the persistent but contradictory white Australian logic that allotted negative behavioural characteristics of 'part-Aboriginal' people as signifiers of a continuing Aboriginality, that considered 'successful' 'part-Aboriginal' people as no longer Aboriginal, and which approved of and understood the 'real Aborigines' still living 'traditional' lives:

> If Aboriginal people from the city ghettos or from the dusty fringe camps of smaller Australian towns attempt to assert some claim to Aboriginality, one area of righteous public opinion sees them as getting assistance under false pretence; they are not real Aborigines, but bludgers cashing in on a touch of the tar brush. (1981, p. 23)

Chase described the social contemporary technologies of remote Lockhart River people in Cape York, emphasising how 'material technologies are subordinate to these social ones' (1981, p. 25). Amidst the changing conditions and the incursions of European material technologies, he reported that to the European eye, Lockhart River people were viewed as people who 'had lost their culture, and had failed to replace it properly from the European reservoir' (1981, p. 25). On the contrary, however, he noted the continuing social technologies or 'Lockhart' 'ways of doing things' (1981, p. 25) that were based on ideologies, which continued to distinguish them from other Aboriginal groups and from Torres Strait Islanders and Europeans. These revolved around ways of interacting with each other and with outsiders that were based in deeply embedded belief systems:

> There is no difference, in Lockhart eyes, between chopping down a tree with either a stone axe or a steel axe (or even a power saw), or hunting a dugong from either a canoe or a dinghy and outboard, providing the honey or the dugong meat is distributed properly among kinsmen. Where European technologies save physical effort without infringing upon the social outcome, they can be readily accepted. (1981, p. 25)

Others added similar cases. For example, Diana Eades, a linguist, questioned the equation of loss of traditional language with loss of Aboriginal identity, arguing that

> [t]his language-equals-culture package and its political consequences are grossly unjustified, naive and unjust. It is a view which often stems from a narrow minded misconception that Aboriginal culture consists only of traditional dancing, ritual, language and technology...Culture is far deeper than the language people speak or the way they hunt. It is right at the heart of how people relate to people, perceive the world and act on it. (1981, p. 12)

Eades (1981) explained Aboriginal language use in south-east Queensland at the time, in terms of adaptation to changed circumstances which evidenced continuity with older languages and the influences of contact represented by the infiltration of other languages. She emphasised that the use of language depended on who was talking. Included were Standard Australian English and dialects of English, including Aboriginal English, and varieties of Aboriginal languages belonging to users' own groups and the groups of those they interrelate with. Language as a social tool was constantly being re-worked. However, even when English was used, communication styles were predominately still Aboriginal, rather than European, expressed through protocols for information exchange, the meanings of silence, the absence of direct questioning and so on, all of which 'subordinated [the use of English] to the ways its speakers relate to each other' (1981, p. 14).

In 1981, this common presumption that 'part-Aboriginal' people were no longer Aboriginal prompted the Aboriginal academic, Marcia Langton an assistant bibliographer at the Australian Institute of Aboriginal Studies at the time, to remark in relation to urban Aboriginal people: 'We were seen as "cardboard cutouts", white in orientation with different coloured skins' (1981, p. 16). She strongly refuted social scientists' inscriptions of urban Aboriginal people [in the literature], from the earlier studies of Reay and Sitlington (1948) through to Eckermann (1977a, 1977b). These, she argued, theorised urban Aboriginal people largely in terms of cultural difference or socio-economic impoverishment and 'most have failed to perceive the insiders' view — how Black people themselves perceive and understand their condition' (1981, p. 16). She did acknowledge that some (Barwick 1962; Beckett 1965; Pierson 1977) had been more 'perceptive in their observations of urbanizing Aboriginal people in their adaptation and orientation to white life' (1981, p. 17).

Langton asserted that an alternative understanding emerges from within Aboriginal experience:

> Many Aboriginal people living in urban centres have refuted the logic of the terminology that has been foisted upon us by successive pieces of legislation, and now by the social scientists: 'half-caste', 'coloured', 'part-Aboriginal', 'detribalized', 'remnant' and so on. We have rejected the notion that we are assimilating into the European population and adopting white lifestyles. We are exploring our own Aboriginality and are finding that the white social scientists cannot accept our own view of ourselves. (1981, p. 16)

She was highly critical of the evolving methodologies of social science research. She argued for research of urban Aboriginal societies that could take an historical perspective and that 'concentrated on the internal social structure rather than the external social structure' (1981, p. 21) and which could produce '[n]ew views of, for example, the Aboriginal family, and kinship networks and, the significance of the Aboriginal desire for externals and material possessions of Europeanism' (1981, p. 22).

Langton further noted the role of anthropologists in constructing notions of urbanising Aboriginal people as people who 'lack culture, have no distinctive culture, have only some truncated version of European culture, or have only a "culture of poverty"' (1981, p.17). Well ahead of later understandings, she asserted 'that identity for any individual is a multivariate composition, non-fixed, situational, and continually maintained and transformed by culture' (1981, p.17).

Langton was responding to both anthropologists and social scientists. The tribal/detribalised dichotomy that she, Eades (1981) and Chase (1981) questioned was giving shape to understandings of 'real Aborigines' that questioned continuing forms of Aboriginality in 'part-Aboriginal' communities of practice. For Langton, Aboriginality was a commonality that connected diverse urbanising Aboriginal groups:

> The history of culture contact and 'chain migrations' of Aborigines to the cities and town have meant that Aborigines have responded to many different European situations, and brought their changing cultures and identities with them,

forming diverse, urban communities with one thing in common, their Aboriginality. (1981, p. 21)

Langton considered the aspects of this common Aboriginality, suggesting it was framed by the Dreaming as the shared philosophical basis of Aboriginal society, as well as 'a simple but highly efficient material culture, the complex social organisation and its acephalous nature and the "metaphysical emphasis on abidingness"' (Sutton quoted in Langton 1981, p. 6).

Langton's argument is supported by the argument of anthropologist Peter Sutton, that

[t]he bones of culture are the principles of things such as how people bring up children, how they pattern their roles as kin, and how they interact in conversation, rather than the details of the forms in which these things are expressed. (1981, p. 6)

ABORIGINAL DIVERSITY IN THE MODERN CONTEXT

In this sense part of the developing conversation emphasises Aboriginality as the persistence of former traditional social practices, now adapted and expressed to fit the 'reality' of changing circumstances in the modern context. Coombs, Brandl and Snowdon (1983), for example, defined Aboriginality as 'the value and patterns of behaviour essential to the Aboriginal world view; in particular their sense of identity with the land' (1983, p. xxvi). They attempted to set out the broad common criteria of Aboriginality which could accommodate the diversity across many local contexts. The criteria they set out would be widely taken up in the discourse of Aboriginality, although developed on the basis of research conducted in remote parts of the Northern Territory. This research informed a policy, the aim of which was to elevate processes for Aboriginal self-determination in its intersections with government policy and program implementation in a range of areas that impacted on Aboriginal family socialisation and education of children, including schooling, health practices, law and order, economic activity and governance.

In the 1980s, Coombs, Brandl and Snowdon argued that '[w]herever in Australia people identify as Aborigines they share certain enduring characteristics' (1983, p. 20). These researchers gathered in numerous authorities (e.g. Brandl 1970; Howard 1978; Stanner 1979; Sutton 1981; Rigsby 1981; Langton 1981; Eades 1981) to support the notion of continuity of traditional principles and the idea that the underlying cultural principles rather than observable forms of culture were what persisted. Further, these persisted not as the surviving 'scraps' of an ancient, collapsing culture but as the 'core of Aboriginality wherever people who identify as Aboriginal are found' (Coombs et al. 1983, p. 30). Aboriginality was suggested to be more than merely descent from the original inhabitants but to be expressed in complex sets of practices anchored in the Aboriginal worldview.

In relation to the experience of colonisation, Coombs et al similarly emphasised that the 'overriding character and quality of the encounters are the same for Aborigines wherever they live and have lived on this continent' (1983, p. 32), and that the mutual recognition of the shared experience by Aboriginal people who have been affected in many and variously different ways is the expression of an Aboriginal value, in itself.

The following seven criteria of Aboriginality were assembled:

1. being and identifying as a descendant of the original inhabitants of Australia;
2. sharing historical as well as cultural experience, particularly that arising from relations with non-Aborigines;
3. adhering to, or sharing, the dreaming, or Aboriginal worldview;
4. having an intimate familial relationship with the land and with the natural world; and knowing the pervading moulding character of this in all matters Aboriginal;
5. basing social interaction on the mutual obligations of kinship;
6. giving importance to mortuary rituals and attendance at them; and
7. speaking and understanding more than one language. (Coombs et al. 1983, p. 61)

CHALLENGES TO PAN-ABORIGINALITY

In the mid-1980s, the concept of pan-Aboriginality was questioned by the anthropologist Stephen Thiele (1984) in a criticism of Tatz's arguments of support for Aboriginal political self-determination. Thiele's criticism provoked a rally of responses and a subsequent reply from him, in which he asserted they had missed the point of his article (Anderson et al. 1985).

Thiele argued that both assimilation policy and the policy of Aboriginal self-determination were reflections rather than analyses of 'the political pressures and ideologies of the day', and that the way forward for Aboriginal people was consequently circumscribed by 'moral and policy positions' (1984, p. 168) in both cases rather than on the basis of substantive social inquiry.

Apart from the moral and policy distinctions surrounding separatism as the basis of action, Thiele questioned the assumptions underpinning Tatz's representation of two homogenous groups — Aborigines and Europeans — that preserved the 'them' and 'us' framework and which continued the analysis of relations between the two solely on the basis of race. He objected to Tatz assuming the nature of pan-Aboriginality without any substantive analysis or interrogation of the difficulties involved in resolving a unitary basis for such a concept. Thiele made similar arguments in relation to Tatz's construction of the collective and equally distributed white mistreatment, racism and guilt, which presupposed a homogenous white society requiring no further analysis. Further, according to Thiele, Tatz's adoption of a moral position ahead of substantiating description and analysis left other structural elements implicated in the Aboriginal position unexamined. Thiele considered Tatz's work atheoretical and circular in its logic. In an earlier article Thiele had expressed his view that '[i]f Aboriginality is what Aborigines do and think there must be many different and contradictory kinds of Aboriginality' (1982, p. 20).

As in Thiele's article, most of the subsequent discussion centred not on the concept of Aboriginality per se, but on the relative strengths and weaknesses in both authors' arguments, which were viewed to have largely fired past each other. Thiele (1984) did make a point when he claims, at that moment in time, that the self-determination approach is an ideology that escaped the lens of substantive social inquiry. In relation to Aboriginality he asserted,

> [f]or example, there has been no attempt to assess comprehensively, at the national level, the nature of Aboriginality — the differing kinds of character, personality, ideologies, activities and structural locations of Aborigines, or of the different kinds of ethos exhibited by Aboriginal communities and groups. (1984, p. 166)

Anderson (1985) reminded us,

> the more important task...is not merely to state whether 'Aboriginality' in any real sense exists, but rather to account for the fact that people think it does, argue that is [sic] does and act as though it does. (1985, p. 42)

At the same time, Tim Rowse pointed out that '[t]he doctrine of "Aboriginality" has a rationale in a particular practice of political mobilisation in the two decades after the referendum of 1967' (1985, p. 46). Even if the concept is not internally coherent, the notion is possible in light of Australian political and administrative practices in relation to Aboriginal people.

As Von Sturmer explained, 'we can never deal *just* with people-people relations; we know that people-people relations are enacted in complex and ever shifting force fields which reside in large measure outside the control of social actors' (1985, p. 47). He came closer to Thiele's point that the self-determination approach defining a moral position to promote a policy position in a similar way to earlier approaches to the management of the 'Aboriginal problem':

> If the language of assimilation actually concealed a discourse aimed at the 'proletarianism' of Aborigines, the language of 'self-determination' may be discovered as concealing a discourse aimed at drawing them inexorably into the corporate State — either directly by recruiting Aborigines...into the bureaucracy, or by means of a more indirect process, namely by the creation of 'Aboriginal' organizations which are required or demand or are invited to participate in government decision-making. (Von Sturmer 1985, p. 48)

Without an understanding of the 'materiality of discursive practices', there is more likelihood of reproducing the historically narrow spaces of colonial Aboriginal identity 'choices' in the hard-fought 'self-determination' policy and regulatory context. The concept of Aboriginality and the contest about what constitutes its evidentiary content or criteria cannot therefore be detached from the legislative and regulatory contexts, which require its continued definition. This is the case even when these legislative frameworks are renegotiated by Aboriginal people in the quest to be 'self-determining' and when regulatory practices are increasingly enacted by members of Aboriginal organisations in de facto 'Aboriginal government' positions. How self-determining Aboriginal people (and their organisations) determine the basis and practices of Aboriginality, identity and identification within the concentric circles of both the legislative frameworks of the nation-state and the merging Aboriginal political structures is a legitimate site for social inquiry and interrogation. That is, the wider context is not irrelevant.

CULTURAL CONSTRUCTIONS OF IDENTITY

In the latter half of the 1980s, discussion emerged of the pan-Aboriginal identity category as a 'cultural construction'. A 1986 meeting at the Australian Institute of Aboriginal Studies in Canberra solicited papers on 'uses of the past in constructions of Aboriginal identity' (Beckett 1988a, p. 1):

> In describing Aboriginality as a cultural construction we are not suggesting that it is inauthentic. It refers to the ways in which Aborigines select from their experience and their cultural heritage to communicate a sense of identity to their young people, to Aborigines of differing backgrounds, and to other Australians. European Australians are also engaged in the construction of Aboriginality as 'experts' and advocates and critics.

The media's role was noted:

> The media devote considerable space to Aboriginal affairs, constructing Aboriginality for the many European Australians who have no direct experience of Aborigines. Aborigines themselves are exposed to these influences and have come to terms with them in their dialogue with European Australia.

As was the misappropriation of the 'past':

> The principal currency in these exchanges is the Past. The memories of old people, anthropological writings, archaeological remains, documentary records, are all ransacked to give authenticity to competing constructions. (Call for session contributions AIAS biennial meeting, 1986 quoted in Beckett 1988a, p. 1)

Geographer Jane Jacobs for example, in a discussion of the articulation of a public Aboriginal identity by Aboriginal land claimants, illustrated 'that Aboriginal groups are not insensitive to the constructs of Aboriginality set by external agents' (1988, p. 31), in this case governments.

Some useful concepts are brought in to the scholarly discourse. The first is the notion that Aboriginality as a cultural construction is a nationalism, and that

> [i]t shares this quality with all other nationalisms...being an example of...the 'imagined community'. This definition does not imply inauthenticity (it is clear that nationalism, ethnicity and Aboriginality remain some of the most passionately felt forms of identity throughout the world), but simply that they are products of the human imagination. This is necessarily so because, as Anderson (1983, 15) observes, 'the members of even the smallest nation will never know most of their fellow-members, meet them, or even hear of them, yet in the minds of each lives the image of their communion'. This image is a cultural artefact, achieved by remembering things held in common, but also by strategic forgetting (Anderson 1983, pp. 14–15).

The second is:

> The 'imagining' of communities' is not arbitrary, but, like all cultural processes, takes place under particular historical experiences. It is these conditions that give the construction its authenticity and also its fluidity. (Beckett 1988a, p. 2)

Also brought into the scholarly discourse is the notion of Aboriginal identity as a process of ethnogenesis. This concept explains the process of building a common culture out of 'the diversity of those becoming a group':

> As to the degree to which past cultural tradition potentially provides the boundaries and norms of an ethnic group, we argue that the common culture of diverse sub-cultures is not 'given' in a situation that is culturally diverse. Commonalities are first conceptualized and then 'constructed'. (Jones & Hill-Burnett quoted in Beckett 1988a, p. 4)

However, ethnicity in Australia in this period was subordinated to nationalism under the policy of multiculturalism, and the inclusion of

Aboriginal people as just another ethnic category has always been strongly rejected by Aboriginal people (see for example, Morris 1988, p. 73). Beckett acknowledged the Aboriginal identity claim was not equivalent to other ethnicities, and indeed was distinguished from all others on the basis of prior occupation and 'the lack of a mother country beyond the seas' (1988a, p. 5); leading Aboriginal people to seek recognition 'in some sense [as] "the same" as those who occupied the country when the settlers arrived' (1988a, p. 6).

Nevertheless, a problem emerges for many Aboriginal people when claiming cultural heritage as a basis of identity because of the extent of the fracturing of traditional heritage. 'Urban' Aboriginal people are able to be positioned as more like white people than traditionally oriented Aboriginal people who still fit within the colonial constructs of Aboriginality, leading to the identification and selection of elements from 'the past' to establish this distinctiveness. Quests to reconstruct and express contemporary forms of Aboriginality emerged in response. These may include elements of traditional pasts and elements of the recent shared past of colonial experience. For instance, examples from Beckett's research demonstrated that Aboriginality 'is in a constant process of creation and it may have many definitions that compete for acceptance, among particular groups of Aborigines or Europeans or in the society at large' (1988a, p. 7).

Significantly, as highlighted by Beckett, Aboriginal identity is constructed in various locations, and according to a range of vested interests, both Aboriginal and non-Aboriginal,

> the process of construction is not achieved through some kind of communal consensus, but in a number of different loci whose output may coalesce, but equally may be in contention. Indeed, competing construction may well be the vehicles for competing political and economic interests, Aboriginal and non-Aboriginal. (1988a, p. 5)

One further concept to emerge has arguably been more difficult to discern, or less developed, in subsequent scholarly and public analysis. This is the notion of differences between private and public identities and the tensions inherent in what Beckett referred to as 'the loci of [identity] construction' (1988a, p. 191).

> At the local level, the most striking line of tension may seem to lie between what Aboriginal people say about themselves and what others say about them. But crosscutting this is another field of tension between the ideas of Aboriginality (and non-Aboriginality) that people of all kinds construct and reproduce for themselves, and the constructions produced at the national level by the state and its various manifestations, the mass media, science, the arts and so on. (Beckett 1988b, p. 191)

The contradiction of Aboriginality between the behavioural and situational 'private' identities and that of publicly recognised forms that seek evidence of 'the past in the present' is that we become 'caught between the attribution of unchanging essences (with the implication of an inability to change) and the reproach of inauthenticity' (Beckett 1988b, p. 194). As Beckett concluded, either we must resist attempts to cut us off from our past or be buried with it.

The changes in this period were substantial. By the time of the 1988 Australian Bicentennial of the European occupation of Aboriginal land, the question of who and what counted as Aboriginal was the site of serious scholarly and committed political struggle. The anthropologists Berndt and Berndt, long-time commentators on the question of Aboriginality, summed up the evolving concepts in this period of transition:

> That identity, however its outward manifestations, has political implications; and Aborigines are well aware of these, as is the federal government. Within the picture is Aboriginal identity as a positive expression of a pride in being Aboriginal and having a common background, however far that may be removed from the actualities of the past. That identity must be seen in a dual sense, as having something to do with the traditional past and also something to do with the struggle for equality, against what often appears to be insurmountable odds. (1988, pp. 528–9)

However, despite the challenges to colonial constructions of Aboriginality, Aboriginal constructions continued to be produced within a web of discursive relations that contained Aboriginal 'self-determination' as a mechanism of governmental incorporation of Aboriginal bodies and which were now implicated in the continuing definition and regulation of Aboriginal identities.

CHAPTER 6
SHIFTS IN THE SOCIAL AND POLITICAL CONTEXT

> Instead of an authorised version of Aboriginality in Australia, there has been a medley of voices, black and white, official and unofficial, national and local, scientific and journalistic, religious and secular, interested and disinterested, all offering or contesting particular constructions of Aboriginality. It is very likely to remain this way.
>
> (Beckett 1988, p. 7)

Instead of an authorised version of Aboriginality in Australia, there has been a medley of voices, black and white, official and unofficial, national and local, scientific and journalistic, religious and secular, interested and disinterested, all offering or contesting particular constructions of Aboriginality. It is very likely to remain this way. (Beckett 1988, p. 7)

The year 1988 marked the bicentennial of colonial 'settlement' in Australia. This period provides evidence of how easily general goodwill on the part of ordinary Australians, as well as on the part of governments, swings between quite polarised positions on a range of fronts in Indigenous affairs. This period also discloses how derivative these positions are of earlier strands of thought around the Aboriginal 'problem'.

During the 1983–1996 period of Labor rule by the Hawke–Keating governments, support for the policy of Aboriginal self-determination peaked, only to then be slowly fractured during the Howard conservative government which followed on from 1996 to 2007, as the social conditions in remote communities, by many accounts, deteriorated (see for example Sutton, 2001). Across these two governments, the Aboriginal and Torres Strait Islander Commission (ATSIC) was established by the Hawke Labor government in 1989–90 and disbanded by the Howard Liberal government in 2005, without contest from the Labor opposition.

ATSIC was a national representative body for Aboriginal and Torres Strait Islander people. It advised government on policy, advocated the recognition of Indigenous rights, and delivered government programs and services for Indigenous people. Whatever its weaknesses, ATSIC presented a consistent Indigenous presence in national political affairs over a period during which concern about persisting Indigenous disadvantage increasingly brought to light the historical circumstances and forms of Indigenous oppression in past policy.

In the same period, governments continued to develop policies for Indigenous people in the major areas of social policy: health, education, employment, housing, law and the arts. Increasing numbers of Aboriginal people worked in Aboriginal-controlled incorporated organisations and in sections of the government's bureaucracies delivering services and programs to Aboriginal people. Increasing numbers of Aboriginal Australians attended university and entered full employment through affirmative actions. Increasing numbers of Indigenous academics and professionals acquired influence in research, policy and social analysis.

EVOLVING RELATIONS AND RECONCILIATION

These developments occurred in the context of evolving relations between Indigenous and non-Indigenous Australians over these two decades. These evolving relations developed not only between an increasingly articulate Indigenous leadership and governments but also between the wider Australian and Indigenous populations. Two major reports kept a focus on the continuing problems in Aboriginal communities. The first was the *Royal Commission into Aboriginal Deaths in Custody*, begun by the Hawke Labor government in 1987, in response to concerns about the rates and causes of death among Aboriginal people incarcerated and those in other police custody. The Commission investigated the wider social, economic and legal factors that underlay rates of incarceration and the custodial practices that contributed to deaths in all jurisdictions. One of the issues brought to light was the effects of the separation and the institutionalisation of Aboriginal children, prompting a further inquiry.

The second was *Bringing Them Home* (Wilson, 1997), the final report brought down in 1997 by the *National Inquiry into the Separation of Aboriginal and Torres Strait Islander Children from their Families*. This report proved shocking to many Australians, as it made public the effects of the history of colonial government policy which up until then had remained relatively unknown. It detailed the inter-generational trauma suffered by Aboriginal children forcibly removed from their families under legal jurisdiction, and represents important insights into the 'part-Aboriginal' experience. The children who were removed were not just those deemed neglected but significantly those who were light-skinned and deemed at risk if raised by Aboriginal parents.

The two reports were produced within the wider context of national reconciliation. The Council for Reconciliation, established in 1991, worked in both Indigenous and non-Indigenous communities encouraging activities to promote mutual understanding. Its focus was on the development of an understanding of Aboriginal and Torres Strait Islander societies, cultures and heritages, the shared ownership of Australian history, and a greater awareness of the historical causes of Indigenous disadvantage. As the then Governor-General William Deane stated in 1996, a year before the *Bringing Them Home* report was tabled:

> It should, I think, be apparent to all well-meaning people that true reconciliation between the Australian nation and its indigenous peoples is not achievable in the absence of acknowledgment by the nation of the wrongfulness of the past dispossession, oppression and degradation of the Aboriginal peoples. That is not to say that individual Australians who had no part in what was done in the past should feel or acknowledge personal guilt. It is simply to assert our identity as a nation and the basic fact that national shame, as well as national pride, can and should exist in relation to past acts and omissions, at least when done or made in the name of the community or with the authority of government...

> The present plight, in terms of health, employment, education, living conditions and self-esteem, of so many Aborigines must be acknowledged as largely flowing from what happened in the past. The dispossession, the destruction of hunting fields and the devastation of lives were all related. The new diseases, the alcohol and the new pressures of living were all introduced. True acknowledgment cannot stop short of recognition of the extent to which present disadvantage flows from past injustice and oppression...
>
> Theoretically, there could be national reconciliation without any redress at all of the dispossession and other wrongs sustained by the Aborigines. As a practical matter, however, it is apparent that recognition of the need for appropriate redress for present disadvantage flowing from past injustice and oppression is a pre-requisite of reconciliation. There is, I believe, widespread acceptance of such a need. (Deane 1996 pp. 19–21)

Deane's sentiments were amplified by the revelations of the *Bringing Them Home Report* and helped position reconciliation as a people's movement over this decade. The report generated collective public expression of sorrow in the May 28th 2000 Sydney Harbour Bridge walk where it was claimed that over 250,000 Australians walked together for reconciliation.

THE INTERVENTION AND 'SPECIALNESS'

By the time of the release in 2007 of another report, the Northern Territory's *'Ampe Akelyermemane Meke Mekarle, Little Children are Sacred* which investigated concerns over the security of children in remote communities, the spirit of symbolic reconciliation was all but extinguished in Liberal government circles, doused by the Howard government's disenchantment with the politics of Aboriginal self-determination. The government's adoption of 'practical reconciliation' was perceived by many as little more than a return to the rhetoric of assimilation, couched in terms of equality with all Australians (Hunter and Schwab 2003). The Northern Territory Emergency Response (NTER) brought down by the Howard government in 2007 in response to the report required the suspension of the *Racial Discrimination* Act, the introduction of the *NTER* Act (Cth) legislation and adjustments to a range of other impacting legislative areas for the Commonwealth to intervene. 'The Intervention', as it became commonly known, split public opinion and caused divisions within the Indigenous community, but it did not split along political party lines.

Under the Rudd Labor government which came to power in December 2007, the Intervention continued, creating enormous division of opinion about the blanket restriction of various human rights and freedoms enjoyed by other Australians as against the appalling conditions in many remote communities which also often fail to uphold basic human rights, especially for women and children (Langton 2007). While the people's movement for reconciliation reflected national desire to see improvements in relations between Indigenous and non-Indigenous Australians and in the conditions of Indigenous Australians, there was no parallel consensus in the Indigenous and mainstream communities or policy arenas to achieve this.

If governments swung between different policy positions in this period so did public opinion, especially where that opinion was manipulated through campaigns of fear. For example, two decades of relative tolerance for Aboriginal Land Rights, although restricted to grants in remote areas or Crown land and granted by governments since 1972, fell away following the Mabo judgement in 1992. The limited recognition of Aboriginal Land Rights was largely understood as a token of redress that recognised the injustices of dispossession. The Mabo case, however, challenged the legal precept of *Terra Nullius* and established that possession by the Crown had not necessarily extinguished the litigants' inherited 'native' title over their land. The subsequent *Native Title* Act established a legal instrument for Aboriginal land claims, causing anxiety and opposition as public opinion was polarised by misrepresentation of the extent of threat to non-Indigenous land ownership. The historical circumstances of dislocated and fragmented family lines became a double disadvantage for many Aboriginal people in this context (Birch 1995, p. 41).

What became known publicly during this period was the historical struggle for recognition that was continuously undermined by government policy aimed at eradicating, assimilating or 'managing' Indigenous people's affairs. As long as this 'specialness' was restricted to the symbolic arena, few Australians objected loudly. But in the practical and *realpolitick* arenas on the conservative right 'specialness' was more easily argued, not in terms of justice or reparation, but as Indigenous 'privilege'. Only if Aboriginal people fitted the criteria of disadvantage that applied to all Australians was their claim on government resources or special provision argued to be legitimate. The case made over the years by people such as Coombs (1976), Stanner (1979) and Tatz (1979) for Aboriginal people to determine the extent and manner in which they negotiated the values and practices of the wider society came under siege.

In 1996, in her maiden speech to the Australian parliament, Pauline Hanson (1996) expressed the essence of this sentiment:

> Present governments are encouraging separatism in Australia by providing opportunities, land, moneys and facilities available only to Aboriginals. Along with millions of Australians, I am fed up to the back teeth with the inequalities that are being promoted by the government and paid for by the taxpayer under the assumption that Aboriginals are the most disadvantaged people in Australia. I do not believe that the colour of one's skin determines whether you are disadvantaged.

These sentiments were not contested by the Liberal Howard government, but rather were upheld as evidence of freedom of speech. Furthermore, especially following the abolition of ATSIC in 2005, the discourse of practical reconciliation undermined the reconciliation process by relating reconciliation directly to policy implementation to overcome disadvantage. Arguments about Indigenous 'equality' with other Australians re-assumed the logic of assimilation. An environment of rhetoric concerning Indigenous issues promoted mutual obligation, a concept referring to Aboriginal people's moral responsibility to engage in certain practices or behaviours in return for provisions made by governments. Political support for self-determination, now seen to be a failed social experiment, also dissipated as the spheres in which Indigenous policy determination could advise and operate were narrowed. The demise of ATSIC in 2005 buried the last notions of Indigenous political representation until November 2009, when the Rudd Labor government provided funds for a new national Indigenous representative body — the National Congress of Australia's First Peoples. This is an advocacy body now charged with providing policy advice to the government.

Nevertheless, in this period, the significance of Aboriginal presence was to some extent accepted in Australian public life, albeit conditional and contingent. It was accepted within the 'sorry' discourse but contained where it was seen to exceed the parameters of this, especially where it threatened national narratives of origin. Aboriginal contemporary cultural expressions, art and dance in particular, entered the artistic and cultural life of the nation. The practice of acknowledging Aboriginal country and the original custodians of the land on which the modern Australian society now stands became accepted practice at public events. The importance of developing policies and services, including health and education, that took into account the cultural dispositions of Aboriginal people was largely accepted as a principle of public service provision, despite a lack of rigorous analysis of the convergence of these in practice.

MEETING AND CHALLENGING THE CRITERIA

Perhaps the most significant event in this period in terms of Aboriginal identity, however, was the revelations of the *Bringing Them Home* report. One outcome of the report was the establishment of Link-Up programs and Aboriginal Family History Units in libraries and archives to facilitate reconnections between lost family members. These units also assisted people whose families were affected by policies for part-Aboriginal people over previous generations, enabling them to verify their lineages and past movements. For many, however, records were not kept or had long disappeared. For many part-Aboriginal people there would either be no answers or a long road to find their way home. These journeys of discovery of lost family and Aboriginal heritage engaged the older questions of 'who is' and 'what counts' as evidence of Aboriginality. The re-emergence of 'lost' Aboriginal identities that sought to claim contemporary Aboriginal identities heightened the contests and struggles over what it meant to be an Aboriginal person in both the Aboriginal community and the wider Australian society.

In this chopping and changing political context, old debates about 'who is' Aboriginal and 'what counts' as the evidence of Aboriginality circulated as they always have around the ambiguity of those with Aboriginal and European ancestry. These Aboriginal Australians continued to be ambivalently located in the eyes of the White community, even when they could prove their descent, self-identify as Aboriginal and be recognised as such by the Aboriginal community according to the three criteria which form the current definition of Aboriginality in Australia.

The value of the three-part definition was that it enabled the recognition of many light-skinned, urban, 'non-traditional' Aboriginal people as Aboriginal, in the wake of the long assimilation campaign to extinguish these people as Aboriginal identities. This recognition was important in the wider Australian social context which often still perceives 'real Aborigines' to be only those unambiguously looking and living like the 'original' 'traditional' inhabitants. However, the three-part definition struggled in this period to resolve these old questions of 'who is' and 'what counts'. A major problem revolved around the difficulty of some people who identified strongly as Aboriginal but were unable to locate sufficient documentary evidence to prove descent. Was community recognition sufficient evidence to carry self-identification in such cases? If the requirement to meet the three criteria were relaxed in some cases, could a person who had proof of descent and self-identified but was not recognised in the community, claim Aboriginality? These issues not only arose but they proved divisive — and not just in the wider court of Australian public opinion but within Aboriginal communities as well (Gardiner-Garden 2002–03).

Gardiner-Garden (2002–03) noted the Tasmanian situation where the Tasmanian Aboriginal Centre, an Aboriginal-controlled organisation, denied access to their resources and services if evidence of descent could not be provided, even if families had long self-identified and recognised each other as Aboriginal. In this case, the findings of a *Final Report of the Community Consultation on Aboriginality in Tasmania* (1996) upheld that all three criteria be satisfied.

In other places during the 1990s, three judicial interpretations were made on the question of the weighting to be given to descent and self-community recognition criteria—*Attorney-General (Cth) v State of Queensland* (1990), *Gibbs v Capewell* (1995), and *Shaw v Wolf* (1998). Determinations in these cases reveal perhaps one consistency at least and that is 'that the emphasis to be placed on the different criteria in this definition will vary according to context' (Gardiner-Garden, 2002–03). As we have seen demonstrated, this is as it always has been. The very need to interpret definitions emerges in the face of the many different administrative regulations, which give force to a range of legislative instruments. Thus the first case in 1990 was able to overturn a previous judgement that an individual was not Aboriginal on the basis of descent alone and determine that for the purposes of the particular inquiry at hand descent was indeed sufficient. Justice French was prepared to conclude that 'the category of 'Aboriginal' could expand or contract according to the context and purpose…' (Gardiner-Garden 2002–03, p. 7).

In 1995 in the second case, also according to Gardiner-Garden, Justice Drummond argued

> that some degree of Aboriginal descent was essential, but that the extent to which the other criteria needed to be deployed might depend on the degree of descent. In the absence of other factors a small degree of Aboriginal descent was not sufficient whereas a substantial degree of Aboriginal descent may by itself be sufficient to establish Aboriginality for legal purposes. (2002–03, p.7)

In 1998, in the third case, Justice Merkel agreed with Justice Drummond and accepted Aboriginal descent as 'a social, rather than genetic construct' (Gardiner-Garden 2002–03, p. 7). As such, Aboriginal identity did not 'need to be proved 'according to any strict legal standard" (2002–03, p. 7).

These continuing cases indicate an ongoing difficulty in determining Aboriginality in the various contexts or purposes implied in discrete sets of legislation. Moreover, the Tasmanian report and the last two cases involved Aboriginal people questioning the identity of other Aboriginal people. Gardiner-Garden (2002–03) contended that

> [a]lthough there have been community disputes over identification in Tasmania, the three part definition has generally been found to help protect individuals from the tendency

among 'mainstream Australians' to consider 'real' indigenous people as people living somewhere else and others as manipulating the system. (2002–03, pp. 3–4)

THE RIGHT TO DEFINE AND CHOOSE ABORIGINAL IDENTITY

However, questions around the legitimacy of light-skinned urban Aboriginal people to claim an Aboriginal identity continue to be associated with the pursuit of perceived benefits. In a sign of the changing times, a recent Racial Discrimination case was brought by nine prominent 'fair-skinned' Aboriginal people against the journalist Andrew Bolt for comments in four of his columns, including one article entitled *White is the New Black*. Bolt was objecting to successful 'light-skinned' Aboriginal people 'choosing' to be Aboriginal when they could have chosen any one of a number of non-Aboriginal heritages. At the heart of his allegations was his logic that such 'choices' were motivated by, or at least conveniently embraced, because of an ensuing public or professional elevation that would not otherwise have been accorded and for private rewards that would not otherwise have been achieved on talent alone. The following excerpt from one of his articles demonstrates more than his logic. It demonstrates an ignorance of the effects of colonial history as Bolt pursued his ongoing quest to compile a growing list of allegedly fraudulent beneficiaries. This is part of only one of several articles in which he exposed and accused successful fair-skinned Aboriginal individuals.

> Meet, say, acclaimed St Kilda artist Bindi Cole who was raised by her English-Jewish mother yet calls herself 'Aboriginal but white'. She rarely saw her part-Aboriginal father, and could in truth join any one of several ethnic groups, but chose Aboriginal, insisting on a racial identity you could not guess from her features. She also chose, incidentally, the one identity open to her that has political and career clout.
>
> And how popular a choice that now is. Ask Annette Sax another artist and — as the very correct *The Age* newspaper

> described her — a 'white Koori'. Her father was Swiss, and her mother only part-Aboriginal. Racially, if these things mattered, she is more Caucasian than anything else. Culturally, she's more European. In looks, she's Swiss. But she, too, has chosen to call herself Aboriginal, which happily means she could be shortlisted for this year's Victorian Indigenous Art Award.

Bolt's tirade continued:

> Shall I go on? Not yet convinced that there is a whole new fashion in academia, the arts and professional activism to identify as Aboriginal?
>
> Not yet convinced that for many of these fair Aborigines, the choice to be Aboriginal can seem almost arbitrary and intensely political, given how many of their ancestors are in fact Caucasian?...Larissa Behrendt has also worked as a professional Aborigine ever since leaving Harvard Law School, despite looking almost as German as her father [author's deletion] name, and having been raised by her white mother. She chose to be Aboriginal, as well, a member of the 'Eualayai and Kammillaroi nations', and is now a senior professor at the University of Technology in Sydney's Indigenous House of Learning.
>
> She's won many positions and honours as an Aborigine, including the David Unaipon Award for Indigenous Writers, and is often interviewed demanding special rights for 'my people'. But which people are 'yours', exactly, Larissa? And isn't it bizarre to demand laws to give you more rights as a white Aborigine than your own white mum? (Bolt, 2009)

Such characterisation of Aboriginal Australians who are seen to be motivated to rort the national resources for their own purposes has its roots in an ignorance of the 'inside' Aboriginal experience of dispossession, colonisation and shifting policies. Instead, ongoing misrepresentations of Aboriginal people and experience which have failed to understand the many varied Aboriginal responses required to survive in such circumstances prevail in popular but misinformed understandings of those who 'choose' to identify primarily as Aboriginal. The success and visibility of Aboriginal people with dislocated heritages adds to questions of legitimacy and Elkin's (1951) old concept of 'intelligent parasitism' continues to underpin this interrogation of contemporary Aboriginal identity. The inference persists into the new millennium that to be a *bona fide* 'real Aborigine' an individual must be disadvantaged, black and/or remotely located.

Bolt's defence for this court case was mounted on freedom of speech but the litigants argued that at a more fundamental level the case was about who has the right to define Aboriginal identity. According to an interview given by one of the lawyers, the argument from the Aboriginal plaintiffs' positions was clear:

> We see this as a really important case. We see it as clarifying the issue of identity — who gets to say who is and who is not Aboriginal. Essentially, the articles by Bolt have challenged people's identity. He's basically arguing that the people he identified are white people pretending they're black so they can access public benefits…We're not seeking to make this a case about freedom of speech, because it's not. The issue is essentially about whether or not other people can define identity, and in particular Aboriginal identity, based on how you look. (Connor, 2011)

Public contests, such as these, point to what Gardiner-Garden (2002–03, p. 8) described as 'the issue of the adequacy of the system for determining Aboriginality', particularly given the increasing rate at which urban Aboriginal identification has been growing. He suggested the struggle emerged from the quest to define an 'all-purpose-serving identity', arguing that '[w]hoever would attempt to define ethnicity confronts the reality that an individual's ethnic identity is always to some degree fluid, multiple, differing in degrees, and constructed' (2002–03, p. 16). The recent public debates over Aboriginal identity engaged with by Aboriginal and non-

Aboriginal commentators are further evidence of the continuing struggle over questions of 'who is' Aboriginal and 'what counts' as the evidence of Aboriginality or identity.

CHAPTER 7
DISCOVERING AND RECONSTRUCTING ABORIGINAL IDENTITY

> The explication of Aboriginal identity requires a theoretical model capable of framing an analysis of ideology within the context of local history and experience.
>
> (Schwab 1991, p. 5)

The 1990s continued to disclose examples of the different strands of identity discourse and of approaches to research, with deepened attention to Aboriginal identity as a social and political construct. The shifts in the debates and conversations saw the emergence of a pan-Aboriginal identity.

In the early 1990s, anthropologist Myrna Tonkinson (1990) published a cogent overview of the struggle surrounding Aboriginal identity. Tonkinson discussed the different investments and outcomes of various attempts to define and classify Aboriginal Australians. Both Aboriginal traditional ways of naming and identifying relatedness to others, as well as the colonial nominations and classifications, were described as significant to the contemporary Aboriginal struggle to maintain a distinct but self-determined identity within the nation-state. In discussing contemporary Aboriginal conceptualisations of identity, Tonkinson made an important distinction between personal and cultural identities formed in the context of a particular group's traditional belief and practice, as distinct from the pan-Aboriginality that supports a collective identity for political purposes. She asserted that the formation of pan-Aboriginality

> build[s] upon the notion of an Aboriginal ethnicity originally imposed upon them. Aboriginality is a tool of contemporary political struggle and is viewed by its proponents as a positive force. Yet this identity was in the past defined

> negatively, institutionalized, and legally codified and enforced by the dominant European society. (1990, p. 192)

Tonkinson suggested that continuities with pre-colonial Aboriginal understandings of inter- and intra-group relations are reflected in the ways that regional, language and smaller kinship-based group memberships are still significant — and valued as a basis for ongoing personal and cultural Aboriginal identity and for identity recovery. Aboriginal groups continue to name and claim distinctiveness in their relatedness to other Aboriginal groups across the country, even where settlement has overseen the destruction of a group's language and culture through dispossession. And Aboriginal individuals, wherever they now live and whatever their history, continue to claim their ongoing affiliation to groups of origin.

Tonkinson contended that a language group or geographically based identity formation did not preclude distinct Aboriginal groups from also recognising a shared collective Aboriginal identity that is distinct from that of all other Australians. She viewed Aboriginal Australians' assertion of a collective identity as a critical response to the shared history of colonisation and the struggle to reclaim inherent rights to land and political rights to self-determination. Together, the common aspects of diverse cultural traditions and the shared experience of colonisation forge this idea of a 'pan-Aboriginality' necessary for distinctiveness and political solidarity at the national level, and for renewal at local levels. Her analysis posited that principles of inclusivity on broader common criteria underpinned this newer conceptualisation of identity.

Tonkinson asserted that Aboriginal people were now involved in a process of identity reassertion that engaged meanings and descriptors derived from the shared history (of traditional cultural patterns and political experiences of colonisation), as well as those meanings and descriptors attached to more specific and local group affiliations, and that 'for many Aborigines both identities are equally important; for some one or the other takes precedence' (1990, p. 193). Tonkinson saw the basis for pan-Aboriginality as a consequence of both national and global forces:

> The identification of common cultural themes and the maintenance of traditions — or their revival (and invention) where they are moribund or absent — are all part of the process. Changes within Australian society and global changes in the position of Indigenous peoples have contributed to

a modern notion of pan Aboriginal identity, which is being institutionalized in political movements, evocative symbols, and personal action. (1990, p. 193)

IDENTITY TENSIONS

In its acknowledgement of global influences affecting Indigenous people worldwide, Tonkinson's work explored the shifting discursive field that produces identities towards the end of the twentieth century. The tensions surrounding the construction of a pan-Aboriginal identity identified in Tonkinson's analysis were clearly discerned in three studies undertaken at the beginning of the 1990s by Schwab (1991), Maxley (1991) and Davis (1991).

Anthropologist Robert Schwab's study, 'The "Blackfella way": Ideology and practice in an urban Aboriginal community', argues for the ethnographical approach to explore Aboriginal identity formations (see Eckermann 1973, 1977a). In his view, 'the explanatory power of the anthropological approach lies in its potential for anchoring the subjective arenas of daily life to the objective realities which structure and are structured by them' (1991, p. 2). Schwab suggested research should focus on 'macroscopic concepts such as Aboriginal identity or Aboriginality' and should be 'grounded in particularistic case studies which focus on single communities' (1991, p. 3). It is at the local level where in-depth analysis can 'examine the tension between ideas, dispositions and social practice within the context of the objective condition of daily life' (1991, p. 4). Schwab also argued that there is an idealised system through which Aboriginal people recognise each other; this is described as 'the Blackfella Way' (1991, p. 4). He claimed Aboriginal people

> are actors in the ongoing construction of their past and present, continually negotiating, reinterpreting and recreating their sense of identity and place within both the Aboriginal and the dominant European communities. (1991, p. 4)

Schwab contended that 'Aboriginality cannot be separated from the political context, social practice or local history. But equally important… Aboriginality cannot be understood apart from the objective conditions of everyday life' (1991, p. 27). He reviewed research into Aboriginal identity and described it as 'vague and impressionistic, supported by inadequate ethnographic detail without grounding in social theory' (1991,

p. 3), and prescribed an approach to identity analysis that merges theory and practice at a 'local history and experience' level (1991, p. 5).

Schwab explored others' attempts to describe Aboriginality, agreeing with Thiele (1984) that 'issues of Aboriginal identity and Aboriginality are precisely the types of notions which are easily asserted but much more difficult to explain' (1991, p. 3) but also agreeing with Langton (1981) that Aboriginality is a concept that non-Aboriginal people are 'unwilling — and perhaps ultimately unable — to understand' (Langton quoted in Schwab 1991, p. 27). He is critical of Coombs, Brandl and Snowdon's (1983) notion of Aboriginality, which they represented as a

> socio-cultural artefact, to be respected and admired but not questioned or examined too closely. Aboriginality…is a coherent system, basic to all Aboriginal people, with an absence of internal tension, contradiction or conflict. (Schwab 1991, pp. 18–19)

In another anthropological study that focused on pan-Aboriginality, Julian Maxley (1991) considered the cultural values attached to a reconstructed common pan-Aboriginal identity. Maxley asserted there are challenges for Aboriginal people in modern Australian society to define their own identity. He included some imperatives in meeting this challenge. He stated, for example, that any definition of Aboriginal identity 'has to have meaning in terms of maintaining and rebuilding a sense of positive group identity that will be significant to their own communities'; 'must serve as a tool to change or challenge non-Aboriginal negative views of Aboriginal culture and identity' (1991, p. 4) and that urban Aboriginal identity must be as 'Aboriginal Australians' (1991, p. 6). He also saw it as important that Aboriginal people circulate positive aspects of Aboriginal culture and the uniqueness of Aboriginal culture to the wider Australian public.

Following Berndt and Berndt (1988), Maxley embraced the notion of an Aboriginal ethos which he described as a 'particular framework of ideas which could be defined as Aboriginal' (1991, p. 5) and suggested that 'the challenge for Aboriginal people is to articulate the ethos…and construct projects that deal with their needs from an Aboriginal perspective' (1991, p. 5). According to Maxley, this view supported Berndt and Berndt's (1988) contention that Aboriginal descent does not mean a person is 'automatically Aboriginal' (Maxley 1991, p. 5), but that abiding by a persisting and shared Aboriginal ethos would demonstrate Aboriginality.

Maxley reviewed literature that suggested that a presence of Aboriginal values and ethos is discernible in urban and rural communities long disconnected from traditional practice (e.g. Stanner 1979; Langton 1981; Berndt & Berndt 1988). He identified the contest around the legitimacy of the pan-Aboriginal identity acknowledging 'there has been a debate between anthropologists as to whether there is (a) a pan-Aboriginal identity, and (b) whether rural and urban Aboriginal people can maintain any kind of Aboriginal identity' (1991, p. 225).

Maxley's study accepted the dual conditions of pan-Aboriginal membership signalled by Tonkinson (1990) to be the common cultural traditions and the common experience of colonisation. But it also focused on common cultural heritage as a legitimate basis for constructing and demonstrating Aboriginality. For Maxley, this was imperative. Although Maxley addressed some of the negative aspects of non-Aboriginal impositions of identity, he argued that Aboriginal people must 'prove to non-Aboriginal people that they have an Aboriginal identity' (1991, p. 25). He acknowledged diversity but emphasised that 'the critical factors regarding Aboriginal identity are that Aboriginal values and lifestyles are important in each type of Aboriginal community' (1991, p. 30). In regard to Aboriginal values and lifestyle he cited the National Aboriginal Education Committee (1986, p. 10), concurring with its view about shared community experience:

> In the main, Aboriginal society is structured around the community…In a general sense, Aboriginal society tends not to be materialistic or competitive, rather it practices sharing of resources and co-operation. (Maxley 1991, p. 31)

Edward Davis in his doctoral study, 'Ethnicity and diversity: Politics and the Aboriginal community' explored the relations between identity and political behaviour. Davis (1991) claimed that pan-Aboriginality was understood as an ethnicity that provided the necessary unity to interact effectively with governments. However, Davis supported it also for its emotional benefits, citing Ted Fields, an Aboriginal contributor to Colin Tatz and Keith McConnochie's edited volume, *Black viewpoints: the Aboriginal experience* (1975). Fields stated that he had '…no living functional group with which to identify…There is nothing in Aboriginal society with which to identify or with which to realise security' (Fields quoted in Davis 1991, p. 33). Davis argued that an ethnic identity would offer the possibility for 'a political community and a psychological shelter within which the individual and the group may find a place' (1991, p. 34). Davis stressed that '[i]n claiming Aboriginal identity or the possession of Aboriginality the individual is placing himself or herself within an ethnic collective' (1991, p. 34). For Davis,

> [w]hen the individual is denied a collective identity there is a separation from an authentic unity which could provide a meaningful existence. The individual is socially and psychologically incomplete and politically irrelevant when there is no sense of belonging. (1991, p. 33)

Davis's study was concerned with 'the diversity that conflicts with notions of Aboriginal nationalism' (1991, p. 8). He focused on three quite different Aboriginal communities within western New South Wales between 1984 and 1990, 'Wilcannia: An Aboriginal town', 'Menindee: An integrated town' and '...An urban setting: Broken Hill' (p. v). He was particularly interested in differences which produce 'conflict, specifically the conflict engendered by various dimensions of Aboriginal politics, which are themselves shaped by various constructions of identity' (1991, p. 6). In this study, the effects of the fracturing caused by colonial policies begin to be considered as a factor in factional politics. Davis's research drew attention to the differences within and not just between communities and asserted that no Aboriginal community was homogenous or harmonious (Davis 1991, p. 3) and that within each community there were many factions and divisions.

Davis recognised the tension between the concept of commonality attached to collective identity and individual perceptions, interpretations and expressions of it. However, he struggled to articulate the meaning of this tension in analytical terms. In describing their Aboriginality, some of Davis's informants commented that for them Aboriginality was the colour of their skin; some made reference to the fact that they were black. Others, Davis noted, made collective claims such as, it is 'the way we as Aborigines think, live and operate' (1991, p. 36). He cited Eckermann's 1977 study to make a point that Aboriginality is about foregrounding aspects of a common identity as distinct from all non-Aboriginal people (1991, p. 37). He concurred with Thiele's view that, 'If Aboriginality is what Aborigines do and think there must be many different and contradictory kinds of Aboriginality' (Thiele 1982, p. 20). Davis viewed Aboriginality as a testament to biological as opposed to cultural inheritance but drew distinctions between practising traditional Aboriginal people and those who, generally speaking, were urban 'non-practising' yet still identifying as Aboriginal.

Davis deployed a familiar strand in the research and popular discourse and asserted that some people identify for material gain, and where there were no obvious physical indicators of Aboriginality they could choose also not to be Aboriginal. This apparent identity ambivalence was represented as the cause of conflict within communities (1991, p. 31). However, the significance of traditional allegiances (or enmities) identified by Tonkinson (1990) are also absent from Davis's discussion about factionalism. Davis also fails to consider the effect of the historical arbitrary creation of mission communities containing groups traditionally in conflict which would have helped explicate identity politics.

The paradox that Davis struggled to articulate was that the diversity of experience within the 'common' colonial experience produces multiple descriptions and possible meanings of Aboriginality that become sites of Aboriginal contest and struggle. The field of possibilities becomes the subject of contested politics that has a tendency to fracture collective unity and reduce the very restorative inclusiveness that pan-Aboriginality seeks to engender. However, this study does help to explicate tensions and conflict within communities in relation to the effects of colonial experience for identity and political relations. And Davis does highlight the tensions between collective and personal identities and the tensions produced in the quest for both political and emotional security.

'INSIDE VIEWS'

In the 1990s and early 2000s, increasing numbers of identity studies were undertaken by Aboriginal people. Many of these attempted to represent the 'inside view' experienced in journeys of re-discovery of Aboriginal identity (e.g. Noble 1996; Boladeras 2002; Blackmore 2007; Bond 2007). Some place more emphasis on the constructed nature of Aboriginal identities, including ways of publicly and privately expressing Aboriginal identity in changing urban or local contexts (Lambert-Pennington 2005; Greenop 2009a; Bolt 2010). Together these studies highlight the precarious position of urban, light-skinned, 'dual-heritage' and/or newly indentifying Aboriginal people, and how they are positioned by discursive practices that continue to regulate and police Aboriginal identities as either Aboriginal or not Aboriginal. The studies provide evidence of the construction and production of Aboriginal identities as conditioned in historically produced spaces (D'Cruz 2001).

Fiona Noble's masters thesis, 'Who do we think we are: People who are learning about their Aboriginality', explored the 'importance and meaning of Aboriginality to people who have lived most of their lives as 'whites' (1996, p. 18). She noted that Aboriginality has been both constructed and deconstructed regularly by non-Indigenous people, impacting on the ways in which Indigenous peoples come to understand their identity:

> For those Indigenous people who are certain of their identities, the deluge of constructions and categories by non-Indigenous society do not threaten that which they know, despite the many negative ramifications that have ensued. Sometimes, for people who are not certain of their backgrounds and identities, the boundaries of cultural or ethnic identity are indistinct. (1996, p. i)

Methodologically, Noble's study looked beyond the dominant discourses of Aboriginal identity to explore alternative stories of those who have been dislocated from their heritage in previous generations. Her methodology included qualitative interviews with participants mostly known to her. This enabled her to make use of what she described as an ' insider position' throughout the research via the opportunity provided to 'access social cues and intended meaning' (1996, p. 9). The study was described by Noble as 'a personal journey', one in which she identifies with her participants in relation to discovering Aboriginality later in life (1996, p. 9). The data generated through her method gives insight into the complexities of the Aboriginal identity question and highlights the minutiae, which have largely been overlooked by many researchers.

The participants in Noble's study described a range of experiences in regard to Aboriginality and discussed the different ways they constructed their Aboriginality, highlighting the difficulties faced in not fitting neatly into the categories of Indigenous/non-Indigenous, black/white, oppressed/oppressor (1996, p. 91). Aboriginal identity issues present particular difficulties when an individual's history does not include an acceptable or recognisable narrative that legitimises a claim to share the common cultural tradition or the common historical experience. These narratives commonly form around mission or reserve experience, urban community experience, or the experience of removal from kin in current or previous generations.

For Aboriginal people who have been intergenerationally disconnected from these shared experiences, the discovery of hidden histories may or may not uncover the necessary detail to construct a similar personal narrative. Noble reported participants' experiences as encompassing the

> search for their genealogies in front of the mirror, how they often become focused on questioning their identities, sometimes chastising themselves for not living up to the expectations that they and others have of Aboriginality. Some have described the process as painful', as they uncovered their family histories, and experienced disbelief and conflict from both people close to them and members of the communities. (Noble 1996, p. 91)

Western Australian author Sally Morgan's story of discovery, *My Place* (1987), featured significantly in Noble's thesis and had been read by most of her participants. The importance of Morgan's book for both participants and the study was that it was the first publication addressing issues of identity for people who become aware of their Aboriginal heritage later in life (1996, p. 30). Morgan's book became what Noble described as a 'political trigger' (1996, p. 30), raising much public debate about Aboriginal identity. Noble speculated that the number of people with similar histories of disconnection from the Aboriginal community had been seriously under-estimated (1996, p. 91). She also contended that the population of people who became aware of Aboriginal heritage later in life were not free to speak of their predicament for fear of being challenged by both Indigenous and non-Indigenous detractors.

Noble's study contributes valuable data to discussions around the diversity of Aboriginal historical experience and Aboriginal identity and recovery. One aspect she could have explored in more detail was the question as to why the participants wanted to claim an Aboriginal identity. So while her study situated everyday experiences and personal stories to complicate understandings of Aboriginal identity recovery, it fell short of situating these narratives in relation to the critical meta-narratives that inform the discursive possibilities for identity construction.

During the 1990s there was an increase in Indigenous people challenging old assumptions about what it meant to be Indigenous and evidencing a variety of experiences. Cheryl Dorothy Moodai Robinson's Masters thesis, 'The effects of colonisation, cultural and psychological on my family', is an example of an account of a personal journey where the discourse of healing emerges as a set of statements surrounding the practices and effects of past policy in the Reconciliation era. It is a discourse that seeks to make sense of, or come to terms with the tragic effects of colonisation through recourse to spirituality. Moodai Robinson discovered her Aboriginal lineage when she was thirty years old. She reveals her frustration about her inability to source information from an older relative and begins her own journey to 'reunite' her family connections, 'reconnect' with her 'rightful identity' and learn about her ' culture' (1997, p. 10). For Moodai Robinson the research conducted to reassemble her family history was her source of healing (1997, p. 110) which, she stated, for her became a never-ending journey:

> For me the theory of indigenous healing is the process of constructing, working and being. The act of participating in the creating is the healing aspect in Aboriginal culture. (1997, p. 15)

Moodai Robinson's research, similarly to Noble's, resonates with the frustration and conflict felt by newly emerging Aboriginal identities as they seek to claim Aboriginality both privately and publicly. She openly discussed the disunity in her own family in regard to their Aboriginal heritage: 'It seems I have become too black for white in my father's eyes, and too white for black in the eyes of some Koori people' (1997, p. 90). Accusations of claiming Aboriginal heritage for economic gain were also levelled at Robinson. In response, she asserted that her identity was ' in' her and that she was 'born of it' and 'it' ran through her veins (1997, p. 90). She claimed that the acceptance and acknowledgement of one's Aboriginality strengthens identity and referred to her 'genetic memory' (1997, p. 97). This essentialist notion of an innate Aboriginality waiting to be acknowledged continues today (e.g. Clark 2008; Phillips 2009).

The theme of the complexities of Aboriginal identity was also highlighted in Jean Boladeras' Masters thesis (2002), 'It's easy to be black if you're black: issues of Aboriginality for fair-complexioned Nyungar[7] people'. Boladeras explored issues for Aboriginal people when they claim an Aboriginal identity and are fair-skinned. When discussing her own proof of

---

7   Nyungar, also spelt Noongar, or Nyoongah, refers to Aboriginal people from the south-west corner of Western Australia.

Aboriginality, Boladeras stated she had 'a sheaf of official documents' that 'prove' her ancestry as Aboriginal (2002, p. 33); however, she also noted that this 'proof' can be irrelevant, with importance being placed on family and acknowledgment by others as 'crucial to acceptance' (p. 33).

Like Moodai Robinson, Boladeras highlighted the complicated lines of tension between personal and community recognition of Aboriginality by identifying the different responses within her family to the discovery of Aboriginal lineage. The notion of 'passing' was explored in Boladeras' work when discussing people who have the ability to pass as non-Aboriginal. She noted that Nyungars readily accept fair-skinned Aboriginal people 'when they are properly identified' (2002, p. 59), whereas those who deny their Aboriginal heritage will typically be resented (p. 59).

Striving to be 'seen' as Aboriginal was a concern for the participants in Boladeras' study who expressed unease at either not 'looking' Aboriginal or lacking knowledge which would identify them as Aboriginal (2002, pp. 118–53). Essentialist notions of Aboriginality as innate and waiting to be brought to light were also indicated. For example,

> I had lived as a white man all my life, and had been thoroughly re-inforced in that identity...I sat down and read those records as a white man. I stood up half-an-hour later as a black man. There was no doubt. (2002, p. 135)

The need to position a 'newly-emerging' identity beyond doubt by appealing to some sort of embodied 'genetic memory', as Moodai Robinson (1997, p. 97) put it, or by asserting a transformation that categorically rejects the former white identity by a commitment not to return to it, reflects the complex political, cultural and emotional investments involved in the process and experience of reclaiming 'lost' identities.

RECONNECTING

Whether these rationales for action reflect an anxiety about the consequences of being perceived to be 'choosing' to be Aboriginal or whether they are responses to the historical contingencies that constructed and positioned ambiguous Aboriginal identities, these positions are able to be understood in the light of the discursive history unfolded in these chapters. Not only do the discursively inscribed politics of Aboriginal identity demand that a commitment to Aboriginality involves a rejection of the assimilating 'white' ethos (see Tatz 1979), but, on a personal level, the emotion of the journey of discovery often engages the metaphor of going home, of return. This return involves a process of turning back and reconnecting to other meanings with significance for 'becoming' and 'being' recognised as Aboriginal. For some this reconnection is negotiated as an extended sense of self that does not require the erasure of existing identities and carries the risk of ambiguity and non-recognition in the public domain. However, the spectrum of individual responses is able to be understood as a range of discursive acts of agency based on the contemporary conditions of possibility.

Ernie Blackmore's doctoral thesis, 'Speakin' out Blak: An examination of finding an "urban" Indigenous "voice" through contemporary Australian theatre' (2007), engaged with the importance of access to cultural knowledge in the process of reconstructing Aboriginal identities. Blackmore explored identity through fictional drama by analysing characters from two of his plays. Despite the use of the third person, Blackmore's thesis blurs the boundaries between reality and fiction, drawing attention to identity as a formation informed in part by fictional texts:

> The overall implications surrounding the identity crisis of the main characters in the play are comparable to that of contemporary Australians living with a secret past that may include their own indigeneity. However, and more importantly, this thesis will explore the 'difficult' although silent spiritual connectedness or attraction experienced by both the younger people to Richard (their father) and the different ways in which the characters in the play act and react to their journey of discovery. The thesis will draw connections between this journey to the reality of contemporary urbanised Indigenous Australians who are struggling to maintain the truth of their own identities and the spirituality of their 'voice' at a time of great silencing. (2007, p. 15)

Blackmore also shared personal insights into the process of identity recovery. As he sought ways to interact with Aboriginal people and access cultural knowledge and activities, his sense of frustration came from the limited avenues to source such knowledge and activities, and the unrelenting policing of Aboriginal identity. He captured this succinctly in the following observation: 'I become very jealous of my identity and get frustrated because I can't get enough or I can't do enough' (2007, p. 301).

Blackmore's use of drama to explore the situatedness of everyday identity struggles for Aboriginal people allowed him to recreate lived experience and to view that, and make sense of it, through the lens of distance from it. His invocation of the 'voice' as a metaphor for expressing Aboriginality opens up possibilities for readers of his plays to understand identity struggles through empathy or relatedness with his characters. The approach simultaneously fictionalises and theorises issues surrounding urban Aboriginality.

Urban Aboriginality and issues related to 'dual heritage' continue to be discussed by Indigenous people offering personal experiences that provide multiple accounts of 'being' Indigenous in Australia. These personal accounts also highlight the conflicting and complex nature of identity politics. Chelsea Bond's doctoral thesis, 'When you're black, they look at you harder: Narrating Aboriginality within public health', argued that epidemiological and health behaviourist applications of identity often produce particular Aboriginalities that convey illness, disease and dysfunction as inherently Aboriginal conditions (2007, p. iv). Bond's argument was that the 'identity narratives of Aboriginality produced within public health contrast significantly against those produced by Aboriginal people' (2007, p. 2). Her interest in the topic was, as she claimed, 'wholly personal' (2007, p. 2) and was initiated by her personal experiences as a practitioner working in Indigenous health,

> I feel compelled to relay my own story of Aboriginal identity, specifically in relation to how it has influenced this research agenda, before I seek to justify it within an academic context. Telling my own story of identity, for me, seems appropriate — it fits — it is the beginning of my learning and reflection upon Aboriginal identity and cannot be separated out from the academic arguments of identity that I position myself within. (2007, p. 3)

Bond discussed at some length her own experiences of identity positioning and what insights her dual Aboriginal-white heritage brought to her role as a researcher:

> As an Aboriginal person, I know the experience of living a policed identity, and for me, it has become a reality of life as someone tarred with the brush of 'part-Aborigine', 'half-caste', 'urban Aboriginal', 'settled Aboriginal', and the many

other labels constructed to challenge the legitimacy of our identification as Aboriginal Australians. (2007, p. 4)

Bond's thesis reveals the anxiety that 'dual heritage' and relatively 'advantaged' Aboriginal people feel as they participate in Australian social institutions such as schools, or negotiate Aboriginal workplaces in the interest of Aboriginal clients or services. For Bond, 'olive' skin is an insufficient physical marker to confirm or authenticate her Aboriginal identity. But, recounting her school experience, her adolescent behaviour and lack of achievement *were* attributed to her Aboriginality. Upon entering a career in Indigenous public health, she was warned by her father of accusations she would confront about 'jumping on the gravy train' (2007, p. 14).

For Bond, the lack of a personal narrative of struggle and tragedy led to feelings of being a 'fake or impostor' (2007, p. 15) She described the policing of Aboriginal identity by other Aboriginal people such as accusations of being a 'coconut', and close scrutiny of aspects of 'common' cultural knowledge (2007, p. 15). Bond also confessed to participating in this process by applying such scrutiny in her judgments of others (2007, p. 18). Bond's experiences generated a desire for an Aboriginal identity authenticated through association and recognition:

> as a bearer of traditional cultural knowledge…surrounded by my own big mob rather than being adopted into others, receiving the shared nod from a coloured stranger that is directed toward my husband instead of me, having a deep spiritual affinity with my traditional country, and being reared in an identifiable Aboriginal community instead of the anonymous white suburb I grew up in. (2007, p. 16)

Both the personal experience and its analysis in her work produced a reassessment of the need to fill what she described as the 'pathetic imaginative space' (2007, p. 17). The result was to accord less legitimacy to the public expectations of Aboriginality, including the use of it as an instrument of social and identity regulation. Posing the question 'what then does it *mean* to be Aboriginal?', Bond claimed she did not know anyone who could answer the question,

> …because there simply is no one answer. And, I'm in fact a little wary of anyone, black or white who purports to be able to answer that definitively and absolutely. (2007, p. 19)

Referring to the aims of her study Bond stated that her 'desires to remedy the identity dilemmas and quandaries' (2007, p. 169) were both naive and not achieved:

> Admittedly, in reflecting back upon the initial objectives of the study which underpinned the aim of exploring and promoting urban Aboriginal identity from an emic perspective, they were developed through an idealistic imagination which would somehow magically salvage 'Aboriginality'. From whom, or what it was to be salvaged, I'm not entirely sure. (2007, p. 169)

COMMUNITY FORMATIONS OF IDENTITY

A different analysis of the meanings of urban Aboriginal identity emerged in Amanda Lambert-Pennington's, doctoral thesis 'Being in Australia, belonging to the land: The cultural politics of urban Aboriginal identity'. She examined the ways and conditions under which urban Aboriginal people from the La Perouse community in Sydney defended their identity when faced with suggestions of inauthenticity, drawing attention to the cultural domains that were created in the process. Focusing on the historical construction of Aboriginal identity, Lambert-Pennington traced evolving conceptualisations of Aboriginality from early colonial, assimilation and self-determination eras. She found that in this community, Aboriginal identity was an exclusive identity defined in its difference from all other cultural identities regardless of the presence of other cultural heritage. From those that were interviewed, a strong sense of Aboriginal identity was evident, as '…the all-or-nothing quality of being "black, but not white" requires that Kooris forge a common indigeneity that connects them with other Aboriginal people' (2005, p. 129).

A political stance vis-à-vis the nation-state, coupled with a strategic essentialism based on cultural understandings, is understood as a loyalty to identifying as Aboriginal, as opposed to having anything in common with what is perceived as white. Any non-Aboriginal heritage becomes inconsequential to cultural acceptance and therefore 'forgotten' (2005, p. 129). Lambert-Pennington claimed her research showed that '[l]inks to whiteness, whether ancestral, behavioural or geographic, are liabilities in constructions of a resolute Indigenous identity' (2005, p. 134). Under the circumstances of this particular urban community where many Aboriginal people are very fair-skinned, requests for proof of Aboriginality were seen to challenge Aboriginal identity. In order to avoid the targeting of fair-skinned football players, the La Perouse football club requested all players to confirm their Aboriginality as standard practice to overcome the potential for divisiveness within the community.

While Lambert-Pennington based her research in a community whose history dates from the early 1880s, Kelly Greenop undertook two studies of Aboriginal identity in relation to attachment to a non-traditional urban place (2009a) and the use of housing (2009b) in a post-war urban community in south-east Queensland that attracted the voluntary migration of Aboriginal peoples from a number of different areas. Greenop's studies explored public and private expressions of re-located Aboriginal identity practices, and how they imposed and preserved Aboriginal memories and new stories of place on a suburban landscape shared with others. These practices and stories provided insights into the way that some Aboriginal people inhabit, respond to and live in the non-Aboriginal world, while remaining continuous with the older, traditionally derived practices of relating in social spaces. What looks outwardly like any Australian suburb is imbued with a range of Aboriginal histories and meanings. Greenop's studies focused on the aspects of continuity as expressions of dynamic and changing Aboriginal identities.

Greenop argued that although Aboriginal identity is familiarly understood in its link to 'tradition countries alone' (2009a, p. 25), her research clearly demonstrated that there were other Aboriginal people who had formed attachments to urban locations which informed a significant part of their identity (2009a, pp. 25–6). She noted that in some instances Aboriginal people now moved to such locations to 'attain an Indigenous identity' (2009a, p. 13), and remarked on the ways Aboriginal people marked Aboriginality in urban landscapes, for example, through the decoration of their homes. External significations ranged from subtle to overt, from garden ornaments to red, black and yellow stickers and the display of either or both Aboriginal and Torres Strait Islander flags. Internally, Aboriginality was displayed through similar items, but also included art works and artefacts (2009a, pp. 6–10). Greenop noted the differing opinions among Aboriginal people in reference to the use of cultural artefacts:

> Some people commented that while certain people heavily decorated their housing now, in the past they went 'drinking with their white mates' and 'didn't identify' as Aboriginal, and such a display is seen as making up for lost ground, or trying too hard to be Aboriginal. Others reject this and see displays as evidence of pride in culture and family, with no one way of being Aboriginal, and reject notions of trying too hard or being seen a 'big noters'. (2009a, p. 10)

Many homes displayed Aboriginal identity through artistic styles associated with desert style dot painting or the x-ray style painting of Arnhem Land. Greenop commented that these styles were not necessarily reflective of the tenant's cultural origins; however, may represent a 'sense of solidarity and unity, a pan-Aboriginality on display, and a desire to demonstrate something which is well known to be Aboriginal' (2009a, p. 11). The extent to which tenants decorated their homes depended on several variants stated by them, including the occupant's history of identifying as Aboriginal (2009a, p. 12).

In the same way Greenop was interested in aspects of continuity as expressions of dynamic and changing Aboriginal identities, Reuben Bolt's doctoral thesis (2010), 'Urban Aboriginal identity construction in Australia: An Aboriginal perspective utilising multi-method qualitative analysis', also invoked community memory and cultural knowledge as processes in the formation of identity. Bolt's study included interviews with mixed-descent Aboriginal people from a town on the South Coast of New South Wales. His participants were known to him, allowing him an 'insider's perspective' (2010, p. xii). His familiarity with respondents demonstrated to them, according to Bolt, that he had 'lived the Aboriginal experience' (2010, p. 193) and was therefore to be trusted with personal information. Bolt used a narrative approach, arguing that 'human identity construction is explicably tied to the *narrative* that individuals author about themselves' (2010, p. 52) as they construct their identities. He asserted that for his participants, 'narrative is the only means of "telling" identity' (2010, p. 52).

Bolt's research identified a number of themes in relation to Aboriginal worldviews. These included Aboriginal identity in the context of a broader Aboriginal collective, and the impact of Aboriginal marginalisation in an Australian colonial context with particular reference to the impact on their sense of self (2010, p. 190). Participants in Bolt's study drew on both positive and negative sources in constructing their identity. In particular, they drew on positive discourses of Aboriginal identity as a means of counteracting negativity (2010, p. 190).

Aboriginal identity, for many of Bolt's participants, is linked to both biology and socialisation within an Aboriginal community. Participants expressed a sense of spirituality that they insisted began at birth and Bolt noted how this spirituality was 'difficult to explain' (2010, p. 180). Drawing on the experiences of two participants who did not grow up within an Aboriginal community yet identified as Aboriginal, Bolt claimed these as evidence that,

> one can learn an Aboriginal identity later in life, showing that the construction of Aboriginal identity does not require a prerequisite process of continual socialisation in an Aboriginal community over the human life course. (2010, p. 180)

On the issue of mixed-descent Aboriginal people identifying exclusively as Aboriginal, Bolt followed Cowlishaw (2004) to explain this in terms of a 'racial loyalty' that is an important strategy to preserve Aboriginal identity (2010, p. 177). However, as Bolt noted, not all mixed-descent Aboriginal people practice 'racial loyalty' by choosing not to deny other aspects of their heritage (e.g. Paradies 2006). Bolt and Lambert-Pennington both offer insights into the ongoing constructions and maintenance of Aboriginal identities enabled by membership of the Aboriginal community through subscription to its ongoing production of cultures and values and ethos.

CHAPTER 8
BEYOND THE DISCOURSE

> [A] specific identity cannot be definitively pinned down in advance of the discourse in which it finds itself effected.
> (D'Cruz 2001, p. 14)

The conversations in the literature explored in the previous chapters reveal the difficulties and challenges faced by those light-skinned or dislocated Aboriginal people without a community history narrative. In particular, those who discover a submerged Aboriginal connection in their family history, and who wish to explore it and re-establish membership of the Aboriginal collective, find themselves traversing a complex terrain. These difficulties are also noted in the ongoing legal interpretations about who is Aboriginal and what constitutes the criteria of the three-part definition.

PERSONAL NARRATIVES OF IDENTITY

Some Indigenous voices in recent years have asserted the meanings of Aboriginal identity through the personal and descriptive narrative (e.g. Behrendt 1994; Gilbert 1995; Holland 1996; Droste 2000; Fredericks 2004). The personalised accounts of such authors have emphasised Aboriginal identity as the persistence of Aboriginal ways and values and resistance to continuing colonialism. Scholar Stephanie Gilbert (1995), for example, drew attention to a continuing Aboriginal victimhood that binds all Aboriginal people, along with Indigenous health worker Marjorie Droste (2000) who condemned the ignorance of 'white' history. Scholar Bronwyn Fredericks (2004) outlined the difficulties of being an urban Aboriginal person who does not fit the physical and social stereotype of the 'real' or 'authentic Aborigine'. Fredericks drew attention to the diversity of Aboriginal experience wrought by colonial history and the dynamics of continuously adapting Aboriginal cultures. Scholar Larissa Behrendt

(1994) also defended and described the unrecognised urban Aboriginal culture but in the process was captive to the binaries of Indigenous and non-Indigenous, asserting good/evil distinctions between her culture and that of the 'white' culture.

While Behrendt and Droste spoke against the negative stereotyping of Aboriginal people, at the same time they invoked generalised, romanticised and stereotyped descriptions of the Aboriginal 'essence'. Droste, for example, deployed the healing discourse that reduces all Aboriginal expression or experience to a commonality of being:

> We as Indigenous people, for our own mental, spiritual, social and emotional health need to reclaim our identity and all that comes with it, our land (where possible), our culture and our spirituality. It is who we are. (2000, p. 13)

Behrendt (1994) made clear distinctions between Aboriginal culture and the 'material' European culture, using oppositions such as communal–individual, egalitarian–hierarchical, co-operation–competition, respect for elders–youth oriented culture and consensus–authoritarianism. Behrendt also emphasised that while her light skin and looks meant non-Aboriginal people 'are often surprised to find out that I am an Aborigine' (1994, p. 59), these and the presence of a white mother offered her no protection from racism and the 'ugliness that white people so easily cast towards an aboriginal person' (1994, p. 59).

Indigenous scholar Wendy Holland (1996) complicated further the terrain of mixed heritage:

> The racism directed towards murris in this society has been a constant reminder to me that I belong to a black family. Yet growing up blonde, blue-eyed, and fair-skinned, I certainly cannot deny my english and irish heritages. Nor can I deny the opportunities I have been afforded as a result of my whiteness and being mis/taken as white in this racist society. (1996, p. 97)[8]

Behrendt and Holland, both fair-skinned and with one white parent and similar experiences of racism, thus applied different understandings of

---

8 Murri is a term used by many to refer to Aboriginal people from Queensland and north west New South Wales

racism that aligned with or produced different identity narratives and claims. Behrendt, for example, claimed,

> [i]n my culture we do not have notions of half-caste and quarter-caste. Those terms are only in white language. In our eyes you are either an aborigine or you are not. If you see yourself as an aborigine and are accepted by the aboriginal community as an aborigine, you are an aborigine. If you describe yourself as 'part aboriginal' or of 'aboriginal descent', you would be considered non-aboriginal, no matter what your skin colour. (1994, p. 60)

Holland, however, took a different view that led her to question the ways Aboriginal identities were always reduced to an 'all or nothing' claim (1996, p. 105). While understanding the resistance to 'any "dilution" of aboriginality' (1996, p. 105), and the strategic politics of allegiance to an unequivocal Aboriginal identity, she argued that the all-or-nothing stand appeals to this 'all or nothing' reductiveness known as essentialism. For Holland, this upheld racism, and importantly was about 'the denial of difference that has always existed and continues to exist within our communities' (1996, p. 106). She offered a different approach, emphasising the relationship between language and subjectivity, and called for 'dialogue' as a way of expanding the conversation about 'who is' and 'who isn't', noting the complexities surrounding identity construction:

> There is a certain silencing that happens around a discourse informed by both historical and contemporary essentialist notions or 'race'…like Marcia Langton I am attempting to open up dialogue in order to move boundaries and undo the restrictions that make it difficult to speak. Subjectivity is dependent on coming into language in a way that enables us to identify ourselves. It is through dialogue with each other that we will come to understand the differences and complexities involved in living in a post-colonial context. (1996, p. 111)

These narratives, although personal descriptions, canvas the themes that take a more theoretical or contextual focus to discussions of Aboriginal identity and Aboriginality. Indigenous scholars, for example, discussed or theorised Aboriginal identity from within personal lived experience and/or in response to the historical or various contemporary contexts in which issues of Aboriginal identity emerge or are discussed (e.g. Anderson 1994, 1997; Dodson 1994; Holland 1996; Oxenham et al. 1999; Huggins 2003; Langton 2003; Nakata 2003; Paradies 2006). On the other hand, non-Indigenous discussion tends to be concerned with the theoretical and/or the difficulties of arguments around Aboriginal identity (e.g. Rolls 2001; Lattas 1993; Ganter 2008). But all these discussions variously cross or emphasise the difficulties around the value and dangers of reductive ideas surrounding identity (essentialism). They also suggest the value and dangers of the existence of authentic Aboriginal identities and the debate about what makes a person 'Aboriginal', and the presence of diverse Aboriginal experience and the implications for expressions of Aboriginal identity.

In other words, all these discussions are intertwined and underpin or inform each other. It is not possible, for example, to speak of essentialism or reductive notions of Aboriginality without raising questions of authenticity. Claims to possess the criteria of authenticity as the basis for representing Aboriginal experience and meanings raise questions of what is to be recognised as 'essential' characteristics of identity. Even so, the diverse and complex expressions of Aboriginal identity that have been produced through varied colonial experiences raise questions and demands to extend the collective right to self-determination to individuals demanding to have their experiences recognised and authenticated as evidence of the 'Aboriginal' experience. These various struggles for 'identification' or recognition are still largely contained within the machinations of the nation-state, which controls the distribution of Indigenous resources and contextualises and constructs the politics of Aboriginal identity. The difficulties in teasing apart all of these entangled scholarly debates and arguments reflect the discursive 'thickness' built up historically across academic, policy, administrative, legal, and public, popular, and private commonsense domains over the last two-and-a-quarter centuries. Resolving the struggles around Aboriginal identity is a colossal and ongoing task.

While the personal narratives of people such as, for example, Behrendt (1994) and Droste (2000) deploy essentialist logic, they do so with little reflection on its historical production via the colonial discourses that constructed Aboriginality. While they demonstrate awareness of colonial constructions of Aboriginal identity, these authors' involvement in constructing a discourse that 'authorises' what 'is' and 'constructs' what 'always has been' is submerged in the textual production of personal narrative. Non-Aboriginal academic Mitchell Rolls asserted, '[t]heirs is not a cultural identity formed from the routes they have travelled, but one based on the roots they imagine they once had' (2001, p. 17). However, in an earlier discussion of discourses of Aboriginality and the politics of Aboriginal identity, non-Indigenous academic and anthropologist Andrew Lattas (1993) argued that to condemn or dismiss these appeals would deny Aboriginal attempts 'to re-value their bodies' and 'the right to any positive imaginary existence' (1993, p. 161).

THE RIGHT TO SELF-REPRESENTATION

Other Indigenous and non-Indigenous academics also put forward varying critical analysis on the essentialist logic of Aboriginal identity discourse. The logic of this essentialist discourse on contemporary constructions of Aboriginal identity is conditioned in the interstices between the 'idea' of Aboriginality (Berndt & Berndt 1988) and the changing lived expression of it over time. This changing lived expression of it has not always been part of the ongoing social/cultural inheritance of many dislocated people now seeking to reconnect. Access to and demonstration of this knowledge becomes critical. However, it also runs the risk of what Berndt (1977, p. 9) called a 'kind of digest or telescoping of the many traditional societies and cultures into a generalised and abstract frame, focused on specific elements in contrast to others', such as can be read in Behrendt's collapsed construction of Aboriginal society as the kinder and more desirable opposite of all that is European (see Paradies 2006 for discussion of this effect as an iteration of an Aboriginal 'moral fantasy').

One strand of more sophisticated Aboriginal analysis draws on the idea of a 'strategic essentialism' (Spivak 1988b) where the reductive 'all or nothing' ideas surrounding Aboriginal identity can be used strategically by Aboriginal people for a particular purpose, for example, for claiming reconnection or continuity. Scholars Michael Dodson (1994) and Ian Anderson (1997), for example, recognised the origins of essentialism in anthropology that unsuccessfully worked to displace the biological essentialism of race that informs ideas about authenticity and who and what is really and truly Aboriginal:

> The 'authentic' or 'real' Aborigine was defined according to the extent to which different individuals or groups conformed to particular racial or cultural characteristics...construed as the essence of Aboriginal people...The emphasis

> shifted through time from an initial focus on racial categories to those of culture. However, these two analytical fields tended to overlay, rather than replace, each other (as argued by Cowlishaw 1987). What remained a constant was a belief that such qualities were fixed. Any contamination of these essences from the other side of the frontier shifted the 'authentic' Aborigine into the ambiguous world of the 'hybrid'. (Anderson 1997, p. 7)

Anderson argued that given the colonial history that rendered many people 'neither one nor the other', 'we might expect that in forming identities Aboriginal people may "essentialise"…[however] the problem is not…with essentialism, but with the type of essentialism' (1997, p. 12).

He acknowledged that 'Aboriginal identities are formed within the context of colonial relations' and so it is inevitable that there are echoes of the hegemonic discourse of race in Aboriginal self-representations (1997, p. 11). However, in defensive theoretical terms, Anderson argued that the very act of naming is an essentialising process and asserts that, '[e]ven the most radical post-structuralist in attempting to dispense with essentialism in identity formation…ends up essentialising non-essentialism' (1997, p. 12).

Dodson (1994) agreed that 'more than enough "fixing" has already occurred' (1994, p. 10) and argued that Aboriginal people must resist '…an essentialism which confines us to fixed, unchangeable and necessary characteristics, and refuses to allow for transformation or variation' (1994, p. 10). Acknowledging the Aboriginal historical experience, both these authors emphasised Aboriginal identity as an embodied experience which 'is not merely a social or idealised abstraction' (Anderson 1997, p. 12) that draws unconsciously from the constructs of colonial categories and meanings, and simply mirrors 'the connotations of a colonial racial framework' (Anderson 1997, p.12). Instead, Dodson stated,

> [t]he right to self-representation includes our right to draw on all aspects of our sense of our Aboriginality, be that our blood, our descent, our history, our ways of living and relating, or any element of our cultures. Certainly, the practice of fixing us to our blood or our romanticised traditions has been a cornerstone of racist practices.

And, Dodson argued,

> [depriving] us of our experienced connection with the past is another racist practice. The relationship we draw with our past is not to be confused with the relationships with the past that have been imposed on us. One is an act of resistance, the other is a tool in the politics of domination and oppression. (Dodson 1994, p.10)

Thus essentialist logic as argued by these authors does not seek to 'fix' Aboriginal identity but to argue for the right 'for Aboriginal people…to represent themselves as coherent people with a sustainable historicised subjectivity' (Anderson 1997, p. 120). They suggest that remobilising colonial categories can be potentially creative and 'challenge and subvert the authorised versions on who and what we are' (Dodson 1994, p. 10). And, as Dodson argued, this ties essentialism to structures of resistance, rather than structures of domination.

However sympathetic some are with Anderson and Dodson's defence of the efforts to reduce identity to an 'essence' of Aboriginality, this does not mean that we should ignore the way essentialism is used for the effects it has on Aboriginal people. Both non-Indigenous and Indigenous scholars have difficulties with its reliance on keeping in place cultural differences or what non-Indigenous academic Mitchell Rolls refers to as 'keeping the colonial binaries alive' (Rolls 2001, p. 11). Rolls articulated a concern also addressed by Indigenous scholars Yin Paradies (2006), Marcia Langton (2003) and Martin Nakata (2007). This concern is not a simple disagreement with neat articulations of difference or deconstructing their effects. These authors speak more to the effects of not acknowledging how such neat definitions of cultural differences do not pay enough attention to the ways these are reproduced by Aboriginal people themselves and do not acknowledge Aboriginality and identity as a social construct rather than some sort of cultural essence that *just is*.

While the sophisticated arguments of Dodson and Anderson might acknowledge this problem, in the circulating popular discourses that generalise from the particular and simplify the complex, Aboriginal identity is more simply tied to the claim of a pure and imagined originary 'essence' based on 'blood' and universalised cultural practices, as seen, for example, in Behrendt's account. According to Rolls, this encourages the 'mystic' essence of an idealised culture and a biologically determined descent to 're-emerge as the hallmarks of authenticity' (2001, p. 11). So Anderson

(1997, p. 12) might use essentialism strategically to argue that blood is not colonialism's 'race' but represents Aboriginal kin relations and that colonial history is an emotional 'internal' experience that produces 'feelings' of being Aboriginal 'within' that are shared collectively. However, Rolls described the problems that this creates and the possibilities submerged in the process:

> If we understand cultures and the identities produced within them as an ongoing and contingent process instead of a hitherto formed accomplished fact, we come closer to allowing for the cultural dynamism apparent within pre-colonial Aboriginal societies. We are also able to allow for the full range of responses — both cultural and individual — to the forces of colonisation and post-colonialism. (2001, p. 12)

Rolls drew from the work of cultural theorist Stuart Hall, who described cultural identities in terms of '[n]ot an essence but a *positioning*' (1990, p. 226). Nakata's work (2007), vis-à-vis the same way Torres Strait Islander peoples are subject to colonial logic, argued that if Torres Strait Islander people are uncritical of the logic of accepted cultural difference that informs reductive ideas about Indigenous identity, they are in danger of accepting an already prescribed position from which to be recognised and identified as 'an Islander' by other Islanders and by outsiders. For Nakata, 'difference' is not meaningless or devoid of content, and it is often critically important in generating new debates and Islander community discussion. But in capturing and rationalising policy and interventions in practice, 'difference' not only redistributes responsibilities for failures of programs onto the shoulder of Islanders but also narrows what it means to be an Islander, for the collective and for the individual.

The possibilities for what Dodson (1994) and Anderson (1997) argued to be the creative potential of essentialism are thus narrowed rather than widened. To think, argue or behave outside the prescribed boundaries is to risk being seen as 'not an Islander', as Nakata (2003) described it, and therefore to be seen as generating unrepresentative or wrong-headed understandings, rather than creative and regenerative ones. Identities perceived in terms of cultural distinctiveness are required to perform that distinctiveness as authorised and demanded by the discursive practices, which produce them as distinct. To Nakata this authorises the colonial logic of us–them, which is based on the assumptions of an undifferentiated and helpless Islander collective. This denies all Islanders their agency and specific histories, and thus their freedom to think and act in response to the complex and contradictory realities of Islander life in the twenty-first century.

ALTERNATIVE WAYS OF PERCEIVING IDENTITY

In speaking about the politics and aesthetics of artistic representations of Aboriginality, Marcia Langton emphasised Aboriginality as 'a social thing':

> 'Aboriginality' arises from the subjective experience of both Aboriginal people and non-Aboriginal people who engage in any inter-cultural dialogue, whether in actual lived experience or through a mediated experience such as a white person watching a program about Aboriginal people on television or reading a book.
>
> Moreover, the creation of 'Aboriginality' is not a fixed thing, it is created from our histories. It arises from the inter-subjectivity of black and white in a dialogue. (2003, p. 118)

According to Langton, a central problem in this dialogue is 'the failure of non-Aboriginals to comprehend us Aboriginal people, or to find the grounds of understanding' (2003, p. 122). Langton contended that the historically shifting policy eras were designed to negate possibilities for mutual dialogue and understanding. However, Langton refuted the idea that representations of 'Aboriginality' by Aboriginal people were necessarily better or 'truer' representations. This logic, she argued, assumes that Aboriginal people are all the same, and denies variations and specificities in what it means to be Aboriginal.

> It is a demand for censorship: there is a 'right' way to be Aboriginal…This thinking is as much based on fear of difference as is white Australian racism. If we only look at that which makes us feel safe, that which tells us that we are what we would like to imagine ourselves to be, we will become naked emperors and empresses… (2003, p. 115)

In an interrogation of pan-Indigeneity, Paradies (2006) asserted that,

> Indigenous constructions of (pan-)Indigeneity also involve elements of boundary construction/policing which seek to

> construct Indigenous and non-Indigenous identities as 'mutually impermeable and incommensurable'…Moreover, the powerful tropes of Indigeneity immobilized during this boundary construction interpellate every Indigenous person, without regard to their individual characteristics, through a plethora of stereotyped images that coalesce around specific fantasies of exclusivity, cultural alterity, marginality, physicality and morality. (2006, pp. 356–57)

Paradies pointed out the ways identity is policed so that Aboriginality can only be understood in reductive or essentialised terms, and suggested that such constructions 'speak' to all Aboriginal people through a vast range of images that are so 'known and recognised' that that they refute any kind of differences between and among Aboriginal people.

Paradies, a 'confessed' diverse Aboriginal-Anglo-Australian-Asian identity, drew attention to an effect of the political quest to build a coherent collective identity around the common Indigenous cultural heritage and shared experience of colonialism. What Holland (1996) calls the 'all-or-nothing' choice, Paradies, following Ang (2000, p. 11), calls a 'prison-house of identity' (2006, p. 356) and refused to divest himself of any of his other identities. He used demographic statistics to muster a case against assertions which support what he called 'fantasies' of Indigeneity: cultural alterity, marginality (disadvantage), stereotypical physicality, moral and epistemological superiority, all of which he classified as stereotypes or fallacies. His aim was to establish the heterogeneity of the Indigenous community to counter the discursive imposition of a singular identity and to provide more space for the multiple identities inhabited by Aboriginal people. So while Anderson (1997, see also 1994) argued the 'hybrid' is Aboriginal, Paradies argued the Aboriginal is hybrid but forced into a singular identity, Aboriginal, by the demands of 'racial loyalty' (2006, p. 357).

At the core of Paradies' argument is the legitimate question of 'what counts' or 'authenticates' the contemporary category of Aboriginal. His solution to the risks entailed in weakening the collective solidarity *vis-à-vis* the apparatuses of the nation-state — a solidarity which hinges on an unambiguous and coherent Aboriginal identification — is to decouple Indigeneity from these colonial 'fantasies' without abandoning the strengthening of cultures or the need for affirmative policies.

> Rather, I am suggesting that we free Indigeneity from the prison of romanticization and recognize that although the poor and rich Indigene, the cultural reviver and the quintessential cosmopolitan, the fair, dark, good, bad and disinterested may have little in common, they are nonetheless all equally but variously Indigenous. (Paradies 2006, p. 363)

Aboriginality, however, has been forged on the appeal to the 'common' heritage and experience. Paradies' interrogation of 'what counts' as the criteria of Aboriginality re-opens a major fault line in the Aboriginal community and in the literature and already in evidence in earlier times through the hostility expressed to those accused of 'passing' or the 'Johnny-come-lately's' (Huggins 2003; Heiss 2003). Wendy Holland (1996, p. 105), for example, noted that for many Aboriginal people, cultural hybridity, as celebrated by post-colonial theorists, is an extremely sensitive issue given the legacy of past classifications of Aboriginal people. Thus, calls to recognise all the diverse Aboriginal experiences of colonialism as the product of colonialism call different positions into contest around the meanings of Aboriginal experience and the evidentiary markers of that experience.

This fault line was starkly evident in Jackie Huggins' (2003) engagement with Bain Attwood's analysis of Sally Morgan's discovery of Aboriginal heritage and Morgan's construction of an Aboriginal identity as revealed in her very successful book, *My Place* (1987). In a scathing criticism of *My Place*, Morgan, and non-Aboriginal intellectuals engaged with research in areas of race, Huggins (2003) drew a stark line between two groups of Aboriginal identity claimants — 'those being the identity-privileged and -socialised *versus* the identity-lost, -seeking or newly arrived' (2003, p. 65). Accordingly, in Huggins' view, Morgan's family history (of attempting to hide their Aboriginality from authorities) was not conceded as an Aboriginal experience of colonialism, and Huggins viewed Morgan and others like her as 'thankfully a minority of Blacks' (2003, p. 61), a claim that may be hard to substantiate according to Paradies' analysis. In short, Morgan was positioned as a race traitor by Huggins:

> Most Aboriginal people never ceded their identity, no matter how destructive, painful or bad the situation was. We vindic-

tively remember those who have passed and…can never forget these traitors. (Huggins 2003, p. 62)

Huggins objected to the assumption by Morgan that biological descent coupled with absorption of romanticised and anthropological constructions of Aboriginality are sufficient to claim to be 'automatically' Aboriginal. As she stated,

> Aboriginality cannot be acquired overnight. It takes years of hard work, sensitivity and effort to 'come back in'. Forgotten people will tell you so. The debt has to be repaid in various ways [to the Aboriginal community]. It's a socialised learned pattern of behaviour and while the blood and spirit are fixed categories, there are protocols and ethics to adhere to when 'becoming Aborigines' again. (2003, p. 63)

Revealing an even deeper contention with the contemporary identity literature, Huggins argued that Aboriginality is fixed — 'if the truth be known, fluidity is nothing less than a cop-out and a sell-out of Aboriginal heritage, values and identity' (2003, p. 63). However, Huggins did not subscribe to an Aboriginal identity dependent on genetic inheritance (2003, p. 64) or 'a diluted mystical vision' (2003, p. 63). Nor did she articulate just what constitutes 'being Aboriginal', beyond her examples of 'acceptance by the community in which one lives and being actively involved to alleviate the disadvantaged positions of Aboriginal people per se' (2003, p. 64). Huggins' position, which effectively denied the diversity of Aboriginal experiences, is not reflected in some recent studies done by various researchers but arguably reflects popular community opinions. As Huggins asked, 'Is identity as Attwood puts it, "a process of becoming" or is it about "already been"?' (2003, p. 63). If the latter, as Huggins seemed to suggest, then a range of 'real' Aboriginal experiences are denied. Indigenous academics Oxenham et al. (1999) explored these questions through a series of personal narratives and discussions and in the process questioned the stance represented by Huggins,

> The indignities our forefathers had to face made it necessary to adopt survival tactics. Who is to be the judge when they were not around to share the lived experiences of our forefathers? One is always much wiser in retrospect. (1999, p. xiii)

According to these academics, Huggins lost her authority to claim what constitutes 'the' authentic Aboriginal identity, by her refusal of the historically contingent nature of Aboriginal identity, expressed through varied Aboriginal experiences brought to light in varying personal accounts of that experience.

Whatever the measure of authenticity, there always remains the question of what is to happen to those 'who are perceived to be living outside the varying notions of authenticity' (Rolls 2001, p. 19). Rolls argued that for these Aboriginal people, '[t]he meaningfulness of their Indigenous cultural experience is deemed illegitimate' and 'the vibrant and dynamic cultures that continue ceaselessly to manifest new forms' are also denied as legitimate forms of Aboriginality (2001, p. 19). Grossman and Cuthbert (1998) see that stereotypical notions of 'authentic' Aboriginality is related to the urban–traditional divide, picked apart by Langton as early as 1981:

> Abiding tensions in Australian cultural paradigms of 'urban' and 'traditional' Aboriginal peoples, communities and practices, and the ways in which these are set against one another as competing terms rather than seen as jointly produced by uneven processes historical agency and accident, have resulted in troubling and disempowering narratives of authenticity and ownership that bear directly on the power of Indigenous Australians to determine and represent their own identities. (1998, p. 111)

With reference to discussion by non-Indigenous academics in different fields (e.g. Muecke 1992; Ferguson 1993; Appiah 1994; Griffiths 1995), Paradies argued that 'fantasies' of authenticity, now enacted through 'border-patrolling' and 'processes of forced inclusion', leave the Indigenous community 'fragmented into those who can authentically perform Indigeneity and those who are silenced and/or rendered outside the space of Indigeneity because they cannot, or will not, perform' (2006, pp. 360–61). Appiah, in a discussion of presuppositions in contemporary multicultural discourse, suggested this as an effect of 'conceptions of collective identity that are remarkably unsubtle in their understandings of the processes by which identities, both individual and collective, develop' (1994, p. 156).

Historian Regina Ganter alluded to the ongoing struggles of ambiguously located identities in relation to evolving discourses of 'who is' and 'what is' to constitute the evidence of being Aboriginal (2008). Despite the politics of identity that now invalidates the middle position once identified as the 'part-Aboriginal' Ganter drew attention to the reidentification in the literature of a 'half-step' position (following Noble 1996). This refers to those members of the current generation 'who see themselves as "being of Aboriginal descent" without being Aboriginal, a position that harbours intensely personal uncertainties, because it is not sanctioned by any socially valid categories' (Ganter 2008, p. 2). For these people, the identity boundaries have been drawn too tight and to cross them entails 'border disputes' (2008, p. 3). Ganter discussed the Northern Australian situation of the previously 'coloured'. These were Aboriginal and Torres Strait Islander mixed-heritage people whose other heritage was not white but Asiatic or Pacific Islander and very often a 'multi-race' mix of these. The following observation in relation to these identities, perhaps sums up the legacy for all of us:

> When binary identity politics gained momentum in the 1990s, in response to legal rights vested in being Aboriginal, people who had counted themselves in the 'coloured' community had to commit themselves either way, at precisely the time when postcolonial consciousness elsewhere in the world asserted 'creoleness' as a viable identity…Some of them have become the victims of binary identity politics, and in view of the complex histories of being, or not being, Aboriginal, cynicism [about their desire or disdain for inclusion] is surely misplaced. (2008, p. 18)

What is referred to here are the ways that either/or constructions of Aboriginality have continued within Northern Territory Aboriginal communities to dictate 'who is' and 'who isn't' long after postcolonial ideas of diversity gained ground. Ganter is arguing that because these ideas have been so thoroughly entrenched, Aboriginal people have become victims of this form of internalised logic. This view adds another dimension to the internalised nature of essentialising Aboriginal identity and the complexities that are experienced by Aboriginal people when seeking to locate a cultural identity within a firmly established discourse of 'who is', 'who is not' and 'who can be'.

PART TWO

CHAPTER 9
CONFIRMATION OF ABORIGINALITY

> What's going on out there? — there's black people fighting black people. As soon as you start to get a good education, then somehow you begin to be 'less black'; the colour of our skin in some areas seems to indicate how black we are and how black we're not. It seems we are buying into what mainstream is imposing on us. Also language — if you don't speak language then you're not black. There's the 'where we live' bit: remote areas are where the 'really black people' live, whereas in urban areas you're not 'really black'…We always push the blame out there to others, we need to take the lead on this instead of sitting back and chopping each others' heads off: We have to change the conversation from one of deficit to one of strength.
>
> (Gorringe, Ross & Forde 2011, p. 3)

As mentioned earlier in this book, in the early 1980s the Commonwealth Department of Aboriginal Affairs introduced a three-part working definition for establishing the identity status of Aboriginal and Torres Strait Islander people:

> An Aboriginal or Torres Strait Islander is a person of Aboriginal or Torres Strait Islander descent who identifies as an Aboriginal or Torres Strait Islander and is accepted as such by the community in which he (she) lives. (Gardiner-Garden 2002–03, p. 4)

The initial purpose of the definition was to establish eligibility for 'special' Commonwealth government funding, programs, benefits and services provided specifically for Aboriginal and Torres Strait Islander people. As the Australian Institute of Aboriginal and Torres Strait Islander Studies (AIATSIS) pointed out, 'any benefit received by being identified as Indigenous is to assist the imbalance caused in the past when Indigenous people did not receive the same educational and work opportunities as that of the majority European population' (AIATSIS, p. 1). However, implicit in the instrumental relation between the definition and its purpose is the need for Aboriginal and Torres Strait Islander people to prove or confirm they are Aboriginal or Torres Strait Islander. The official process is known as Confirmation of Aboriginality.

Over the decades Confirmation of Aboriginality has become the accepted process for determining eligibility to benefits from an increasing range of sources, including: government benefits and services at national, state and local levels; various assistance measures from charitable funding bodies; and programs and assistance that support the education and employment of Aboriginal people in private, public and Aboriginal organisations and institutions. While a range of government and other institutions or organisations require Confirmation of Aboriginality documentation as proof of identity status, it is Aboriginal community-controlled organisations that bear the responsibility for determining whether an applicant is Aboriginal or not (Heiss 2003). This is to facilitate Aboriginal community wishes to hold control over the decision-making processes and supports the principles of Aboriginal self-determination.

The establishment of community-controlled organisations is an outcome of a Federal government initiative in the 1970s (Coombs 1976) to provide a means for 'the local Aboriginal community to be involved in its affairs in accordance with whatever protocols or procedures are determined by the community' (NACCHO 1995). The Aboriginal community Confirmation of Aboriginality process is thus vested in Aboriginal organisations that are incorporated as 'community-controlled' organisations. Any government, agency, employer, service or benefit provider which requires proof of Aboriginal identity to allocate a government benefit or service can accept a Confirmation of Aboriginality document from an individual only if it has been verified by an Aboriginal organisation, and only if that organisation has been formally incorporated under State or Territory legislation.

The Confirmation of Aboriginality is accepted as a pseudo-legal document by institutions and their officers, and demonstrates due diligence process for meeting any required exemptions to the Commonwealth *Racial Discrimination Act 1975* to positively discriminate in favour of Aboriginal people. Although requirements may vary, it is usually satisfied with a signed statutory declaration from the applicant declaring factual information has been provided. The information required must verify Aboriginal descent, self-identification and community recognition. There are various ways of providing this documentation, and how individuals present the evidence often depends on the relative ease or difficulties of establishing lineage, and the ability to have other recognised Aboriginal people confirm this. Where community recognition is well established it is relatively easy to achieve official sign-off in the formal process. In other cases, where individuals have to appeal to the organisation for community recognition on the basis of the documentation they are able to supply, it is not as easy. Once personal documentation is lodged in the latter case, the applicant awaits resolution from the Aboriginal community organisation's governing committee. If resolved in favour of the applicant, the resolution is recorded and the Confirmation of Aboriginality certificate is then fixed with the organisation's common seal and signed by the governing committee. The primary responsibility for an Aboriginal organisation is to ensure that all the elements of the three-part definition are met. Through this process, the applicant is either deemed to have met the requirements, or to have failed to satisfy the three-part criteria.

Like any regulatory process, Confirmation of Aboriginality has both positive and negative implications. On the one hand, it supports the distribution of resources and development of targeted programs. It prevents those ineligible from fraudulently claiming benefits intended for Aboriginal people. On the other hand, those who cannot provide documented proof of Aboriginality may be refused access to a range of services, including the fundamental needs of health, housing, legal aid and welfare supplements to which they may be legitimately entitled. Official refusal by vested Aboriginal community organisations to confirm Aboriginal identity can have real material effects. Many mainstream and Aboriginal organisations, for example, require a Confirmation of Aboriginality certificate for employment in an identified Indigenous position. Likewise, most tertiary institutions require Confirmation of Aboriginality forms for special entry into courses and for Indigenous scholarships.

EMERGING TENSIONS IN THE CONFIRMATION OF ABORIGINALITY PROCESS

Following the colonial/historical governmental imposition of definitions of 'who is' and 'what counts' in the determination of Aboriginal status, the new definition and the removal of the nation-state in determining status is perceived, in the main, as a step forward. The contemporary method of requiring documentation and communal corroboration is viewed by many to be a vast improvement from the early periods of determining blood quantum with categories such as 'half-caste' and 'quarter-caste' and the like (see Dodson 2003; Lamb 2007).

However, the current Confirmation of Aboriginality process is constituted by and constitutive of particular tensions in the relations between the nation-state and Aboriginal people. Not only does the link between Aboriginal identity status and access to resources demand a regime for 'proving' to governments and other assorted agencies and people who (every)one is, in return for access to 'special' benefits provided to overcome the effects of past neglect, Aboriginal people must now determine and regulate who is and who is not Aboriginal to assist the nation-state in distributing 'special' resources. The price of self-determination carries with it a regime of community surveillance and regulation. In this partnership, the Aboriginal community must now ask questions of and pronounce judgments on its members. Aboriginal people, through our organisations, have become complicit in the apparatuses of the nation-state, from which we seek escape through mechanisms for self-determination. Mick Dodson is not wrong in his argument that by refusing the imposition of colonial inscriptions of identity and defining ourselves, we can 'transform that identity creatively' and have the 'freedom to live outside the cage created by other people's images and projections' (1994, p. 5). But how we impose our own inscriptions of Aboriginal identity onto Aboriginal bodies and lives now becomes a new site of tension in ways similar to those between the Aboriginal collective and the nation-state.

Nowhere is this tension felt more than in the requirement to be recognised by the Aboriginal community in which one lives. Community recognition is increasingly a key site of both anxiety and tensions within internal Aboriginal community relations. These tensions are conditioned in the historical events of colonialism but emerge in the contemporary community space as a struggle between competing and emerging accounts of Aboriginal experience and what it means to be Aboriginal in the self-determination era. Emerging Aboriginal and non-Aboriginal accounts of colonial and historical experience indicate a wide range of individual, family and group experiences and circumstances under these regimes. Ongoing contests over what should constitute the criteria for 'recognition' of Aboriginality increases the challenges in determining and confirming Aboriginal status. All these tensions and conditions were evidenced in the scholarly studies and conversations that I discussed in earlier chapters. Here, however, I focus more on the ways in which some of these emerge in the Confirmation of Aboriginality process at community levels.

SOME PROBLEMS IN THE CONFIRMATION OF ABORIGINALITY PROCESS

The problems that arise in the Confirmation of Aboriginality process are generally related to the challenges that many Aboriginal individuals face in providing the necessary evidence, and the challenges for organisations in establishing a fair and consistent process for dealing with applications for confirmation. Part of the problem of establishing such a process for community recognition is the lack of community consensus over what counts as indicators of Aboriginality. The greater the challenges on each side the more likely determinations are made in capricious, arbitrary and potentially unjust ways. The parallels with the past would appear to arise from the definition itself, as an instrument applied to support a process of inclusion/exclusion.

The process for individuals to acquire evidence of their Aboriginality can be complex, tedious, and invoke considerable emotional pain and anxiety. Those from remote Aboriginal communities or relocated and/or reconstructed Aboriginal communities formed in the mission and reserves eras generally have an easier time gaining confirmation in the communities to which they have always or long belonged. Those individuals who are descended from Aboriginal people who moved away, or were moved in previous generations, can have a much more difficult time providing evidence. Aboriginal people who were able to escape the control of colonial and government administrations and live relatively independently have the most difficult time of all, particularly when this is used in community discourse as evidence of choosing to abandon Aboriginal kin and values. There is also a lack of consistent historical documentation around Aboriginal births, deaths and marriages, and the movement of Aboriginal people for survival, work or forced relocations, as well as a lack of census-taking in relation to Aboriginal people in earlier periods contributes to difficulties in confirming identity. The historical accounts of the variety of individual Aboriginal experiences under colonial and Australian administrations are still emerging. The fact that many Aboriginal survivors were young children at the time of relocation and dislocation further complicates the situation for those trying to find their way 'home'. The oral memory of older Aboriginal people is often needed as evidentiary testament of lineage and/or origins, but this too is not always available.

The three-part definition legislated to determine Aboriginality did not seem to foresee the difficulties this definition entails for those Aboriginal people who were removed from or no longer live on their ancestral lands. Further to this, there are no set guidelines to assist a person acquire a Confirmation of Aboriginality certificate when there is no available documentation to support their claim, nor any guidelines for community organisations in how to respond in these circumstances. The Australian Institute of Aboriginal and Torres Strait Islander Studies (AIATSIS) accepts documentation that may be in the form of certificates or records from reserves and missions, photographs, or corroborated oral testimony that clearly demonstrates lineage to an Aboriginal person. For many Aboriginal people fulfilling the Confirmation of Aboriginality requirement of being 'recognised as Aboriginal' by the community to which they have relocated also often demands documentation from a community organisation in their ancestral home. The local organisation in both places must then be satisfied that the 'right' evidence has been provided. This brings about other problems. Recognition by the original community does not always suffice as evidence for the community the applicants now find themselves in because, as will be evidenced below, community organisations can impose their own criteria for recognition.

PROBLEMS FOR ORGANISATIONS

The problems that community organisations have in determining Aboriginal status are not entirely of their own making. They are constituted in the tensions with the nation-state over the allocation of resources and in the regulations that govern incorporated organisations. Their situation must also be considered according to the history of colonial fragmentation of Aboriginal communities and families, and in the colonial acts of removing Aboriginal people from their ancestral country onto country belonging to other Aboriginal groups. Further, these situations are constituted in the debates through which we have come to understand and resist the colonial constructions of Aboriginal identity. The question that has to be considered therefore, is to what extent Aboriginal community organisations have become part of the problem they were designed to overcome.

> The problem and practice of classifying Aboriginality has been something 'given' to and 'expected of' Aboriginal people. It is something we seem to have accepted and run with and our organisations have accepted the requirement of a 'certificate' of Aboriginality. (Heiss 2003, p. 18)

Community-controlled organisations, particularly as instruments of collective Aboriginal self-determination, suggest a basis for cooperation, collaboration and consensus in the interest of shared Aboriginal goals. However, community organisations are both immured in Aboriginal politics and involved in reconstructing and 'officially' controlling the meaning of Aboriginal community and, by default, people's Aboriginal identity. These practices are constituted in and reflective of both the tensions in the relations between the Aboriginal collective and the nation-state and the internal tensions within the Aboriginal collective about the meanings of being Aboriginal. Such tensions converge, merge and reemerge in the processes of confirming Aboriginality. Some Aboriginal organisations privilege their construct of 'the community' and police its borders through practices of decisionmaking and access to resources. These in turn rest on particular views about what constitutes the criteria for recognition of other Aboriginal people.

CONSTRUCTS OF 'COMMUNITY'

Since the introduction of the term 'community' into the public lexicon, Aboriginal organisations have taken charge of the meaning of the term, particularly in urban settings where it has specific connotations of official 'authority' at local levels (see Yamanouchi 2007, 2010). Further, 'community participation' is recognised by participation in events hosted by Aboriginal organisations and by attendance at meetings (Yamanouchi 2007, p. 140). Conversely, '[i]t is within organisations' activities and events that people have their strongest sense of being part of an experience they call community' (2007, p. 144). As part of her doctoral research, Yuriko Yamanouchi interviewed participants from south-west Sydney who reported that Aboriginal people who do not participate in organisations' activities 'do not have much to do with the community' (2007, p. 144). The inference is that community organisations *are* community, when self-identification as a member of the Aboriginal community can mean, reflect and be expressed as many different investments. For example, self-identification might be embedded in an individual's commitment to working in the Indigenous sector, to volunteering in different settings, to caring for immediate or extended family, to understanding family history and rebuilding relationships, to improving opportunities for future generations of the family, or to understanding Aboriginal knowledge or traditional philosophy, and so on. Therefore, the notion of Aboriginal community and Aboriginal identity applied only through the lens of community can be quite restricted in terms of everyday experience. The relations between 'community recognition' as applied in the definitional criteria and an Aboriginal individual's public visibility in community organisations and activities — themselves products of Australian government largesse — denote a further layer of tension. Layers emerge between the nation-state, Aboriginal political principles of collective self-determination, and the freedom of Aboriginal individuals to determine the way they live and participate as Aboriginal people in both Aboriginal and the larger Australian society. Many questions emerge at these discursive boundaries and intersections as to what constitutes 'community', and who can speak for or confirm an individual's identity (Lamb 2007).

The notion of Aboriginal community is complex. Aboriginal writer Frances Peters-Little suggested that government policies and community organisations have been largely 'shaping "who" and "what" constitutes an Aboriginal community' (2001, p. 198). While throughout colonial history new Aboriginal communities emerged through enforced relocation and dislocation from ancestral country, the axiom 'the Aboriginal community' has only become entrenched in popular discourse since the 1970s to streamline government funding to Aboriginal people. One effect is what Peters-Little referred to as 'The Community Game' where 'prominent and dominant' (2000, p. 10) families seize power and regulate the 'game' to their own advantage. The community, although a nebulous group as she suggests, is a powerful force and in many local urban communities has considerable input into all things related to local Aboriginal politics.

In this way, the role of community in relation to the authorisation of Aboriginal identity is intrinsically political, with particular implications for the requirement of community recognition for determining Aboriginality. In the practice of confirming Aboriginality, community organisations become part of the ongoing historical 'problem' of defining and regulating Aboriginal individuals. One area of concern emerges around the often-contested form of identity politics that plays out in the constitution of community organisations and which has repercussions concerning who gets to make the decisions about whom. The other area of concern is the way that the notion of community recognition is wielded around unresolved arguments about what counts as the criteria for Aboriginality.

COMMUNITY POLITICS, IDENTITY POLITICS AND THE PRACTICES OF COMMUNITY ORGANISATIONS

Aboriginal community politics and Aboriginal identity politics are mutually constituted. Aboriginal people who are involved in community-controlled organisations, or who utilise the services provided by such organisations, are generally familiar with the 'divisive politicking' that characterises many of these organisations (Bond 2007, p. 14). As Peters-Little (2000) has highlighted, it is not uncommon for factional groups or dominant family groups to control Aboriginal community organisations. This often results in the exclusion of other groups and individuals in decision-making processes and at times restricts the services provided to certain groups in the community (Peters-Little 2000; Bond 2007; Yamanouchi 2010). The way that community organisations function or do not function to provide constructive or effective 'community-based' decision-making processes can be contingent on individual personalities or self-interest groups. This does not always reflect the broader community's interests or an organisation's ethical credibility (Lumby 2004).

Attempts to describe and explain the problem of Aboriginal community factionalism have been reported in various studies and scholarly conversations in earlier chapters (see, for example, Barwick 1962; Eckermann 1973, 1977a). While there is a range of theories, there is agreement that the contemporary situation has been conditioned by the historical elements of both traditional social relations between Aboriginal groups and the forced restructuring of these relations through dispossession from ancestral country, and the social relations engendered through colonial administrations. For example, there were traditional enmities between groups who were placed on reserves by governments who did not recognise any social, economic or political relations between Aboriginal groups, let alone the significance of them for community cohesion (Eckermann et al. 1998, p. 105). Community cohesion may be engendered in those circumstances that demand resistance to the nation-state but may fracture when that common purpose is not the critical community imperative. But as well, these historically reconstructed communities on missions and reserves now also engender their own allegiances and loyalties vis-à-vis the broader contemporary Aboriginal community in ways that can work against Aboriginal 'outsiders', who also reside in these larger communities. Anne-Katrin Eckermann et al. explain factionalism in its contemporary form, as something that

> persists today in areas where people closely intermarried and share the same environment. It becomes most vicious when individual and immediate family interests are, or are perceived to be, threatened by those of other family interests. (Eckermann et al. 1998, p. 108)

Eckermann et al. (1998, p. ix) have suggested that the term 'community' sutures over everyday politics when applied to Aboriginal constituencies and obscures the primary focus of factional loyalties.

Myrna Tonkinson (1990), however, attempted to shed more light on the significance of traditional social, economic and political relations between Aboriginal groups. In this view, the survival of small groups required an emphasis on internal group relations as cohesive, loyal and inward looking. Co-operation with other Aboriginal groups was also necessary for survival, and particular forms of exchange and dispute resolution existed. Together these practices embedded sets of inclusionary and exclusionary practices and relations that, while adapted, still bear visible traces in contemporary Aboriginal relations and politics.

Whichever way the causes and meanings of factionalism are theorised, the historical traces emerge in contemporary Aboriginal communities in ways that ensure some community organisations form around quite narrow sets of seemingly personal or family interests to the exclusion of other legitimate broader community interests. In the relations with the nation-state, community organisations are embedded in the politics of self-determination, a positive principle for collective political action. With regard to relations between various interests and concerns at the local community level, community organisations are often embedded in principles for action and decision-making that deny the principles of collective self-determination.

Aboriginal communities are thus invested in a political struggle with the nation-state, ostensibly over resources and other issues of control, in which differing 'factions' or 'interests' within communities compete against each other. The regulations surrounding community-controlled organisations do little to diffuse factionalism and, inadvertently, often support it. Within Aboriginal community-controlled organisations, the management position(s) are accountable to a board of directors. Such boards are comprised of elected representatives of the local Aboriginal community. At a board's annual general meeting there is a call for nominations as required by all incorporated bodies for community representatives to become a board member (Lumby 2004). In my observations of a number of community-controlled organisations, whoever applies to become a community representative and whoever votes on the list of nominees is subject to political orchestration by those who are already members of established community factions, or by those wishing to avoid or confront and contest them. The politics is similar perhaps to factional politics within the pre-selection processes of major political parties. A major consequence of factionalism as it plays out from communities and into the membership and decision-making processes of community organisations is its capacity to obscure the wider political aims of organisations working in the interests of self-determination.

In this way, the empowerment of the Aboriginal 'community' to decide the question of who is or who is not Aboriginal has become part of the everyday problematic of Aboriginal Australians (following Smith 1987). Who gets to decide, and what qualifies particular community organisation board members to make these decisions fairly and justly? Decisions about an individual's Aboriginal identity status may have shifted from the nation-state to the Aboriginal community, but many Aboriginal people are still the recipients of arbitrary practices. The arbitrariness of any decisions to confirm or not confirm Aboriginality in the Confirmation of Aboriginality process resides both in the processes followed in organisations, or lack thereof, as well as in wider contests over the criteria for establishing 'what counts' as evidence of being Aboriginal. The latter reflects the issues discussed in the scholarly conversations around Aboriginal identity in earlier chapters.

THE QUESTION OF LEGITIMACY: COMMUNITY CONTESTS AND THE CONFIRMATION PROCESS

The legitimacy of the Confirmation of Aboriginality process is often contested, beginning with a lack of consensus within the Aboriginal community on the need for self-identification through the acquisition of a Confirmation of Aboriginality certificate. One of the main objections is that the certificate symbolises a return to the days of 'exemption certificates' derisively referred to by Aboriginal people as 'dog licences' or 'dog tags' (Broome 2002, p. 175). In the 1940s, Australian citizenship was granted to Aboriginal people who held exemption certificates; these were authorised government identification documents issued to Aboriginal people deemed of 'good character and industrious habits…[and who had demonstrated] the manner and habits of civilised life' (Flood 2006, p. 227). Those who held an exemption certificate were entitled to receive 'benefits' afforded to non-Indigenous citizens of Australia in the same way a Confirmation of Aboriginality certificate entitles the bearer to apply for Aboriginal benefits today. It is noteworthy that where earlier periods required certification that denounced Aboriginality, the situation today is one where Aboriginal people *have* to have documentation to prove that they *are* Aboriginal.

The need for community recognition as part of the Confirmation of Aboriginality processes takes the identification process beyond the formalities of the document and into the informal realm of the community gaze. Aboriginal self-surveillance today is operationalised via the scrutiny of the Aboriginal community gaze, which now enacts the practices of former colonial regimes. Given these conditions, a critical question arises: on what basis does 'the community', via its 'community-controlled' organisations, determine the criteria for the recognition of Aboriginal individuals with quite different personal and family histories?

Previous chapters attest to the difficulties faced by Australian courts in providing a consistent interpretation of the definition of Aboriginality (see for example, *Attorney-General (Cth) v State of Queensland* (1990)[9], *Gibbs v Capewell* (1995)[10] and *Shaw v Wolf* (1998)[11]). Determinations in these cases were often made according to the intentions of the particular

---

9 *Attorney-General (Cth) v State of Queensland* (1990) — https://jade.barnet.com.au/Jade.html#!article=194280
10 *Gibbs v Capewell* (1995) — https://jade.barnet.com.au/Jade.html#!article=213204
11 *Shaw v Wolf* — http://www.austlii.edu.au/au/journals/IndigLawB/1998/49.html

Acts under which the regulations being applied and/or contested were framed. Where lineage was seen to be weak, judges considered the evidence that an Aboriginal individual self-identified as well as evidence of community affiliations. Where self-identification was long held and community recognition strong, a lack of documented Aboriginal lineage or weak or distant lineage could be less critical in determinations. Further, Justice Merkel concluded that identity is linked to self-determination, and therefore best left for bodies with Aboriginal representation (Australian Law Reform Commission 2003, p. 27).

The representativeness of community-controlled organisations, however, is a matter for debate and already problematic. In this sense, the transparency and consistency of the processes used to confirm an individual's Aboriginality become more critical to the issues of fairness and justice. While the Confirmation of Aboriginality certificate provides defence from accusations of 'fakery', it is not a guarantee against such accusations. There are many instances where paperwork has been questioned and its owner accused of 'conning' those who authorised the document (Yamanouchi 2010, p. 225). What is important to understand is the extent to which 'proof' is valued in the context, and even more crucially the historical antecedents of such demands for 'proof'. The issue of how community organisations determine the evidence of criteria in order to confirm community recognition is therefore a matter for interrogation. Quite apart from the issue of process, however, the criteria for Aboriginality are also hotly disputed.

CHAPTER 10
CONFLICT, COMMUNITY AND THE REGULATION OF ABORIGINAL IDENTITY

> People are blaming things like Native Title for the trouble that is happening in our communities, but it's got nothing to do with Native Title. It's to do with us, about us taking responsibility around the way we talk and relate to each other.
> (Gorringe, Ross & Ford 2011, p. 5)

The issues surrounding Aboriginal identity are a topic of discussion for Aboriginal people and this discussion has been a subject for community reflection, both privately and publicly. A concern increasingly emerges around the destructive effects on individuals, as well as on community cohesion, of current ways of talking about and responding to questions of Aboriginal identity.

Academic and author Anita Heiss has reflected that '[i]n our own Aboriginal community, comments in discussions around who is and who is not Aboriginal can range from "They're not black enough" to accusing individuals of being "Johnny-come-lately's"' (2007, p. 51). She noted that '[c]riticism of Aboriginal people by Aboriginal people is strong, and no one escapes' (p. 53). The idea that no one escapes criticism from within Aboriginal communities connotes our surveillance of each other within and between communities. It also illustrates the polarisation of the discussion around who is and who isn't Aboriginal and what counts and what doesn't. These ways of talking strictly categorise the particular and diverse historical narratives of Aboriginal individuals in an oppositional relation where one stands in a devalued relation to the other. The opportunities to recognise and include different narratives, including irrecoverable ones, as a reflection of the shared history of colonisation, are lost. Instead, some narratives become privileged and others discounted, unless individuals are prepared to undertake particular forms of identity work to be recognised and brought into the fold of community (see, for example, Huggins 2003). Those individuals who have not been disconnected and have been socialised within Aboriginal communities are 'the identity-privileged' (Huggins 2003, p. 65) — they do not have to prove their identity. Those who are 'identity-lost, seeking or newly arrived' (Huggins 2003, p. 65), on the other hand, must prove themselves.

The unfairness of such categorical proscriptions for the processes of community recognition as a definitional criterion of Aboriginal identity has been discussed by Aboriginal health professional Natasha Lamb (2007). From her position, the working definition of Aboriginality is inherently racist and community recognition has become the cause of many problems for individuals and communities alike: 'Aboriginal people are mandated to have an organisation or group assess their identity (the last criterion), and this presents various issues related to power, acceptance and perceived identity/ancestry' (2007, p. 178). Lamb constructed the divisive practices within Aboriginal communities in terms of 'in-groups' and 'out-groups' (2007, p. 180). Being part of the in-group means you have to the Aboriginal community acceptable attributes and qualities, which are rewarded with 'inclusion' into the Aboriginal community. Acceptable narratives, acceptable qualities and acceptable attributes for inclusions into the Aboriginal community are constructed by those privileged through their own specific historical narratives. As Huggins contended, 'If you haven't walked the walk how can you possibly talk the talk' (2003, p. 62).

However, if considered as part of the out-group,

> [I]t is difficult to gain access and acceptability in a community, and to be part of the information sharing networks essential to progress in Aboriginal communities. Being part of the in-group, is like having a 'cultural passport', granted to you based upon your family connections, or through being viewed as having the right amount of 'colour' and therefore 'culture' and therefore acceptability. (Lamb 2007, p. 180)

Lamb also described the language of denigration and reported the devastating effects on individuals,

> ...there are a number of terms that Aboriginal people use against each other. Terms like 'coconut', 'upper-class black' and 'Johnny-come-lately black' are often used to denigrate another Aboriginal person and to eradicate that person's identity... usage of words like these underpin attempts to sabotage and undermine a person's respect and acceptability in a community, and they work to marginalise some Aboriginal people... The impact of removing identity results in many individuals feeling demoralised and devalued, not only as Aboriginal people but as individuals. (Lamb 2007, pp. 179–80)

However, as we have already seen, the purpose for which an 'unrecognisable' Aboriginal individual may seek identity confirmation is an important community rationale for scrutiny and exclusion. Gregory Phillips, an Indigenous medical anthropologist, suggested that in the cases where people do claim 'their innate Aboriginality...[merely to claim financial benefits they do] ride the gravy train, and need to be weeded out' (2009, p. 8). However, Phillips introduced another criterion of Aboriginality that extends beyond the context of participation in community organisations or events. This is the more nebulous criterion of 'belonging' that resides in what he called 'our blood memory' (2009, p. 2). This appeal to 'feeling' Aboriginal as a criterion of belonging to the Aboriginal 'world' harnesses a 'strategic essentialism', which serves to legitimise an Aboriginal identity (e.g. Anderson 1994; Dodson 1994).

The Aboriginal concept of belonging to the land is understood to separate and distinguish Aboriginal people from non-Aboriginal people and signifies our constitution within Aboriginal knowledge systems:

> Our ontological relationship to land, the way that the country is constitutive of us, and therefore the inalienable nature of our relationship to land, marks a radical, indeed incommensurable, difference between us and the non-Indigenous. This ontological relation to land constitutes a subject position that we do not share, and which cannot be shared with the post colonial subject whose sense of belonging in this place is tied to migrancy. (Moreton-Robinson 2003, p. 31)

In identity terms, the appeal to various discourses of belonging invokes the need to demonstrate Aboriginal belonging in recognisable ways.

However, in the context of the identity confirmation processes of community recognition, the notion of belonging is situated in a complex web of relations with the nation-state, the corpus of Western knowledge about Aboriginal people, and our own understandings of ourselves passed down over generations. The interface (Nakata 2007) between these sets of now entangled meanings constitutes the significance of 'belonging' in complex, contradictory spaces rather than singular or generalisable discursive frames. Nevertheless, how to demonstrate what is essentially something 'felt' becomes a matter for comment and discussion within the Aboriginal community and enters the community discourse. As a form of 'cultural authorisation' in claims to Aboriginality, such narratives seek to establish an individual's belonging in terms of the shared cultural heritage (see, for example, Tonkinson 1990).

The ontology of belonging is well accepted by Aboriginal and non-Aboriginal people, and embedded and naturalised in contemporary Aboriginal discourse. However, in the context of community recognition, this notion can effectively exclude Aboriginal people who have no surviving connection to land other than in an imaginative or simulated sense (Paradies 2006). There can be, in the process of community recognition, unfair and uneven judgments of appeals to cultural authenticity. For example, people may claim connection to ancestral country and be recognised as 'belonging' when they have never had the opportunity to be culturally socialised into the specific meanings of country. On the other hand, people who have been socialised on country that is not their ancestral place of belonging can be accused of inauthenticity or viewed as appropriators of others' stories. And yet again, those who simulate the meaning of 'belonging' by selective subscriptions to generalised cultural meanings often subscribe not to cultural meanings embedded in particular country but to those 'signs' that demonstrate difference from non-Aboriginal people and identification with Aboriginal people, and which are discursively constructed as significant (Paradies 2006).

Rigid interpretations of the connection between Aboriginal identity and land fail to consider the many people who are of Aboriginal descent but without connections to traditional lands and who must find alternative ways to demonstrate this signifier of Aboriginal identity. What counts as significant in urban settings and significant to community organisations is subject to political struggle over the meanings of Aboriginality as well as over the divisive community contests that affect individuals. For those who have no 'real' connections to land, redefining oneself according to this criterion involves embodying the discourse.

The outcomes of community divisiveness on issues of identity, which affect many Aboriginal people, have drawn attention to the problems of the identity discourse itself. Two community workshops, in 2009 and 2011, at the Australian Institute of Aboriginal and Torres Strait Islander Studies in Canberra sought to address 'a matter of growing concern to many Aboriginal people — the prevalence of an erosive mindset of deficit which pervades many Aboriginal communities and its attachment to notions of identity' (Gorringe et al. 2011, p. 2). The participants of the first workshop acknowledged that 'issues surrounding identity were of fundamental and increasing importance and had a real impact on community and individual relations' (2011, p. 6). The 2009 workshop focussed on two prominent issues — identity and community — noting that, '[i]ssues surrounding identity [can] produce destructive relationships in the Aboriginal community' (Gorringe et al. 2011, p. 6).

The familiar language and meaning of 'erosive mindsets' sums up the negative effects of community identity discourse and processes on community cohesion and on individuals:

> Words which undermine Aboriginal identity are commonly used as insults and tools of social exclusion (such as 'coconut', 'text book black' or 'air-conditioned black'), as are accusations of supposed privilege and favouritism applied to those perceived as (or accused of being) 'real blackfellas'. In doing so, a sense of division is created between individuals, groups, communities and even geography — thus the language/no language, remote/urban or north/south 'divide'. (Gorringe et al. 2011, p. 5)

In juxtaposition, the terms 'community' and 'identity' narrow the way in which individuals can express their identity and produces a self that can be surveilled by community technologies of control, where indiscretions can incur penalties, and where those privileged as authorities are expected to be involved in

> the withholding of access to perceived benefits or privileges, questioning of Aboriginal identity, personal and professional attacks in the workplace and the questioning of motives for

working with Aboriginal people which can lead to disassociation with one's family based on a perceived lack of cultural attributes. (Lamb 2007, p. 177)

COMMUNITY RECOGNITION AS A TECHNOLOGY OF SURVEILLANCE AND SELF-SURVEILLANCE

For the French philosopher Michel Foucault, 'power produces reality, it produces domains of objects and rituals of truth' (1979, p. 194). The current definition of Aboriginality and the Confirmation of Aboriginality process are forms of power/knowledge relations that operationalise and reify particular 'truths' about what it means to be Aboriginal, in order to regulate who can and who can't 'qualify' as Aboriginal. It names, relates, divides and surveils all within.

In other words, the definitional criterion of 'community recognition' subjects an Aboriginal individual to the gaze of the Aboriginal 'community'. The community is thus installed as the central point or the panoptic position, and as the nation-state's substitute for the once all-powerful Aboriginal Protector who stood as the truth interpreter and regulator of Aboriginal identity in colonial eras. Here, where the 'truth' of an Aboriginal identity can or cannot be confirmed, all Aboriginal individuals now regulate according to the 'self-determined' community gaze. However, what is not always recognised is the way in which the community gaze is produced in complex discursive convergences. These are already constituted in a matrix of knowledge/power relations conditioned in much wider sets of knowledge/power and social relations, which obfuscate the many other 'truths' of Aboriginal identities and constrain the discursive spaces in which they can be recognised.

In his book on the birth of the prison, Foucault wrote of the effects of surveillance on those subjected to institutional power. He marked the historical shift from surveillance by the State to processes of self-surveillance where institutional regulations are internalised and individuals and groups begin to subject themselves to scrutiny and self-regulation.

> He who is subjected to a field of visibility, and who knows it, assumes responsibility for the constraint of power; he makes them play spontaneously upon himself; he inscribes in himself the power relation in which he simultaneously plays both roles; he becomes the principle of his own subjection. (Foucault 1979, p. 202)

Community surveillance in the same way impedes our thoughts and actions, causing us to examine our every move through a process of ongoing surveillance and regulation whether we deem ourselves to be thus subjected and regulated or not. Foucault's dictum of the simultaneous occupation of 'surveiller' and 'surveilled' fits well with practices deployed by Aboriginal communities. Those 'identity-privileged' surveil for the evidence of their own privileged narratives among the 'seeking or newly arrived'. Those 'seeking or newly arrived' are scrutinised and upon recognition and authentication by the community, embody the gaze as scrutinisers of themselves and others.

EXAMPLES OF TENSIONS AND CONTESTS IN A COMMUNITY-CONTROLLED ORGANISATION

At a local community organisation meeting I attended, the Confirmation of Aboriginality process and the issues it raises for local Aboriginal people were discussed in relation to access to Aboriginal dental services. A local Elder suggested that light-skinned Aboriginal people be asked to provide a Confirmation of Aboriginality certificate as they were the ones that might not be Aboriginal. Another objected as her grandchildren were fair-skinned. She suggested Aboriginality be identified through family name. It was then argued that surnames do not always denote Aboriginality and that many Aboriginal people are married to non-Aboriginal people. It was suggested also that many recognisable Aboriginal names are not exclusively Aboriginal and many people who are neither related nor Aboriginal share these names. The conversation returned to skin colour and it was proposed that those with dark skin be exempt from providing a Confirmation of Aboriginality certificate. A member stated he knew that Tongan people had used Aboriginal services; but while they were dark-skinned they were clearly not Aboriginal.

The debate continued and the members began to explore other characteristics as examples of definitive proof of Aboriginality. It was suggested at one point that Aboriginal people have a particular gait in the ways they walk. When no conclusion could be reached at the meeting on the appropriate criteria for identification, an older lady of fair complexion suggested that the Confirmation of Aboriginality certificate was the only unbiased way to determine if someone is 'really Aboriginal'. Another Elder challenged this woman's right to speak because she was not Aboriginal. At this point, the fair-skinned woman reached into her bag and pulled a document out for all to view, asserting with confidence that the document was her confirmation of Aboriginality. The Confirmation of Aboriginality certificate thus gave her 'the right to speak' as an Aboriginal person.

I recall this practical example as a way of marking out the layered and competing tensions and complexities that arise from debates about 'who is' and 'who isn't' Aboriginal. Issues of identity are still implicated by skin-colour, gender and physical characteristics such as walking style, and can be further complicated by personal histories and the knowledge of family historical experience that might not be 'provable'. This example illustrates the continuing difficulties in the everyday at the local level, where issues of personal distrust are central to the exercise of having to prove one's identity for official purposes. It also evidences the onerous burden placed on Aboriginal organisations in the name of self-determination and the problem of determining Aboriginal identity for official purposes without an easy method of official identification.

The various statements from participants at the meeting relayed above also reflect a contemporary discourse in the Foucauldian sense, where sets of statements define the regulation of what can and can't be said about a particular object of knowledge, in this case the unstated rules and regulations that prescribe 'who can' and 'who can't' be Aboriginal. These statements call to mind the presence of an intelligible commonsense that has been constructed through relations to 'knowledge, once used to regulate the conduct of others, [that] entail constraint, regulation and the disciplining of practice' (Foucault 1979, p. 27). This discourse of Aboriginality also reveals the specificities of overlapping and intersecting 'regimes of truth' that emerge at the interface of different knowledge systems and which make it difficult to make sense of their contradictions (Nakata 2007). Aboriginality is discursively produced within the limits of particular understandings, which are constituted within an already established order of things, policed by individuals in the everyday, and regulated by the community.

However, what these statements also reveal is the collapse of the issue about how to police access to public services into the criteria for authenticating and judging Aboriginality as an embodied inscription. A discussion that is ostensibly about policing access to restricted services shifts its focus to the policing of Aboriginal bodies, and in this process judges Aboriginal people according to the same criteria as colonial governments and indeed, to the same criteria as hostile non-Aboriginal commentators, such as Andrew Bolt, whom we decry as racist (see discussion in Chapter 4).

The criteria of community recognition falls prey to its discursive antecedents as it purportedly seeks to support and express the practice of political self-determination. The concept of community recognition as evidenced above assumes that all Aboriginal people are mutually recognisable when there is an abundance of evidence that suggests this is not so, at least not for the purposes of official recognition. Socially, the test of community recognition still proceeds through understood and informal protocols of announcing who one is, where one comes from and who one is connected to. This protocol fails miserably in its translation into the formal arena.

CHAPTER 11
COMMUNITY DISCOURSE ON THE CONFIRMATION OF ABORIGINALITY AND ABORIGINAL IDENTITY: A CASE STUDY

The *Koori Mail* is a fortnightly Indigenous newspaper that is distributed nationally. 'Your Say' is a forum in this publication where people can write in and raise areas of concern or interest, publish poetry, search for lost relations, as well as voice opinions over issues which are generally of interest to Aboriginal and Torres Strait Islander readers. In 2006, a series of contributions to this column focused specifically on issues surrounding Aboriginality and the Confirmation of Aboriginality process. Here I present an analysis of some of these contributions to evidence the tensions and problems as expressed in public community discourse, many of which resonate with the range of positions described within the scholarly conversations in previous chapters. These contributions speak to the meaning of both Aboriginality and community and the legitimacy of the Confirmation of Aboriginality process.

THE CONVERSATION

Welsh, a contributor to the column, opened this conversation, suggesting that he wrote in to 'Your Say' to 'generate discussion about Confirmation of Aboriginality, as it appears to be in some cases a booming industry' (2006, p. 26). He then moved to name and authorise himself through announcements of his membership of a number of community-based organisations. As an 'active' community member he was favourably positioned to speak as someone well-informed on the issues. He raised the rhetorical question of who can or cannot be Aboriginal to highlight the issues that are, according to him, 'constantly discussed by community-oriented Aboriginal people' who are particularly concerned about 'Uncle Toms, Johnny come lately's [sic], and, last but not least, the "nine-to-fivers", (2006, p. 26).

The use of the 'Uncle Tom' label describes Aboriginal people who are deemed assimilated in their thinking and their actions and are assumed to not share Aboriginal community values. The 'Johnny come lately' tag applies to Aboriginal people who have just 'found out' about their Aboriginality. This term is also used for those who are accepted as Aboriginal but have never actively participated in community activities, utilised community organisations, or been vocal or active in regards to issues which concern the community. The reference to 'nine-to-fivers' is used for people who occupy identified Aboriginal positions but do not work for the community beyond those hours. He suggests there is concern about people who 'turn up in a community, claim some relation for five minutes, ascertain a Confirmation of Aboriginality, and suddenly they become ghosts' (Welsh 2006, p. 26).

Welsh's concern expressed a wider perception of, and a resentment towards, Aboriginal individuals who do not participate in Aboriginal community organisations and events. These people are often assumed to have not grown up as community-oriented Aboriginal people, nor faced hardship, nor participated in identified historical struggles. This locates a particular space for the identity discourse where Aboriginality implies a particular narrative of low socio-economic status, restricted access to skills and education, or disadvantage (see for example, Eckermann 1977a, pp. 12–13). Conversely, the absence of such a narrative calls into question an individual's claim to be Aboriginal.

Welsh raised the following questions to other readers, noted here in detail because they generate a significant level of response over ensuing weeks:

> Should there be a cut-off point — e.g., Aboriginal person marries non-Aboriginal — they have children — then the same circumstance happens for the next three or so generations. Should they be able to claim Aboriginality?
>
> Is being Aboriginal claiming a parent or some other kin, or is it about self-identification?

> When someone is accepted as a member of an Aboriginal corporation, does that entitle them to a Confirmation of Aboriginality form, or should they be made to attend general meetings for 12 months prior to giving them a Confirmation of Aboriginality form?
>
> What is the legal process and how much would it cost for people to challenge a confirmation of Aboriginality, for those that have been provided under the table and /or under false pretences. (Welsh 2006, p. 26)

The responses to this initial contribution point to the unresolved questions about what counts as the evidence of being Aboriginal as well as to the concern about fraudulent processes. The first response gave a view from the other side. Under the heading, 'Lost…and accused of supplying fake documents', a contributor claimed to have been refused treatment from an Aboriginal health service as his documentation was deemed 'fake' (Melohn 2006, p. 26). This respondent thought the situation could have been resolved easily if the local aboriginal health service looked up his uncle's details, as his uncle was previously the chairperson of a local Aboriginal organisation. The writer asked what should he do? 'It's just like discrimination to me. I'm lost. What should I do, forget about my heritage? I've never asked for anything' (2006, p. 22). To establish his credentials as an Aboriginal person he aligned himself to the three-pronged definition: familial links to his Uncle perhaps because he was the more identifiable authority in the community, his links to the community by claiming to know some Aboriginal Elders, and conveying that he identified with the community.

In a subsequent article a contributor 'admit[s] that I am not a purebred Aboriginal person. I am of mixed race' (Brown 2006, p. 22) and then offers a list of Aboriginal attributes:

> Love and respect all other Aboriginal community members,
>
> Crimes of any kind will always be met with punishment,
>
> Shamelessness and any other depraved act is prohibited, treat others how you would like to be treated yourself,
>
> Forsake all other gods, excepting Biami,

> Value traditional lands and be a good custodian so that your children will grow strong in this belief,
>
> Teach moral lessons through dreamtime stories to educate,
>
> Refer to your Elders and treasure the young, faithful leadership means being a community role models,
>
> Pollution of the Spirit is a pollution of the sacred heart. (Brown 2006, p. 22)

Another 'mixed descent' participant in the debate claims, there are

> two different groups among the persons who are white, living in mainstream society, and know of Aboriginal ancestry…One group are descendants of women who were traded into white families to cause that long-term family reciprocal obligation to exist between Aborigines and those who invaded and farmed our land. [And the second]…who simply prefer being mainstream whitefellas; who don't care much about 'the blacks', as they call all identifiable Aboriginal population regardless of skin colour. (Copas 2006, p. 25)

Although this contributor acknowledged that her 'grandmothers and their grandmothers certainly "passed as white"' (Copas 2006, p. 25) as a survival strategy to protect their children, she highlighted the varied and often irretrievable circumstances of previous generations to distinguish herself from Aboriginal people who 'conspire with invaders to their own advantage' (2006, p. 25).

Another contributor (Hinton 2006, p. 25) asked, 'How do we sort out the real from the "wannabes"?' Her concern was that high paying identified positions within government departments are not always occupied by people she would consider Aboriginal and that these are people who do little for the community — 'we have some coconuts (black on the outside and white on the inside)' (2006, p. 25). The writer cautions that '[m]ost Aboriginal people can pick an Aboriginal person out of the crowd whether they are black, white or brindle' (Hinton 2006, p. 25). Of equal concern were those who 'pass themselves off as being white' and who work in 'high-profile jobs' (Hinton 2006, p. 25). The people who can 'pass' in these roles 'didn't have to put up with the name-calling, the bashings and everything else that comes with being distinctly Aboriginal' (Hinton 2006, p. 25) and were therefore accused of not understanding racism.

In the next edition an anonymous contributor who knew Hinton wrote in to accuse her of 'hypocrisy' (Anonymous 2006, p. 24), and as occupying one of those many 'high-paid government identified positions' (2006, p. 24). The contributor questioned Hinton's contribution to the community and implied that she merely 'grandstands her ideas and imposes barriers on Aboriginal people who have worked hard to educate themselves and obtain positions within government to help our people' (2006, p. 24).

In following weeks, a challenge was put up under the heading, 'Proof of Aboriginality' (Briggs-Smith 2006, p. 24). The author was a well-recognised Aboriginal woman who had made contributions to the documentation of local Aboriginal history, archives and library services. She discussed the 'booming industry' of providing Confirmation of Aboriginality certificates to people whom she considers to not be Aboriginal. Her concern was that 'many have gained Confirmation of Aboriginality just through claiming one descendant who dates back to the colonial days' (2006, p. 24). She suggested certain parameters must be reached:

> You must be of Aboriginal descent through immediate Aboriginal genealogy blood lines.
>
> Name your ancestors who have identified, lived and were known and accepted in their Aboriginal community.
>
> Name yourself and immediate family members, who currently identify, live, are known and accepted as being of Aboriginal descent.
>
> You must currently live as an Aboriginal community-orientated person, and be known and accepted by the Aboriginal community where you live and work. (2006, p. 24)

To police such criteria, Briggs-Smith proposed a 'special unit' be set up by 'the Government to investigate those whom we challenge that have not met the full requirements' (2006, p. 24) and suggested it could be similar to the Native Title Units. In this vision, it is suggested that the investigations should include retrospective challenges to those who have already received a Confirmation of Aboriginality document 'be they on the top of the table or under' (2006, p. 24). Briggs-Smith's solution sought to abandon all notions of self-determination, preferring the colonial practices of government administration. She sutured over the Tasmanian precedent where challenges to the identity status of many claiming to be Aboriginal could not be resolved by the Tribunal charged with the investigation and the Tribunal concluded Aboriginal identity confirmations could only be done by the community (see Guilliatt 2002, pp. 18–23).

Not surprisingly, in a later article, an Aboriginal academic responded with some candour, 'is it me or are there other Indigenous people out there that are disgusted about that little piece of paper that is supposed to prove our identity' (Green 2006, p. 24).

Another contributor added a change of focus to the conversation, directing it towards those more readily accepted as traditionally oriented Aboriginal people:

> [W]e should also have the right to query the many non-thinned down blooded people who by the very nature of their Aboriginality are de-valuing our culture and identity: Those who condemn advancement for monetary gain, those who sell culture and claim ownership solely instead of accrediting their knowledge to community and the carriers of culture, those who sit back and take perks, cash in on the lurks and gain the benefits of their Aboriginality selfishly. We should have the right to question the injustices and the inequalities attributed to the many falsities that arise from 'Aboriginality'. (Bartlett 2006, p. 24)

A further element of Aboriginality was brought into the discussion. This contributor had been searching for over a decade for 'proof' of her Aboriginal heritage. During this time, she made it clear that she neither wanted a Confirmation of Aboriginality document nor sought any benefits related to her claim of Aboriginal heritage. Her motivation was a spiritual connection to her 'people, country and [my] soul' (Bartlett 2006, p. 24).

THE CHECKMATE

These statements mirror other community positions. But what do all these community positions reveal about community discourses on Aboriginal identity, the meanings of being Aboriginal, and the problems and contests about the Confirmation of Aboriginality process? It cannot be said these views are representative of any consensus 'community' position. But they do provide evidence of the convergence of tensions, contests and the authorities of delimitation in which the discourse and discussions about Confirmation of Aboriginality are embedded.

What is also very evident is the degree to which internal community surveillance forms part of the regulation of Aboriginal identity. Further, the questions of 'who is' and 'what counts' is unresolved but still seeking resolution. However, rather than express the possibilities of 'freedom to live outside the cage created by other people's images and projections' (Dodson 1994, p. 5), the discourse evidenced in these articles and letters is constrained by its own limits and would appear to offer few spaces for moving forward in the present moment. Rather, it appears to work to impose its own cage by restricting the acceptable narratives through which Aboriginal people can 'transform that identity creatively', as Dodson hoped (1994, p. 5).

Throughout the 'Your Say' discussions, nearly all authors attempted to demonstrate their Aboriginal identity as the source of authority that enabled them to question others. And why wouldn't they, given the constant surveilling of each other? The contributors illustrated an understanding of what it meant to be able to demonstrate an acceptable narrative that conforms and complies in the face of surveillance. More importantly, they understood the penalties for not doing so. All contributors tried to relay what is expected of them, knowing that even in the written form expressions of Aboriginal identity are being observed, evaluated, assessed, discredited or acknowledged in the community. Only one individual expressed disgust with the need for certified Confirmation of Aboriginality processes.

The close association between participation in community organisations or events and a legitimate claim to be Aboriginal is particularly underlined by the conversation. The non-recognition of people in 'high-level' identified positions as contributors to the Aboriginal community persists, drowned in a discourse that associates good pay with self-interest, unless one works in a community organisation. The accepted narrative of Aboriginality associated with disadvantage — a disadvantage that must be able to be narrated through generations and place — authenticates identity status only so far as individuals are recognised as participating at grassroots 'community' levels. The appeal to spiritual connections attempts to decouple identity claims from financial benefits and attempts to situate

Confirmation of Aboriginality requirements in an emotional context rather than in terms of access to material benefits and services.

Contained in many of the arguments made in this conversation is a subtext of fear that announcements of a diversity of Aboriginal experiences will diminish the hardship experienced by many Aboriginal people and erode the collective solidarity built around 'shared' cultural heritage and colonial experience. The idea that all Aboriginal people share a collective experience is common among Aboriginal as well as non-Aboriginal people, and is accepted as a primary signifier of authenticity. Some of these community arguments contradict and invalidate their own assertions. For example, Briggs-Smith's concern was that people were aligning their Aboriginal backgrounds singularly based on distant relatives, and not necessarily fulfilling the requirements of identifying and being accepted by the Aboriginal community (2006, p. 24). Yet people who appeal to some distant past ancestor as their claim to Aboriginality, in nearly all cases she asserted, were not able to prove this as there is incomplete archival documentation to verify family stories passed down. If written documentation does not exist, authenticating one's descent through this process is thus impossible and Briggs-Smith was able to checkmate those separated from their heritage, in support of her views.

There is little thought, on the other hand, to how this serves to discount the many undocumented histories of the first people being brutally taken from country, from families, from parents, from brothers and sisters. First disconnected from country and kin, now many Aboriginal people seeking to reclaim Aboriginal identities continue to be disconnected because they do not have the right paperwork. Thus the Aboriginal community can condemn as colonial racism the events and governments that oversaw the destruction of families but not so the community's roles today in requiring this same paperwork of each other. To argue support for a lack of documented evidence, however, would be to risk being accused of not being Aboriginal.

THE SILENCE

Such attempts in the everyday to 'fix' the meanings or 'essence' of Aboriginality appear punitive but can be understood as the desire to have clear and distinct boundaries between Aboriginal people and other Australians. Surveillance arises to reinforce these boundaries, which are then maintained through exclusionary practices that go on to restrict inclusion of those who upset a privileged community sensibility about what it means to be Aboriginal. In the process, the similarities between community surveillance and colonial regimes of classification and the denouncements of Aboriginal individuals by the popular mainstream media appear to escape notice. In this sense the Aboriginal community constitutes and regulates the social spaces in which Aboriginal identity can be claimed and confirmed in very similar ways to past regimes through a constant surveillance by groups and individuals to weed out those 'who are not Aboriginal enough'. In the ways that this occurs, many Aboriginal people appear to gain more legitimacy by exposing or 'weeding out' the perceived imposters, with little regard for the difficulties in confirming Aboriginality in the current discursive conditions.

CHALLENGING THE DISCOURSE

The difficulty for Aboriginal people who may want to challenge the community discourse publicly is illustrated in the following example. Loretta Kelly, an Aboriginal lawyer who contributes a column in the *National Indigenous Times* conducted a survey at the Aboriginal Legal Service conference (Coffs Harbour 2010). She asked delegates, 'Do you agree with the 3 part legal definition of Aboriginality? (1. Descent 2. Self-identification 3. Aboriginal community acceptance)' (Kelly 2010, p. 24). Over thirty Aboriginal Legal Service staff members were approached and were interested in making comment but the condition for participants was to put comments 'on the record'. Despite the initial interest, only ten agreed to be identified publicly. Kelly reported that many did not want to go on the record due to 'fear of reprisal in their community' (2010, p. 24). Nevertheless, in many Aboriginal community public, private and institutional spaces, the popular community discourse is mediated and/or resisted or contested, albeit often 'silently'.

Under the rubric of 'Aboriginal identity' there is evidence of a constant dilemma that demands both freedom and fixity of identity. Throughout the public discourse and inter-course presented in my analysis, there is not only the evidence of a constant process of negotiation but also the evidence of suppression and contradiction. In other words, it is also through the absences and gaps in community positions that the public discourse is able to be produced in the forms it takes. In this sense, it is as much *what is not said* in the community discourses as it is *what is said* that regulates Aboriginal identity. However what *can be said* is limited and regulated by the discourse and what *might be said* to shift the discourse, in testing the limits of the discourse, must risk community censure of the individuals who dare to say the 'un-sayable', the unintelligible, the incomprehensible, or the 'unpopular'. These gaps and silences arguably accumulate in those 'uncertain' and less 'fixed' meanings that unsettle the certainty and fixity of polarised antagonistic op-positions. To follow Macherey's line of thought, the community discourse

> cannot speak of the more or less complex opposition which structures it; though it is its expression and embodiment. In its every particle, the… [discourse] manifests, uncovers, what it cannot say. This silence gives it life. (1990, p. 217)

The 'profoundly antagonistic, conflictual and even incommensurable' (Bhabha 1994, p. 2) dialogues in this 'contested terrain' (Nakata 2007, p. 197) of Aboriginal identity are hard to make sense of by those contained/constrained within the limits of the discourse. Aboriginal identity — as it is enacted and expressed in the everyday through both the spoken and written word — is played out daily through constant community and self-surveillance. Although the commentary in the Koori Mail newspaper has in many ways raised more questions than answers, it has demonstrated the complex nature of Aboriginal identity politics in 'the reality as it arises for those who live it' (Smith 1987, p. 110). The constant tug-of-war between authenticity and diversity of trajectories and experiences operating at the Cultural Interface (Nakata 2007) provides early insights into the cracks and leaks in corporeal borders that seek to contain a 'true' and mostly 'exclusive' Aboriginal identity.

The process of Confirmation of Aboriginality is both a demand imposed by the nation-state and an instrument of Aboriginal collective political self-determination. The Confirmation of Aboriginality certificate has come to be one of the more powerful means of authentication possible for a person's claim to Aboriginality, especially when there is an absence of any typical sign of Aboriginal heritage. While it provides a defence for Aboriginal identities it does not necessarily provide protection from accusations of 'fakery' for those who have them. This is because the legitimacy of the process is itself a site of community contest. The requirement to confirm Aboriginal identities according to definitional criteria also produces and harnesses a divisive community politics and an Aboriginal identity politics with sometimes devastating effects on individuals. As one Aboriginal woman put it: 'It's not easy being Aboriginal, out there. It is not easy' (Kickett 1999, p. 74).

CHAPTER 12
RESEARCHING THE POLITICS OF IDENTITY

> [I]dentification is in the end self hiding inside the many other, more superficial or artificially imposed 'selves' which a people with a shared history and ancestry hold in common and which can stabilize, fix or guarantee an unchanging 'oneness' or cultural belongingness underlying all the other superficial differences. It accepts that identities are never unified and, in late modern times, increasingly fragmented and fractured; never singular but multiply constructed across different, often intersecting and antagonistic, discourses, practices and positions. They are subject to a radical historicization, and are constantly in the process of change and transformation.
>
> (Hall 1996, pp. 3–4)

In 2011, I completed a Doctor of Philosophy, and this book is one of the outcomes of that study. My aim was to gain an understanding of what sustains the process of making and remaking Aboriginal identity in contemporary times. To this end, I conducted interviews with Aboriginal people who were prepared to speak about their Aboriginal identity. There was a balance of both male and female interviewees, and they ranged in age from nineteen to seventy years old. The participants in my research included people who claim to have always known of their Aboriginal descent and others who have recently learned they had Aboriginal heritage. Some who had always known they were Aboriginal had Confirmation of Aboriginality certificates, or the evidence and means to acquire this document. Those who were employed were primarily working in 'identified Indigenous positions'. Participants' comments are included in this section, and are identified with the codes they were given during data collection, for example 'P26'.

Given the popularity of online social networking sites I also explored participants' online profiles and engagements as well as other public sites where questions of Aboriginal identity are posed or counterposed. I was particularly interested in how Aboriginal people represented and negotiated the issues of Aboriginal identity and community recognition in the online space, more specifically Facebook. (Chapter 18 explores Aboriginal identity and community online.)

THE POLITICS OF IDENTITY: MY RESEARCH

My research aim was to illuminate how particular Aboriginal identities are produced and come into being and/or how they are maintained and expressed in ways that affirm a positive sense of Aboriginality as an embodied identity, while often inadvertently consolidating and reifying colonial inscriptions and practices. Another aim was to illuminate the spaces or processes through which some of these Aboriginal identities are enabled to resist these constraints and work towards questioning or widening the meanings or spaces in which they can define themselves as Aboriginal and/or be recognised as such.

As creative 'self-determining' agents in this particular historical moment, how do participants know, define, construct, affirm, negotiate and express their Aboriginal identity in the face of various discursive and material constraints? The discursive constraints might include, for example, understandings from a range of knowledge sources (both European and Aboriginal) *about* Aboriginal people, or about the *meaning* of being Aboriginal, as evidenced in Part One of this book. Material constraints might include, for example, not looking or sounding Aboriginal, not having a narrative of disadvantage, or not being able to demonstrate connections to or knowledge of country, kin and culture. The convergence of such constraints emerges in the ways that individuals narrate their experiences of discovering, knowing, becoming, transforming, expressing and performing what it means to be Aboriginal.

An intention of the interview process was to allow participants to bring their own reflections to the surface of the conversation. However, as a researcher who also has experience of this journey, which informs the focus of my research inquiry, I guided the process through a series of broad, loosely sequenced questions which revolved around:

How participants came to know they were Aboriginal and how they identified;

What being Aboriginal meant to them and what they thought was important to know and value;

How participants experienced being Aboriginal, for example, whether they were recognised and/or called to defend their Aboriginality;

How participants expressed their identity in personally meaningful ways, and what sort of things they did to publicly signal they were Aboriginal; and

Participants' views on the legal definition and Confirmation of Aboriginality process.

For this research, I focused primarily on those intergenerationally disconnected Aboriginal people who must still 'struggle' to secure their identities in the midst of this long history of government policies and practices that positioned their forebears and now seek to position them. Aboriginal people with intergenerational dislocations in their personal histories, it seems, must narrate a history and personal commitment to a larger Indigenous narrative. They must fit themselves into the space — and where and when they do not fit, they must reconstruct a suitable narrative, a body of knowledge, and demonstrate a political commitment as a condition of membership of the Aboriginal community. This means that in the present, as in past historical periods, these individuals are positioned to deny their full sense of self, as official impositions and personal choices are once again marshalled to parade and posture as one and the same, through the binary Aboriginal politics of identity.

In contemporary Australia Aboriginal people are often positioned to regulate themselves and others, as the agents of governments, social institutions and colonial administrators once did. We define and determine just who can and cannot be considered Aboriginal, referring our disputes to courts of Australian law. Where once the plethora of definitions and categories produced ambiguous and shifting identity positions that resulted in confusion and uncertainty, now the categories are reduced to two — Aboriginal or not-Aboriginal. But arguably the criteria used to evidence and confirm Aboriginal or not-Aboriginal status are as unforgiving and contrived, but also as discretionary as ever, perpetuating confusion, insecurity and uncertainty.

While all Aboriginal identities can be called into question in this regime, it is Aboriginal people without officially recognised personal narratives, and who do not look recognisably Aboriginal, who carry the heaviest burden of the history of colonialism. They are arguably weighed down further by the burden of identity 'work' that requires them to construct and perform 'authentic' identities in the public space — the public space that fails to recognise and acknowledge their personal histories as ones forged though colonial practices. The space for the expression of more meaningful personal identities that reflect the more fluid and complex experiences of identity production are closed off to many by the political imperatives of resisting the apparatuses of the nation-state and persisting with an Aboriginality defined within essentially cultural paradigms. However, the struggles over 'who is' and 'what counts' is an ongoing process that increasingly involves contestation within the Aboriginal community. A large question arises around how to deal with the historical experience of those who for various reasons have been intergenerationally disconnected from the 'collective' experience of being Aboriginal.

THEORETICAL POSITIONS ON IDENTITY

The study of identity is not a new field of research. From the early psychological studies by James Marcia (1966) on adolescent identity and Erik Erikson's studies (1950, 1968, 1979) of identity formations over a lifespan, scholarship has been contributing to and developing understandings of psychological identity, namely how individuals see themselves as a person and/or in relation to others (e.g. Ricoeur & Blarney 1995). As well, drawings from anthropological studies of kinship and social organisation have been brought to bear on understandings of identity as also constituted through membership of a collective, fixed by a common ancestry and thus inherited (e.g. Beckett 1958, 1988b). Other social theorists have contested such a standpoint and instead have asserted that identity is not fixed but negotiable and adaptive (Langton 1994). Edward Said (1993) reminds us also of the presence of particular identities that are inscribed as 'other' to serve someone else's interests in the world. The possibility that a sociological identity could be much more than an identification of 'sameness' but rather constantly changing, and potentially everything, has brought mixed scholarly reactions, including calls to do away with the term altogether (e.g. Bayart 2005).

Charles Taylor (1989) and Stuart Hall (1990, 1996) conceptualise identity as a process that occurs within a dynamic of changing times and circumstances. Postcolonial theorists (e.g. Ashcroft, Griffiths & Tiffins 1989) are also oriented to the diverse and changing social experience and the space it provides to foreground a political framework to consider colonial influences on Aboriginal people's identity. Indeed, their identification of marginalised people as Gramscian subalterns,[12] along with Gayatri Spivak's call for 'strategic essentialism' (1988a), affords a space for colonised people to unite and speak as a collective while using a clear and unambiguous image of identity as 'solidarity in resistance'. However, Spivak cautions that the subaltern identity should not be confined singularly to a narrow politics of representation that 'must traffic in a radical textual practice of difference' (1988a, p. 27). Homi Bhabha (1994) goes further to challenge the assumed harmony ascribed to groups whose histories may be common:

> How do strategies of representation of empowerment come to be formulated in the competing claims of communities where, despite shared histories of deprivation and discrimination, the exchange of values, meaning and priorities may not always be collaborative and dialogical, but may be profoundly antagonistic, conflictual and even incommensurable? (1994, p. 2)

To understand the mutability and problematic of Aboriginal identities in colonial societies, it is helpful to first consider Fredrik Barth's (1969) work in the 1960s on ethnic boundaries. Social groupings, such as subalterns, Indigenous people, in-groups, out-groups and so forth have, and maintain, boundaries that can be inclusive as much as they can be exclusive (Tajfel & Turner 1986). As Frantz Fanon (1963, 1967, 1970) and Roland Barthes (1970) noted, group divisions can lead to a sense of self and representational types that can mirror, even in resistance, the language, culture and histories of the colonisers — what Jacques Lacan (1977) alluded to as a completeness in the body of others. Hall (1996) points out that in contemporary times forms of cultural identity have been reduced to a politics of location, where representational types no longer operate within their original meanings and

---

12 Following Gramsci's (1971) work in critical theory and postcolonialism, 'subaltern' is the social group who are socially, politically and geographically outside of the hegemonic power structure of the colony and colonial homeland.

where subjectification processes of identification is sutured over. The challenge in the field of identity studies today is not only the difficulty in locating appropriate analytical tools with which to theorise the shifting nature of 'self' in contemporary times, but also more about what Martin Nakata (2007) describes as the challenge of defining the area for study and the question one needs to ask when one arrives there.

Influenced by feminist theorists (see Smith 1987; Polhaus 2002; Harding 2004), Nakata (2007) recognised the need for an alternate theory that could provide a way to analyse the varied and diverse experiences of Indigenous peoples under colonial regimes. For him, an Indigenous standpoint theory must provide the means to 'help understand our varied responses to the colonial world' (2007, p. 217).

INDIGENOUS STANDPOINT THEORY

Indigenous research methodological frameworks have given power to Indigenous standpoints that more accurately and sensitively guide future research towards more diverse, appropriate and valid representations of Indigenous perspectives, voices and experiences (Morton-Robinson 2014; Rigney 1997; Nakata 2007; Martin 2008; Tuhiwai Smith 2012). I drew on the work of Indigenous scholars in developing a theoretical framework that provided a critique of those Western methodological frameworks that have (often knowingly) continually perpetuated and accentuated the negative impacts of colonisation for Indigenous peoples. Specifically, I utilised the work of Nakata and in particular his notions of an Indigenous standpoint, as both an entry point for inquiry and a tool for analysis. Within contemporary academic dialogue there are many interpretations and understandings of Indigenous standpoint theory. For example, at a conference I attended while completing my studies, Indigenous standpoint theory was discussed as a personal perspective, a collective perspective and as a defining characteristic of the Indigenous researcher. Closer attention to Nakata's work on Indigenous standpoint theory reveals that it is

> a distinct form of analysis, and is itself both a discursive construction and an intellectual device to persuade others and elevate what might not have been a focus of attention by others. It is not deterministic of any truth but it lays open a basis from which to launch a range of possible arguments for a range of possible purposes. (2007, p. 214)

This does not mean a personal perspective or an Indigenous standpoint simply because one is Indigenous. An Indigenous standpoint theory 'is not an Indigenous way of "doing knowledge" (2007, p. 214). Rather, as Nakata suggested, it provides a way for Indigenous researchers 'to explore the actualities of the everyday and discover how to express them conceptually from within that experience, rather than deploy predetermined concepts and categories for explaining experience' (2007, p. 214).

Nakata identifies three useful principles for an Indigenous standpoint theory. Firstly, that the researcher's position in the everyday is 'discursively constituted within and constitutive of complex sets of social relations as expressed through the social organisation of…[the] everyday' (2007, p. 216). Secondly, as a researcher, one must recognise 'Indigenous agency as framed within the limits and possibilities' (2007, p. 216) of what can be known from this constituted position. The third principle is an incorporation of the 'tensions' he refers to as the constant 'tug-of-war' that informs as well as limits what can be said or known in the everyday. The 'constant tensions' (2007, p. 216) in such locales lie in points of emergence and becoming, in spaces where Indigenous knowers shape and reshape their engagements. These engagements do not necessarily seek or reflect unity in the everyday world but can reflect and provide evidence of the contradictions and ambiguities of the constituted Indigenous space.

Foucault (1979, p. 60) also reminds us that individuals are self-determining agents capable of challenging and resisting the structures of domination. He argued that although agents necessarily exist within regimes of power/knowledge, these regimes do not determine the experiences they have, the ways they can exercise their reason, the beliefs they can adopt or the actions they can attempt to perform. Following Foucault, Nakata's standpoint theory sees Indigenous peoples as having agency, as creative subjects, even if the given social contexts in which the agency occurs is restrictive.

Drawing on the work of feminist philosopher Gail Pohlhaus (2002), Nakata suggested that an Indigenous standpoint theory can assist a way to theorise

> knowledge from a particular and interested position — not to produce the 'truth' of Indigenous position but to better reveal the workings of knowledge and how understanding of Indigenous people is caught up and implicated in its work. (2007, p. 215)

Nakata suggested that an Indigenous standpoint theory offers a method of inquiry useful for analysing experiences, which are 'excluded or subjugated within intellectual knowledge production' (2007, p. 213). This form of analysis, following Nakata, is ongoing, always in production, and a discursively constructed intellectual tool to focus attention on particular aspects of the data; and for the purposes of my inquiry, the production and consumption of standpoints on Aboriginal identities. Nakata's conceptualisation of a standpoint theory for Indigenous research and researchers provides a way for understanding the complexities of Indigenous experience and Indigenous struggles within contemporary times. Indigenous standpoint theory is complemented by and perhaps best understood alongside his concept of the Cultural Interface, a term he coined to denote the everyday site of struggle that continues to confine colonised people.

The Cultural Interface represents a site of negotiation, resistance and interaction whereby the specificities of the everyday articulations of Indigenous people can be understood in both productive and non-productive ways. The Cultural Interface is located at

> the intersection of the Western and Indigenous domain...the place where we live and learn, the place that conditions our lives, the place that shapes our futures and more to the point the place where we are active agents in our own lives — here we make decisions — our lifeworlds. (2002, p. 285)

As can be seen from earlier chapters, representations of Aboriginal identities have become increasingly problematic. Their different forms have become embedded in histories of colonialism, policy discourse and practices, and as they converge with Aboriginal lineages and customary ways, they become the constitutive elements for a site filled with tension and confusion. In terms of its usefulness to my study, the Cultural Interface disrupts the intelligibility of mainstream academic thought that situates experiences and representations of experiences uni-linearly as well as simplistically as cause–effect, us–them, centre–other, white–black, and so forth. It helps me as researcher to understand that

> there are spaces where people operate on a daily basis making choices according to the particular constraints and possibilities of the moment. People act in these spaces, drawing on their

own understandings of what is emerging all around them…in this process people are constantly producing new ways of understanding and at the same time filtering out elements of all those ways of understanding that prevents them from making sense at a particular point in time and trying in the process to preserve a particular sense of self… (Nakata 2007, p. 201)

The Cultural Interface allows us to consider that although Aboriginal people have been subjugated this does not mean that all Aboriginal people were uniformly oppressed in the same way or experienced their oppression in the same way. But neither does this imply that although some Aboriginal people were able to work positively from within their particular experiences or escape more extreme practices and effects of oppression, that the experience of colonisation was, in all or part, a 'positive experience' for any Aboriginal person. The Cultural Interface makes problematic the space of everyday Aboriginal negotiations without applying limitations singularly to the canonical lens, and enables me to arrive as a researcher knowing in advance that limits are already in place in the debates around identity.

A RECONCEPTUALISATION OF MULTIPLE MODES OF ABORIGINAL SUBJECTIVITY

Variations in identities — or variant selves as I have utilised the term for the multiple and often conflicting modes of subjectivity that Aboriginal people negotiate daily — are not merely random adoptions of identity that suit particular contexts. Variant selves is a term I am using to depict the complex nature of Aboriginality without resorting to the uncomfortable term 'mixed descent' which, to my mind, as noted, implies a quantum of Aboriginality that can be measured and reduced according to colonial discourses. Terms such as 'dual heritage' and 'mixed descent' have become more acceptable ways of reducing Aboriginality to a limited fraction of possibilities for a 'self' or 'selves'. The term variant selves, on the other hand, conjures up the possibility for additional selves, or multiple ways of being that cannot be neatly diluted into manageable compartments of disciplinary knowledge. In relation to urban Aboriginal identities, the connotation of variant selves allows for a wider expression or manifestation of *being*, to use that western metaphysical term. The term variant selves represent the possibility and availability of multiple subject positions; to my mind, it says for Aboriginal people what the term identity says for non-Aboriginal people. That is, they are not limited by the dominant discourses that ascribe and dictate their identity. Variant selves give Aboriginal people the possibilities to name terms, discard already given terms, and reposition themselves in the everyday.

Variant selves is a concept that enabled me to see strategic intent by Aboriginal people. In other words, the term enabled me to see with more clarity that, at the Cultural Interface,

> we have developed a reading of ourselves at the interface of colliding trajectories…we are fighting against the odds: and we are making and re-making ourselves in the everyday…we have some agency in history. (Nakata 2007, p. 197)

The multiple identities in all their variations can be made sense of through a lens of possibility, rather than through an interpretation that sees only a chameleon-like set of 'selves' donned for particular occasions. Variant selves are often political constructions of 'self' that speak to — but are not limited to — the identities prescribed by colonial discourses. We are alert to how we have come to 'define ourselves primarily in our difference to others and [how] the descriptions and characteristics of this difference have been firmly developed within the Western knowledge tradition' (Nakata 2007, p. 198).

I was keen to explore what conditions the possibilities in the ways we sign ourselves as Aboriginal in the everyday. The Cultural Interface offers a way to contextualise and understand the formation of variant selves in a 'space that abounds with contradictions, ambiguities, conflict and contestation of meaning' (Nakata 2007, p. 199). The Cultural Interface thus is a space informed by particular variables, including time, space, memory, competing discourses and social, political and economic organisations from both Aboriginal and non-Aboriginal beginnings.

> All of these elements cohere together at the interface in the everyday to inform, constrain or enable what can be seen or not seen, what can be brought to the surface or sutured over, what can be said or not said, heard or not heard, understood or misunderstood, what knowledge can be accepted, rejected, legitimised or marginalised, or what actions

can be taken or not taken on both individual and collective levels. (Nakata 2007, p. 199)

Within this interpretative frame the variant selves emerge informed by what can be recalled from their lived experiences, as they simultaneously negotiate the myriad competing and contesting discourses. The Cultural Interface then is a site of 'possibility as well as constraints' (2007, p. 200) and it is in these everyday negotiations that people draw upon their knowledge, that is what they have learnt, experienced or have come to understand as their subject position. It is here that subjects make and re-make the meaning of their lives. As Foucault observed:

> Whenever one can describe, between a number of statements, such a system of dispersion, whenever, between objects, types of statement, concepts, or thematic choices, one can define a regularity, (an order, correlations, positions and functionings, transformations), we will say, for the sake of convenience that we are dealing with a discursive formation. (2004, p. 41)

In other words, in the everyday space of the Cultural Interface, Aboriginal identities are imagined, formed, tried on for size, negotiated, reworked and/or discarded as Aboriginal subjects function in both productive and destructive ways to enact their lived realities. The Cultural Interface enables a configuration of the everyday not just as a contested space but also one that is constantly being negotiated. Nakata sees this space as 'a productive theoretical space…a re-theorisation of the lived position as the space where…people make and remake themselves as they encounter competing and changing traditions' (2007, p. 12).

EVERYDAY LIFE AND AGENCY

According to French Jesuit scholar Michel de Certeau (1988), locating human agency in everyday life begins with challenging the idea that cultural subjects are passive onlookers, controlled by a force of established rules. For him, they are not simply faceless consumers but active producers, 'poets of their own acts, silent discoverers of their own paths in the jungle of functionalist rationality' (1988, p. xviii). De Certeau was interested in everyday activities and behaviours, which can manipulate or subvert the discursive order in what he refers to as 'a network of antidiscipline' produced by the 'dispersed, tactical, and makeshift creativity of groups or individuals (1988, p. xv). He offered a useful framework for understanding how strategies and tactics are deployed in the everyday, and how cultural subjects utilise knowledge in a variety of ways that influence the making and remaking of everyday culture. For de Certeau, many everyday activities were considered tactical, 'ways of operating' (1988, p. xix). And for him a tactic

> does not have a place, a tactic depends on time — it is always on the watch for opportunities that must be seized 'on the wing'. Whatever it wins, it does not keep. It must constantly manipulate events in order to turn them into 'opportunities'. (1988, p. xix)

Tactical opportunities are momentarily satisfying but do not necessarily change the imposed order in any significant or lasting way. De Certeau suggested that tactics are 'clever tricks' used when one knows that it will result in getting away with things. He likens this behaviour to 'hunter's cunning, manoeuvres, polymorphic simulations, joyful discoveries, poetic as well as warlike' (1988, p. xix). Strategies, on the other hand, are a manipulation of power relationships requiring the subject to be discursively competent. Strategies carve out a space from where threats to the balance of power can be planned and managed. As he suggested, strategies are an 'effort to delimit one's own place in the world bewitched by the invisible powers of the Other' (1988, p. 36).

De Certeau did not neatly divide tactics and strategies as manoeuvres belonging to particular groups. In fact, he acknowledged that marginality was not limited to minority groups, which is why his work was of particular interest to my study. He recognised that strategies can turn into tactics as '[p]ower is bound by its very visibility' whereas 'trickery' is a manoeuvre of the weak (1988, p. 37). Trickery, he explained, is often used as a last resort or where one is backed into a corner.

De Certeau's interest was in how people use, utilise, change and rearrange all sorts of cultural signs and artefacts to suit their own needs. As he suggested, people can manipulate situations to better suit their intentions, 'Sly as a fox and twice as quick: there are countless ways of "making do"' (1988, p. 29). He recognised that there are numerous ways of operating within regulated systems and that people have the ability to, and do, find ways of turning it to their advantage. As he suggested, '[t]he imposed knowledge and symbolisms become objects of manipulation by practitioners who have not produced them' (p. 32). It is important to note that De Certeau's approach to agency was not merely as a rational choice based in Enlightenment thought, but more profoundly as the actions, subversions and meaning-making processes of those to whom imposed knowledge and symbolisms do not fit with everyday experience or cultural frames of reference.

Philosopher and gender theorist Judith Butler's work on 'performativity' where she argued that gender is a set of repeated acts within a highly rigid regulatory frame is also useful as a way to understand the everyday performances of identity. For Butler,

> [s]uch acts, gestures, enactments, generally construed, are performative in the sense that the essence of identity that they otherwise purport to express becomes a fabrication manufactured and sustained through corporeal signs and other discursive means. (1999, p. 336).

Despite her focus on gender and sexuality, I wanted to draw into my interpretative framework her work on the performance of identity as it relates to the Aboriginal acts and gestures utilised in the everyday. Butler rejected the notion of an authentic or fixed identity. Gender was for her 'the repeated stylization of the body, a set of repeated acts' (1999, p. 33). These acts are performed over a period of time and ultimately produce the 'appearance of substance, of a natural sort of being', thus making gender performative' (1999, p. 33). She explained, 'gender is not something one is, it is something one does, an act, or more precisely, a sequence of acts, a verb rather than a noun, a "doing" rather than a "being"' (cited in Salih 2002, p. 55). Gender is an act that brings into relief what it names. The proposition here is that no gender identity precedes language. As Salih explained, 'it is not that an identity "does" discourse or language, but the other way around — language and discourse "do" gender' (p. 56). Salih, following Butler, gave a wonderful example of how, through language, particular statements are in themselves performative: when a doctor announces 'It's a girl/boy' at the birth of a child, the doctor is not simply referring to what they see, they are in fact 'assigning a sex and a gender to a body that can have no existence outside discourse' (p. 61). The crux of

Butler's argument was that gender is performative. It is real only to the extent that it is performed:

> Performativity must be understood not as a singular or deliberate 'act', but rather, as the reiterative and citational practice by which discourse produces the effects that it names. It is always a reiteration of a norm or set of norms, and to the extent that it acquires an act-like status in the present, it conceals or dissimulates the conventions of which it is a repetition. Moreover, this act is not primarily theatrical: indeed, its apparent theatricality is produced to the extent that its history remains dissimulated. Within speech act theory, a performative is that discursive practice that enacts or produces that which it names. (1993, p. 13)

Aboriginality, by contrast, is often accepted as a sort of essence or innate feature, as something those who say they are Aboriginal possess, and those who are not, do not (e.g. Phillips 2009). Aboriginality, as with gender, is manufactured through an unremitting set of acts, a particular process, what Butler referred to as 'a set of repeated acts within a highly rigid regulatory frame' (1990b, p. 33). With the notion of variant selves, the emergence of Aboriginal identity can be seen as a set of performative acts that function according to discourse: they produce Aboriginality through the iteration of speech acts, the visible display of signs, through association with group members where performative iterations are recognised and understood. This does not imply that performativity of Aboriginality is not 'real' or less meaningful, in the same way that gender could not be said to be not real or meaningful. Indeed, its repetitiveness can ameliorate exclusion or ridicule and can guarantee validity, as Butler noted,

> iterability implies that 'performance' is not a singular 'act' or event, but a ritualized production, a ritual reiterated under and through constraint, under and through the force of prohibition and taboo, with the threat of ostracism and even death controlling and compelling the shape of the production, but not, I will insist, determining it fully in advance. (Butler 1993, p. 95)

In manifestations of variant selves, many newly discovered Aboriginal people learn to identify through wearing the colours of the Aboriginal flag on jewellery or in clothing as a statement of style. There may be identification through an association with certain sporting terms, or through using a particular vernacular. Following Butler, these manifestations of culture can be seen as performative acts by those who seek identification, and as imbued with the discourses that prescribe what constitutes recognisable signs of Aboriginal culture.

Butler's assertion of the corporeal fabrication, while confronting to some, gives a sense of the repetition required by Aboriginal people in the process of gaining cultural acceptance and recognition. In fact, it opens the possibility of liberating us as Aboriginal people from the prescriptive and restrictive constraints of the pervasive notion of 'essence', which assumes one is supposed to innately 'know' how to be Aboriginal. In understanding identity as a performative act we can begin to make sense of the multiple iterations of self and their various manifestations.

Marcia Langton has written that '[t]he term Aboriginal, and the colonial and post-colonial implications of the concept, began to take shape in Australia to some extent in 1770, but more so in 1788' (Langton 2005). While she spoke of the imposition of Aboriginal identity as a product of colonial factors, she does highlight that 'Aboriginality' is discursively constructed. In other words, the way in which Aboriginality has been manufactured post-1788 has seen the development of a fabricated reality in which those who claim an Aboriginal identity are then expected to perform.

Butler's concept of performative operates on many levels for Aboriginal people. For example, Darren Godwell has shown in his doctoral thesis that, in rugby league, '"[a]cting black" is important for Aborigines who have voluntarily moved into the all-white world' (1997, p. 58). As Butler suggested, iterative acts 'bring into being that which they name' (Butler 1990a, p. 33). Michel Foucault made this even more clear in his studies of discipline and punishment where he examined how people are regulated and normalised through the operation of disciplinary power: 'it is not that…the individual is amputated, repressed, altered by our social order, it is rather that the individual is carefully fabricated in it' (1979, p. 217).

THE CONTEXT OF THE INTERVIEWS

My interpretation of the data collected in my research (presented in the following chapters) highlighted for me my blurred position as both researcher and an individual with personal experience and personal views of the issues which are at the centre of this book. This is partly because the rationale and the process for Confirmation of Aboriginality are imbued with the politics of Aboriginal identity. It is my experience and observation of local community politics in regard to Aboriginal identity confirmation that motivated my research inquiry, and subsequently this book.

Confirmation of Aboriginality is a point of convergence for individuals, local Aboriginal communities, the national Aboriginal community and Australian government imperatives, where a whole range of discourses and meanings culminate to produce very strong feelings and responses that constitute and reinforce the politics of identity. At the local level such identity politics, in my experience, can be destructive rather than supportive of those Aboriginal subjectivities that have been forged outside of local community experience and/or the more privileged narratives of the pan-Aboriginal historical experience. These politics also characterise the wider national Aboriginal discussions of identity issues, as the literature discussed in earlier chapters reveals.

Participants' data revealed a muddle of positions, logic and argument, all of which are evidence of the conditions of this discursive and lived space and the investments of individuals trying to make sense from within entangled discursive intersections. Here we see just how difficult it is for individuals, including myself as an Aboriginal researcher, to make sense of the ways discourses of Aboriginality — generated via the colonial, historical, government and now Aboriginal administrative apparatuses — enable individual agency in Aboriginal identity production even while they constrain, regulate and 'legally' police what it means to be Aboriginal and who can call themselves Aboriginal.

It has been a challenge to produce a coherent analysis of this 'muddle' in the Cultural Interface that is both constituted by and constitutive of the politics of Aboriginal identity. Revisiting the context for understanding the participants' responses helps to situate the data. For example, it is helpful to understand that it is not mandatory for Aboriginal people to have a document that confirms their Aboriginality. However, as discussed in previous chapters, in some circumstances an individual may be required to prove or confirm that they are indeed Aboriginal for the purposes of receiving benefits or accessing services designated for Aboriginal people only, or to be considered for an identified position, or to defend against being questioned about their Aboriginal status. In these cases, an official Confirmation of Aboriginality document can be required or prudent.

However, it is not always necessary to have documents of 'proof' to access services or benefits because there is also a tacit acceptance that some Aboriginal people are, without question, 'known' to be Aboriginal. For some individuals, there is an effect that emerges in reality which works not unlike a self-fulfilling prophecy: the more an individual is known, recognised and accepted as Aboriginal in the community in which they live, the less likely their Aboriginality is to be questioned and the less likely they will require an official Confirmation document to 'prove' they are.

It is, therefore, those individuals who do not know or cannot prove their Aboriginal lineage, and/or are not known to 'the community', and/or who do not demonstrate accepted ways of looking, being and/or expressing Aboriginality who have most need for a Confirmation of Aboriginality document. Yet often it is these people who have the most trouble in obtaining one. Moreover, those individuals who want to access services, or benefits or work in identified positions are often those more likely to need them. Therefore, not needing services and benefits also makes the confirmation process irrelevant for some individuals, as does having a long history of connection to the community in which one lives. However, not needing or not using services and benefits can also be perceived as evidence of not being Aboriginal or of living too much in the 'white way'.

In the light of all this, many of the participants in my study did not have a Confirmation of Aboriginality for a variety of reasons: their Aboriginality had never been in question; they had never been asked to produce one; it was not possible to obtain one; or they opposed the requirement to have one on political grounds. Some participants, however, had never heard of the Confirmation of Aboriginality process. Some had heard of it but did not know what it involved, and/or did not know what the definitional criteria for proof of Aboriginality were. However, all participants had opinions about its legitimacy and about its relevance for them personally, whether they had an official Confirmation of Aboriginality document or not. Some held opinions on its relevance for others as well.

THE NEED FOR A CONFIRMATION OF ABORIGINALITY

It was quite easy to discern from participant data those who were strongly against the need for a Confirmation of Aboriginality, those who thought it a good thing, and those who had mixed feelings about it, who were in the majority.

Some participants strongly disagreed with it, whether they had one or not. For example, one participant put her objections less than succinctly: 'Oh, the three bits of paper? They can shove it up their clackers, honey' (P14). Asked if he would ever consider getting one, he replied: 'No, no I won't. I will never do it. I am not buying into that ridiculous bloody thing.' On the other hand, another participant who had been required to get one to be eligible for a grant expressed similar feelings: 'I was mad you know. Like, I'm opposed to it, totally and absolutely opposed to it' (P13).

But some others against it were less adamant and less political:

> I don't think you should need one, there are so many people out there from so many different backgrounds that live in so many different communities who would not have one but are still Aboriginal, um, they are still born of the same blood, same background, same history, same heritage and just because you have or don't have a piece of paper, I don't think that is really relevant. You either are or you are not. (P1)

This participant's personal experience of being born to an Aboriginal mother in New Zealand and having New Zealand citizenship, shaped this view. It appears to be the case that computer databases such as Centrelink and Medicare cannot accept as Aboriginal a person born outside of Australia. The two categories are mutually exclusive. For this participant: 'The fact that they need hard proof to confirm you are Aboriginal just made it way too hard. I just didn't bother with it at all' (P1). However, this participant touches on the major fault lines evident in community and scholarly discourses. What is to count and who is to decide given the range of differences in 'blood' and experiences of being Aboriginal? The irony of his statement — 'either you are or you are not' — emerges in this logic. However, this position signals the frustration of those who cannot comply with the three definitional criteria but who understand themselves as Aboriginal because this identity has been formed in the personal domain of immediate family, even when that family lives in another country.

Some participants supported the Confirmation of Aboriginality process. For example, a recently identifying participant, who hadn't known about it, strongly endorsed it as a good thing: 'I think it's important to do because it's important to be part of the culture and the community' (P24). Another took a similar view:

> I think that claiming Aboriginality [through the Confirmation process] is one step in forming, you know, your identity. 'Cause when [you] set out to claim your Aboriginality you are in essence claiming a connection to that culture and those people and it's the same as saying, you know, I'm an Australian but my parents are British you know. (P4)

Of course, it is clearly not the same. People can claim British heritage without ever being called upon to conform to any criteria of 'Britishness'. Nor do they have to confirm British heritage for any official purpose other than extended visa purposes, for example, or perhaps an Anglo-Australian exchange of some kind. It is the need for official Confirmation of Aboriginality to access services or benefits which are provided from the wider public purse that positions Aboriginal community organisations as gate-keepers of the meanings of being Aboriginal. Another participant, who did not identify until he was well into adult life, helped to make this point: 'It is fair because it [community service] is a free service and people need to prove who they are to get the benefits and free services' (P16).

Interestingly, only one participant directly stated that Confirmation documents were important for defending accusations from white people. Indeed this person had the papers for only this purpose because she was accepted in the Aboriginal community:

> I thought I might need them in the future, mainly [for] white people who question whether someone is Aboriginal or not. And if I had to apply to a white person I could say, 'Excuse me, my community recognises me so who are you to question me'. (P17)

Most participants, however, talked of Confirmation of Aboriginality in more qualified and ambivalent terms. Often agreement with the requirement was qualified by acknowledgement of the difficulties it posed for some people. Similarly, disagreement with it was often qualified by talk of why it was needed. Most talk about it soon wound back to explanations for having it on the one hand and the difficulties it posed for some people on the other. One participant, for example, described it as a 'necessary evil' (P11). Many referred to the difficulties involved in getting one: 'I can see why it's needed to weed out the "Johnny Come Lately" but I still think it's a hard thing. It's a hard process to go about' (P8).

However, the various positions and arguments did not emerge in a strict relation to the degree of difficulty involved in getting Confirmation or the personal need for one. Those who could easily establish their Aboriginality often had the least need for official Confirmation and some felt insulted by the official imposition on them. But this did not necessarily mean they disagreed with the need for others to prove they were who they said they were, especially if individuals were from outside the local community. And even if participants were against the official requirement absolutely, it did not necessarily mean they were in disagreement with the definitional criteria as measures of Aboriginality.

As well, those who had difficulty assembling the proof for Confirmation were often most in need of it, but some of these participants were equally insulted by the imposition and refused to undergo the process. However, some who could not get one still thought it a reasonable requirement or were pragmatic about their own need for it. Some who objected to the requirement had obtained one and some who didn't have one agreed with the requirement. This variety of responses has led my analysis to focus on opening up the issues for further contemplation and inquiry and to resist reductive deductive analysis. What follows in the next chapters are some of the major themes that emerged from the interviews.

CHAPTER 13
IDENTITY JOURNEYS: WHEN ABORIGINAL HERITAGE WAS ALWAYS KNOWN

> It's not just about that piece of paper. I think to be Aboriginal you need to identify with a group of people. Actually that could be really hard to identify too because you don't know that family. So you have to trace back and, as I found, it's really hard to trace back even though I am living in the community. (P10)

> Yeah, it's a journey now, a good journey, a journey on knowledge. But it can be hard and you have to work at it all the time. (P9)

In my analysis of participants' interview data, I worked from within Martin Nakata's notion of the Cultural Interface (2007), as explained in the previous chapter. I took a position on Aboriginal identity as a process of ongoing individual negotiation in the everyday world in which participants live, work and grow. In this sense, 'being' Aboriginal assumes some process of negotiation of the *meanings* of Aboriginality by individuals, either over time and/or at particular points in time or place, in order to be firstly 'self-realised' and secondly to be recognised and legitimised by others as Aboriginal.

NEGOTIATING AN ABORIGINAL IDENTITY

This idea of Aboriginal identity as a negotiated process also holds open a common space for analysis when the individual experiences of participants are quite varied in terms of age, gender, family/Aboriginal country heritage and connections, early experiences, and recent and historical movement from place to place. For me as a researcher, one unexpected strand of discussion that emerged from some of these interviews was the reference to Aboriginal children's identity construction. I have included this to highlight the significance of reconnecting the broken inter-generational links in participants' journeys to reconstitute the meanings of being Aboriginal in the contemporary space.

Approximately half of the participants said that they had always known they were Aboriginal or had Aboriginal heritage. But for these participants, the knowledge of Aboriginality held various meanings depending on the particularities of their lived experience. The other participants all found out they had Aboriginal heritage at varying stages in life and through a range of circumstances. Given the ages of participants ranged from nineteen to seventy years, the participants' experiences reflect the eras that have shaped those experiences. So, due to the particularities of individual circumstances, a young participant can be in the process of discovering Aboriginal heritage, through similar processes as older people did some decades ago at a similar age. Two people a generation apart can be undergoing similar processes of discovery or learning about their Aboriginal heritage at the same point of time. A young fair-complexioned person of dual Aboriginal and other parentage can be more secure in the knowledge of her Aboriginality than an older person recognisably Aboriginal but who has endured the effects of removal or dislocation or of being unable to find family. Also, an individual can grow up knowing they are Aboriginal but without awareness of its meaning while young, and so find themselves learning about the meaning of Aboriginality at a similar age in life as someone who has only recently found out about their Aboriginal heritage. In light of these varied circumstances, the idea of Aboriginal identity as a process of negotiation holds as much for the participants in this study who grew up always knowing they were Aboriginal, as it does for those who found out they were Aboriginal later in life, whether recently or some decades ago.

In this way, there emerges from the data a sense of an identity 'journey' for all participants as they either move from 'unawareness' of Aboriginal heritage or, in the case of those who had always known, from a 'taken-for-granted' or 'less reflected on' awareness of the meaning of being Aboriginal in younger years to a consciousness of what it means to be Aboriginal as an adult in the contemporary everyday world. These 'journeys' are all personal and particular to individual circumstances, and all lead to varying personal interpretations and public expressions of Aboriginality. There appear to be commonalities, patterns and even sequence in how people negotiate their Aboriginality in the sense of it being a journey.

However, in the way participants talk about their everyday negotiations, there also emerges inconsistency, contest, contradictions and uncertainties that evidence not only individual agencies but some of the personal limits that individuals place around some of the meanings of the accepted discussions about Aboriginality. In these limits can be understood the tensions that emerge from the convergences at the interface of Aboriginal, Western, colonial, historical, academic and popular discourses — all of which Aboriginal people negotiate daily as a condition of being Aboriginal.

AWARENESS OR DISCOVERY OF ABORIGINAL HERITAGE

Participant responses to interview questions around whether they had always known they were Aboriginal, and how they discovered they were, reveal both the patterns and diversity of the Aboriginal historical experience of colonial and subsequent administrations. In participants' statements, the family histories of the present generations reveal not only how it has always been difficult to be Aboriginal in urban and regional Australia, but also how it has been impossible for some to be Aboriginal, and how challenging it has been to hold Aboriginal families together in everyday life in such circumstances. For all participants, making sense of their own experience involves looking back over the incidents in their early life and the experiences of their parents and grandparents. For some, this means not having grown up with wider Aboriginal family networks; for others, it is about working around not being recognisably Aboriginal in the wider Aboriginal and non-Aboriginal communities, an awareness that was often confronted for the first time at school. For yet others, it means working around the silences and disconnects within the older generations, before being able to narrate what it means for them to be Aboriginal today.

ABORIGINAL HERITAGE: ALWAYS KNOWN

Those participants who had always known they were Aboriginal or had Aboriginal heritage nevertheless have diverse backgrounds and stories that shaped how they approached identity issues. These participants revealed how knowing one is Aboriginal does not necessarily carry with it clarity about what this means. The meaningfulness of Aboriginality is closely entwined with life circumstances and parental histories as well. A range of factors impact, including where a person grew up, proximity to the extended Aboriginal family, whether the custodial parent was Aboriginal, which historical policy era they grew up in, and so on. For example, growing up away from the Aboriginal community conditions identity for the following participant:

> Well I have always known myself to be Aboriginal as well as Danish but I was born in New Zealand so I…you know, I was a Kiwi and that was it…but since I have been here [Australia] I have just sort of taken more notice of it I think. (P1)

While his identification as Aboriginal was unequivocal and there is an acknowledgement of his Aboriginal mother, this participant's personal history led to some qualifications of its meaning:

> I think it means acknowledging…my ancestry and just knowing who I am in that respect. Not necessarily being what I am doing or where I live…not necessarily being part of community involvement and all that stuff. (P1)

However, dual heritage did not mean unequivocal identification as Aboriginal for all participants. One participant with an Aboriginal mother and white father identified as both, despite her Aboriginal mother emphasising all through her life she was not 'half-caste' but Aboriginal. Acknowledging both sides of heritage produced conflict and required defence of both heritages in different situations:

> Yeah, I have [experienced conflict] but, for me, am I supposed to not acknowledge my Dad's side? And it is obvious I am not fully Aboriginal, like look at me, I can't say, oh yeah, I am Aboriginal and nothing else because people will be like, that is bullshit. Mum says, yes I am Aboriginal but that is not right because I am both. There was this one time when this woman…says to me you are not Aboriginal and I said, I am, and I felt shame speaking up cause everyone was looking and I know they was thinking, she looks white to me. (P25)

Identification conflicts for this participant were closely linked to her fair complexion and looks:

> She was pretty constant about us saying we were Aboriginal but it is easier if you are darker to feel that and because she never knew [she was Aboriginal when] growing up she wanted us to know and say who we were. (P25)

This participant reveals the tensions in her everyday world that position her between one set of discourses that question those who do not look Aboriginal and/or have a white parent and those other sets of tensions emerging from the historical experience of her Aboriginal mother, who now, in a different historical era, has the possibility to reclaim and reinstate once again family continuity with the Aboriginal line. The agency of this participant is revealed in her refusal to be categorised in a way that would force her to deny her other family side, even if it means experiencing conflict and positioning from both sides.

For some participants, it was school that played a part in shaping a sense of being Aboriginal and the need to defend Aboriginality. For example, one participant with a white mother and Aboriginal father had always known she was Aboriginal because half of her extended family was Aboriginal, but she did not become aware of the distinctions between Aboriginal people and other Australians until she went to school:

> [W]hen we started to say we were Aboriginal it was a case of you can't be Aboriginal 'cause you have white skin'. That's when we had to assert, yes we are, yes we are, then go home and ask our Dad what is it that's different about us? Like if we're the same as all the other kids but you tell us we are Aboriginal, what is it about us that's so different?...'cause it was very much we battled with 'no you're only half Aboriginal' 'cause once kids accepted that we were...it was very much about, well, how much of you is Aboriginal. So after we got past that identification stage it was only like half of you is, it was really a battle explaining to kids... (P4)

Her Aboriginal father answered questions about part-Aboriginality with Aboriginal humour: 'you tell him that your little pinkie's Aboriginal and your next one's not, that's the white part of you' (P4). However, on a more serious note, not looking Aboriginal meant siblings had different experiences of these battles that went on to become significant personality as well as identity constructs in their lives. This participant spoke of one sister who had dark eyes like herself and looked like their Aboriginal family, while the other sister was blond and blue-eyed like their non-Aboriginal mother. In reference to the very fair sister:

> as she got older she used to find these very bizarre ways of asserting her identity which would mean, you know, getting into arguments with people by taking this really hardline stance on Aboriginal issues. And people would be shocked… they would 'what are you talking about this stuff for you're not Aboriginal', and she'd say 'yes, I am, just 'cause I don't look like an Aboriginal person it doesn't mean I'm not'. (P4)

However, for Participant 4, defending her Aboriginal identity at school was situated within broader schoolyard challenges and she was able to use it as a strengthening agent when being teased for being a large girl:

> So I was really able to take hold of my [Aboriginal] identity and say well this is who I am. You're already giving me crap about everything else so I don't care if you give me shit about this as well. (P4)

She said that her Aboriginality:

> really helped me through some of that 'cause it was something that I could have that other people no matter how much they give me crap about it, it was something I really believed in. (P4)

Another participant who had always known and thought of herself as Aboriginal because she grew up with her Aboriginal mother also commented on the difficulties of not looking Aboriginal and how this only became an issue as an adult when she moved away from the community she grew up in:

> It was really hard at times because I am not dark or don't really look Aboriginal so I get judged about that sometimes but back home everyone just knew so it wasn't an issue but here I was on my own and this fair-skinned person was wanting to be part of the community. There is discrimination against fair-skinned Aboriginal people; it is easier if you look a certain way. (P22)

For others of dual heritage, fairness and a lack of 'Aboriginal looks' have little to do with identity. Cultural orientation at family and community levels was much more significant. Nevertheless, one participant with an Aboriginal mother and French father also referred to the absence of other ethnicities in her school years and how she became aware of the identity choices as being Aboriginal or Australian, when she went to school. As an adult, she reflected that 'I can't just say I am Aboriginal because I am half French as well and it is not fair to diss one side' (P3). However, even though her father spoke French at home, she grew up being Aboriginal because there were few avenues to learn about and express 'Frenchness' but many avenues for being and expressing Aboriginality. As well, she was part of an extended Aboriginal family, which reinforced her sense of being Aboriginal. So despite acknowledging her French heritage, in her everyday life it meant much less than her Aboriginality. When asked about how she would define Aboriginality, she noted the difficulties of doing so but reflected,

> I think it is acceptance within yourself about your culture and your people, those you have been brought up with. Like my Mum and all my Mum's side, they have always said, yeah, we are Aboriginal…like there hasn't been any sort of contested, like you're a half-caste or anything, like you not really an Aborigine are ya…you should always say you are and not pretend not to be. (P3)

The importance of the presence of Aboriginal family was also emphasised by another participant with a white father and Aboriginal mother:

> I have always known about my heritage on both sides of the family, probably more on my mother's side. I think Aboriginal people have got a bigger clan as they are really into the family side of things, so I have always known where I have come from. (P7)

For this participant,

> [Aboriginality] means basically belonging to here and family. I guess association to the land and culture as well as knowing where I come from…It's the search of wanting to know that deep meaning of where they've come from. (P7)

For some, dual parentage did not impact at all and if raised the Aboriginal way there was no question of their Aboriginality. For example, one participant of dual heritage grew up without either parent and with Aboriginal grandparents:

> I never seen my father in my life, but I was fortunate too, as he was white, I was fortunate to grow up with my Koori family, so I've got that knowledge there. (P23)

This knowledge of being Aboriginal involved continuity with traditional knowledge, for example, as expressed in the following statement: 'When I was a kid my great grandfather was a traditional fisherman so he taught us all them ways' (P23). It also involved knowing about the hardship of the past:

> Aboriginal people have had it hard and that is what makes us Aboriginal in some way, we all know about our past and what it means to be Aboriginal. So that is why, when people aren't really Aboriginal because they haven't faced these things, it isn't right they can say they are Aboriginal. (P23)

A political solidarity with the collective concept of Aboriginality as something forged from a shared cultural heritage and the shared experience of colonisation shaped this participant's view of what it meant to be Aboriginal and, significantly, what excluded others from the membership.

For another, estrangement from her Aboriginal father who is part of a well-known Aboriginal family, and being raised by a non-Indigenous mother enabled her to trace the different meanings her Aboriginality held for her over time. In early years,

> the only thing I knew about Aboriginal, Aboriginality, was from external influences…it could have been through being asked questions [at school], 'What are you? What nationality you are'. It could have come through being teased, being called an 'Abo' which was very common…It was seeing other Indigenous people and often saying 'Am I like them? Why aren't I like them?' (P21)

This participant began to establish her Aboriginal identity through information seeking and community participation in her teenage years. Now an adult and raising the children she has had to Aboriginal fathers, being

Aboriginal means many things to her. However, she emphasises the importance of community and the threads between past, present and future:

> [T]here's a real emphasis on public identity and community. It's a collectivist society still, so the urban identity is grounded...in family groups, community groups...and a shared sense of dispossession and colonisation, and how that lives out today...A strong sense of urban identity can also be characterised of finding out your roots...A lot of Indigenous people don't know their cultural roots, so there's a strong sense of urban identity of wanting to find that out. So perhaps merging the past with the present and redefining the future is a very strong sense of urban Aboriginality. (P21)

Thus we see how for some participants the personal/private meanings of Aboriginal identity are given emphasis and, for others the collective and political meanings are held central in personal understandings of what it means to be Aboriginal. How individuals position themselves within the discursive and 'real' lived tensions is contingent upon complex spaces of historical, personal and everyday manoeuvrings of family, community and wider social relations.

In another dual heritage family, for example, silence about Aboriginality also affected a participant's journey but in a different way:

> I guess we knew but it didn't have any meaning...I always sort of knew, but no-one talked, alright? Always sort of knew, but we weren't allowed to live it or act it. No-one actually came out and said it, I had the belief that I always was...[but] it was probably fifteen years ago when people started admitting it... (P19)

For this older participant, a combination of a racist white father and an Aboriginal mother who was stolen led to a silence by his mother who 'was worried about us being taken because we never had much money' (P19). Across his mother's immediate family, there was also silence, with some only learning quite recently that there was Aboriginality in the family: 'I don't know about other families, but I know in my family it was very hush, hush. Don't talk' (P19). For this participant, who once had drug and alcohol problems, being able to admit and talk about his Aboriginality and have his Aboriginality recognised had changed his life and sense of self: 'that made me whole as a person. And now I can walk quite happy and proud, quite everything' (P19).

For another participant, her family not talking about Aboriginality meant she could not be sure where her Aboriginal side came from. She stated she had been raised Aboriginal even though her Aboriginal mother deserted, because her white father remarried another Aboriginal woman. In remembering her childhood she stated that her father 'never once said, you know, that you're not black, you're white' (P20). Although this participant married outside of the Aboriginal community, she raised her children as Aboriginal. For her the meaning of being Aboriginal is

> what you are inside you, and how you conduct yourself and your lifestyle, and recognition, you know by the Elders, and respect for the Elders, and you know, seeking advice from the Elders. (P20)

Two participants who had always known they were Aboriginal related that life circumstances meant they grew up without a sense of belonging, and this now shaped their current lives and commitment to their Aboriginal heritage. For example, one whose mother had left her community and moved to Sydney in the 1930s, where he was born, spoke of himself as 'part of that Diaspora of almost lost and forgotten Aboriginal Australians' (P13):

> I live in a world in which I don't belong in the sense that I was born in Leichhardt [suburb of Sydney] which is in Gadigal country but I have no connection to Gadigal people [apart from growing up there]. (P13)

Nor did he have any connection to his mother's country, for she never went back. This older participant's account reveals the significance of different eras in identifying as Aboriginal. With his father's red hair and European looks, he related how he was still known as 'Black Mary's kid' when picked up by truant officers as a child, in an era when there was no expectation of Aboriginal children to attend school. But as he grew, he realised that skin colour and Aboriginality were significant, and his looks meant that he could do a lot of things that his recognisably Aboriginal friends could not. When working in the trucking industry, for example, 'it was to my advantage to keep my mouth shut and I did' (P13). While identifying as Aboriginal in some contexts and situations, he could also not identify and receive the advantages of not being recognised at that historical moment. It took a change of eras before he found his way to mobilise a less ambiguous identity in his later life. Part of this journey was the refusal to acknowledge his white father, and his close links to and identification with his Aboriginal mother:

> Well I think why would I want to identify anything with my father, he was a drunken mongrel. He bashed kids up…
>
> Yeah, I don't want anything to do with bloody English, I identify with my Mum. I grew up with my Mum. I was in touch with my Mum. My links were with my mother. My spirituality were with my mother, they were never with my father.
>
> I'm a blackfella, I'm gay, I'm left-handed, you know I'm a writer. These are the elements of my identity. These are things that I'm proud of, these are the things of who I am…I'm not some bloke trying to be white, I'm not some bloke trying to be illiterate. You know all those things have gone, I'm free! I'm free! (P13)

This personal identity was still situated within a broader narrative that connected Aboriginal people to the narrative of the nation-state and the Aboriginal past to an Aboriginal future. In this way, a narrative of resolution of a disrupted Aboriginal history was enabled.

> I believe in the ongoing dream of society that this is a Dreaming story and we're involved in it and it's ongoing you know and it's part of who we are and we will continue on and we will adapt and we will change and we do a whole different range of things. We've got a job to do. (P13)

Another older participant who grew up white but whose father was Aboriginal began to reconnect after his father's death, through a concern about losing that last link.

> So I am endeavouring to get a connection back with culture. I was brought up in a white society, a white culture and I probably relate more to white society than Aboriginal society. But yeah, I feel there is an imbalance now, and I want to get a balance in my life with my Aboriginal side of the family. (P16)

In common with some other participants who 'grew up white' and reconnected with their heritage later in life, this participant, in his talk about being Aboriginal, placed some emphasis on the familiar stereotypes of Aboriginal people in white society and emphasised how he works against it:

> There is a tendency for white Australians to have experience or know of worst-case-scenario Aboriginals, and therefore judge all Aboriginals and put them in the same basket. I find that very unfair, because they put me in that basket too and I'm trying to be a representative of the other side, for Aboriginals who try hard and are responsible, so yeah, I find that difficult to cope with at times. (P16)

This participant seemed to express some conflicts between being Aboriginal and having been successful living in white society before he knew he was Aboriginal and the difficulty of finding a place:

> I consider myself a modern Aboriginal. I work in a white society as an Aboriginal. I endeavour to work my best to set a good example for Aboriginals that want to make it in white society…But there's not many of us, or we're low profile, so we don't know where we are. (P16)

This participant understood that finding the balance between his white and Aboriginal frames of reference would be a 'slow process'. However, his view of Aboriginal society, at least as it is revealed in the interview process, is firmly grounded from the standpoint of the colonial and popular discourses of what it means to be Aboriginal, though the disjuncture with the internal Aboriginal view did not appear yet to be fully recognised by him.

Another participant who grew up with a strong sense of being Aboriginal located the historical reasons why her Aboriginal mother 'wanted us to have a strong sense of culture' (P10):

> She wasn't able to show her Aboriginality because around the time of growing up it was very hard. Aboriginal people were stereotyped, like basically if you showed you were Aboriginal people would put you down and you wouldn't be able to live a successful life. (P10)

This participant's mother had grown up believing she was Spanish and emphasised the importance of culture and Aboriginal spirituality. While her mother instilled Aboriginality through her own stories and acquired knowledge, for her daughter, however, there were difficulties explaining in words what she thought made her Aboriginal:

> Just the, I can't explain it. It's just a feeling, I guess. It's a feeling you know you belong to a particular group where you won't be shinned upon with each other or most of the time. Yeah, just the feeling of knowing that I am Aboriginal and knowing that my culture is over 40,000, 50,000 years old, so I'm just proud that I'm still here. (P10).

For many participants whose parents had had a difficult time, this sense of Aboriginality as survival was strongly felt and associated with pride.

CHAPTER 14

IDENTITY JOURNEYS: DISCOVERING ABORIGINAL HERITAGE

> I just always kind of knew, like it is something in you even if you can't prove it. It's like some sort of blood memory, in your bones, your DNA, who you are. (P6)

The participants in my study who had not always known they were Aboriginal indicated many similar positions and tensions to those who had. Through interviews, these participants revealed a range of ways in which they found out they had — or may have — Aboriginal heritage. My aim with these participants was to attempt to understand their varying entry points into what often become personal quests to reconnect with the wider Aboriginal community or to be secure in their personal knowledge of their links to Aboriginal heritage.

ABORIGINAL RELATIVES IN THE FAMILY

A number of participants related how Aboriginal relatives appeared at times in their lives but how their Aboriginality was either not clear, not an issue or their connection to them not explained to them when young. This often appears to be related to the historical era or the legacy of earlier policy eras. For example, one participant with an Aboriginal stepfather had always thought she was Aboriginal and had a lot of 'Aboriginal input' (P14) in her life. Her non-Indigenous mother would not speak of her parentage, however, and the reasons were understood as historical, 'fear of having your children taken away and fear of all sorts of things' (P14). Only later in life when her older sister was dying did she find out the name of her real Aboriginal father. This led the participant to find her father's family and reconnect. The impact of colonial history was entwined in this participant's meaning of being Aboriginal, which for her was

> [k]nowing who I am, knowing my place…Having the absolute right to claim it. That's my right and no-one has any business of trying to deprive me of my right to claim my heritage. Being strong enough to do that but certainly at last understanding all the skeletons in the closets…understanding and having clearly understood their official histories and the unofficial histories and…the impact of that on people… It turned good honest people into people who would hide their true identities, would hide truths in order just to survive, in order not to have their children taken away, in order to get a job or to be deemed OK. Those policies made people believe that Aboriginality was a shameful thing. (P14)

For this person her Aboriginal identity was defined by 'claiming my spirit… and without it I'm not me…it's my spirit that makes me this whole person who emphatically and self assuredly identifies as an Aboriginal person' (P14) but this emerged through knowledge of how her story was conditioned in the wider relations with colonial authorities and the nation-state.

Another participant had a similar experience of 'sort of' knowing but of not understanding it. Her grandfather would not talk of it and after his death Aboriginal heritage was traced by her father and uncle, but even then not spoken of to her as a child. It was not until the participant was in high school that her father began to encourage involvement in the Aboriginal community through participation. This participant identified as Aboriginal and with her Welsh heritage as well without any sense of internal conflict. Other family members were happy to know and identify as Aboriginal, but 'some of them don't feel they have the right to identify… because they haven't grown up knowing, I suppose' (P5). So for this participant, being Aboriginal meant connecting and participating in community events in order to feel she belongs.

For another participant, visits in childhood by clearly Aboriginal relatives led him to ask questions of his father: 'Dad told me pure and simple my Uncles were Indian Sioux [be]cause you are going back to…[g]rowing up in the fifties and sixties and that' (P2). When later in life this participant found his name on a Native Title Claim, this proof enabled him to identify so that 'my children wouldn't miss out on what I missed out on with it being hidden' (P2). The awareness of the impact of historical policy on family was evident once again. His father had himself been told by his parents that the family were Indian Sioux. As a ten-year-old this participant had a dream where he was dying and had been told to turn back by an old Aboriginal woman who was later identified in his father's photos as his grandmother. Although not growing up with awareness, this participant felt more at home in the company of Aboriginal people and interpreted this as a 'spiritual thing' (P2). Despite proof of Aboriginality, this participant only identified himself as Aboriginal to Aboriginal people.

In another example, a participant recalled family reunions where 'dark-skinned' (P26) people were identified as Aunties. When in her adulthood they were confirmed as relatives, she thought about its meaning for her:

> I thought about it and over the next few weeks thought, well, it is who I am, so I may as well be that then. And then I was saying out loud, I am an Aboriginal and you know that it was really natural, you know, it was just natural to say, 'Yes I am an Aboriginal'. (P26)

This identification is recent but fully embraced and it led to a changed orientation in her family life, through study and connection to community events and the identification of her children as Aboriginal at school. Her husband is also exploring his as yet un-researched Aboriginality, but this participant was strong in the belief that he was also Aboriginal: 'I mean you just have to look at him and you can see it in his face...his nose and eyes, he is definitely Aboriginal' (P26). As a recent identifier, her Aboriginality had not been questioned 'because I am not wanting anything for being Aboriginal' (P26).

Being Aboriginal,

> [f]or me, it isn't about getting things for free, it is just about me, you know, who I am, and that I am more interested in giving back to the community, you know helping the people and helping with the health side of things. (P18)

This participant demonstrates an awareness of the popular discourses of public opinion and the grounds on which Aboriginal people may be challenged or accused of taking advantage of benefits for Aboriginal people only.

One participant became aware of Aboriginal heritage as a ten- or eleven-year-old when called names. Once again, his grandmother and mother hadn't known that they were disconnected members of a well-known Aboriginal family. All he knew of what it meant to be Aboriginal came 'through television and what people have told me through reading' (P18). As an adult he has found meaning in working for the community and learning language and cultural knowledge to transmit to his children. His Aboriginality has been challenged many times, but this is able to be situated within the wider historical and ongoing relations with the nation-state. Challenges to Aboriginality reflect these tensions, which are expressed in the anger and assumptions of some Aboriginal people that some have had it easier than others. An interesting interpretation on the concept of being 'stolen' was articulated:

> There are many ways of being stolen, like even having your Aboriginality withheld from you for safety, or for racism, so being stolen is lots of things. It is having your past stolen, your right to be Aboriginal and your culture. (P18)

From most of these participants, a much stronger sense of historical injustice emerged to give shape to self-understanding and to the meanings forged through an embracing and reclaiming of their Aboriginal identity. Identity narratives also often involve retrospective sense-making of earlier experiences through attribution to significant but unrecognised signs of Aboriginal connections, including spiritual claims.

ACCIDENTAL DISCOVERY OF ABORIGINAL HERITAGE

Making up for lost 'historical' time and retrospectively making sense of earlier experiences or identifying inner feelings does appear to emerge as a theme for those who find out in later life they are or possibly are Aboriginal. A number of participants discovered accidentally that they were Aboriginal, or were possibly Aboriginal. One participant, who was adopted as a child, reconnected with her Aboriginal father in her middle-age years after her daughter had researched and located him. She discovered that certain physical habits and traits made sense.

> I thought all this time I've been picked on [for physical and language traits] and it comes from somewhere. I'm not stupid and the way I feel, the feelings you have, you know, you feel different, you don't belong… (P9)

This participant identified straightaway. For her it was a story of completion, of closure: 'I just feel complete now' (P9). However, her father had concerns:

> Dad was hesitant because he said he didn't want me to go through what he went and I said, 'I don't care, you should be proud of it Dad, you know, stand up, I said. Stick your head up and be proud of it you know.' (P9)

The possibilities for this participant's understanding of what it means to be Aboriginal in the current policy era were in contrast to those of her father in an earlier one. Here the meanings within the community and scholarly discourse of Aboriginality are being expanded and the boundaries pushed out to include those who have little history of 'being' Aboriginal: 'It means I say it with pride, with honour for my Dad and right back through the mob and I also say it in heartache that I wasn't along that journey' (P9).

Another participant who stated she had 'grown up white', related how she found out she was Aboriginal when she had a child and was told by doctors that 'bruises' on the child were a sign of black heritage on both parents' sides. The possibility that this information was not correct or misinterpreted was not explored. She stated that the father of her child was Polynesian, and that she was told that 'Mongolian spots' or 'bruises' are common in Polynesian and East Asian people. This participant stated that she was convinced that she must also have black heritage and after searching her family lineage she did confirm Aboriginality on both sides of her parents' families. Once again, there was some retrospective analysis that enabled some sense that there had always been a deeper unconscious awareness:

> I'd had dreams most of my life where these old Aboriginal women would come to me in my dreams and told me things and danced around the fire and stuff, and I never understood those dreams neither, but all of a sudden when that information was given to me, it all started clicking into place, why I behaved in certain ways, why I didn't fit in where I didn't fit in and why I did fit in, yeah, so it all sort of clicked into place, like the fact that I used to love going bush…I never like to wear shoes, and I still don't. It's really weird, but my feet get really hot and uncomfortable wearing shoes. That might be a bit of a trait too. (P17)

Like other participants this woman connected particular behaviours or 'traits' with being Aboriginal. For example, 'going bush' or not wearing shoes. Many participants drew on limited understandings of what 'being Aboriginal' means to find their connection to an Aboriginal identity. Often such ideas were drawn from stereotypes or media representation of Aboriginal characteristics. This participant did try to locate further information' however, her parents were reluctant to talk about or acknowledge their Aboriginal connections due to the historical context of being stolen and of being disowned for marrying 'interracially'. This participant did not embrace her Aboriginal status right away but after a few years began to study, learn about and participate in Aboriginal events.

One participant who had understood she was not Aboriginal described how it was suggested to her that she might be. She was employed in an Aboriginal organisation and an Aboriginal community member commented to her that she looked Aboriginal and should investigate her heritage. This participant was able to locate documentation, which provided proof of Aboriginal descent, when she was in her late thirties. This participant identified via both her Aboriginal and English heritages, and how she identified herself depended on who she was talking to. Interestingly, she felt the need to add her English heritage as a way to account for the colour of her fair skin: 'most people think that Aboriginal people should be dark-skinned people, and that is not the case…' (P15). She was aware of not always knowing which was 'the white side of me thinking, or the black side of me thinking' (P15) but talked about the meaning of being an Aboriginal person for her as:

> [I]t's a lot about family, it's a lot about being a good person in society, not just in the eyes of white people but being a good role model to others. It's about where I was born. It's about how I feel towards the country itself, to the community. (P15)

Like others who had discovered their Aboriginal connection later in life, she was proud of the survival of Aboriginal people, of the survival of language and cultures in many places, and sad for those on the east coast who had lost these things.

Another participant was told by his mother when he was seventeen years old that he was Aboriginal. This occurred when filling in a form that asked for formal identification of Aboriginal or Torres Strait Islander heritage. The participant asked his mother, expecting 'no' as the answer, 'Well am I?' The reply was 'yes'. He 'ticked the box' (P8). His mother explained to him that

> [s]he was brought up being taught to deny it...just because the way we were treated back then. She grew up in Forbes and that, well, you understand now why my grandad said he was Spanish. (P8)

Being Aboriginal for this younger person meant

> [j]ust being proud of being an Indigenous person. Being proud of where I'm from, proud of my heritage. Having that connection to my people...my passion for being involved in the community...(P8)

SELF-BELIEF IN ABORIGINAL HERITAGE

In other cases, participants had held a strong belief they were Aboriginal even when unable to confirm the family line. Among these participants there is poignancy about their commitment to this belief without knowing genealogical connections. One participant in her thirties always 'knew that there was something there...I always knew I didn't fit in that I was different, not the same as the white kids' (P24). In her thirties, while researching, she found a family photo of her father's mother 'and you could tell straightaway that she was an Aboriginal, she has the features and was really dark...' (P24). This photo is the participant's only connection to her Aboriginal past and for her constitutes the truth of her identity: 'Well, I have the photo to prove I am Aboriginal and I have showed the photo to Elders and they agree that my father's mother is Aboriginal' (P24). In this situation, community recognition is paramount and as this participant volunteered at a community organisation and went out on the land with Aboriginal people, 'the community can see I am part of it'. This participant is the only one of her family to identify, no others acknowledge it, and after learning about what happened to Aboriginal people she understands why 'everyone is still in that denial stage for fear of the consequences, so I do understand now but I didn't before, but now I do' (P24).

The *feeling* of being Aboriginal was very strong for these participants. Another participant claimed she has always

> felt in my bones I had black in me somewhere, black roots somewhere, I didn't know where, I felt maybe some connection to Kenya or something. That is all I could think of, but I felt it in the marrow of my bones. (P6)

This participant had a public profile and quite out of the blue was 'recognised' as Aboriginal at a protest by an Aboriginal woman who did not know who she was and assumed her to be an Aboriginal woman. She describes what followed this event, employing a retrospective analysis of feelings of awareness held for a long time:

> You spend fifty-two years of your life having been brought up to think you are white or whatever that means, to suddenly find you're Aboriginal or some kind of mixture, you know, a bit vague but it is hard to work out, it is confusing. Now so much else is happening. I thought about it, I asked about it, I sensed actually when in the company over a period of time and I could relax with Aboriginal people — my face relaxes and then the bone structure which is definitely Aboriginal starts to show. It is interesting but when my face is taut and tense I look like European. So this is, there has been many things since but that is where I started and I ran into a lot of dead ends…and it has been a much interrupted journey but I attempt to try and trace my roots which have been very difficult. (P6)

Although tracing roots has been difficult, this participant had four elements which she drew on as the 'truth' of her Aboriginal heritage: her European surname which is also an Aboriginal family name, her looks, her memory of a song and her father's way of relating. An Aboriginal woman explained to her the survival of the Aboriginal way of relating and this participant recognised this in her own father:

> [I]n a culture where human relations isn't considered very important the genocide completely missed out the question of the Aboriginal way of relating because the bastards couldn't see it — so it survived and I recognise it through my father and you know I was trying to trace it where and of course I could see it through my father and my grandmother who was by then dead…so the Aboriginal way of relating, the Aboriginal way of seeing things, a different way of seeing things, those things and without realising it he was passing this on to me even though he wasn't aware of his Aboriginality either. (P6)

The issue of her looks was a major aspect of how she was able to view herself as Aboriginal and she talked about this in her discussions about challenges to her Aboriginal identity:

> That has happened, although I think that is just too bad, because I know I have got [Aboriginal identity] in my blood and in my bones and I know that part of the reason [I am not recognisably Aboriginal] there was deliberate changes, umm four perfect teeth were taken out of my mouth and then braces put on which pulled my face back which actually had the effect of narrowing my nose changing the shape of my lower part of my face to make me look European. Well I know that. (P6)

The memory of a song was also critical to her self-belief in the face of challenges to her Aboriginal identity:

> [T]here is a song, it is an old song, they can't take it away from me, so when I am, you know, whatever. Particularly whitefellas, how would they know, you know, that kind of stuff? They wouldn't know, I mean it just has no credibility. Who are they to say, you know? But even when Aboriginal people say it and it really hurts I just say to myself, you know that song, they can't take it away from me. You know it is a good song. It relates to something quite different, it still has meaning. This is what I am, bugger it. (P6)

This participant was also told by a doctor friend that she 'had Aboriginal feet' (P6). This sort of appeal to physical traits is common. For example, Participant 11's question about whether he was part-Aboriginal was answered by his Pop with 'oh well, your legs look Aboriginal, maybe you are' (P11).

However, in the circumstances of people like Participant 6, the evidence of the tensions experienced are also to be found in the response of other Aboriginal people who challenge:

> [W]hen I called myself [Aboriginal name], she got up and walked away in disgust and used the word in a very derogative way, derogatory and then also criticised me, because at that point I wasn't sure what I should do, so I would say Part [Aboriginal], that is self-evident that part of my genetics roots are Aboriginal and part European non-Aborigi-

> nal, so I thought nobody could question that and then she was disgusted that I would say part-Aboriginal rather than just Aboriginal… (P6)

She betrays her lack of knowledge of the Aboriginal experience by not knowing the objection to using a colonial category, in a way that is qualitatively different from those individuals in Aboriginal families who know they are understood to be Aboriginal but who consciously wish to acknowledge their heritage from a non-Aboriginal parent. These make up the evidence of different subjectivities being forged and emerging in communal and social spaces, from different personal histories. One who knows she is Aboriginal tries to find a space for her other heritage (P25), while another (P6) who believes she is Aboriginal but has no experience of it reveals her lack of knowledge of Aboriginal sensitivities on this matter. Nevertheless, for Participant 6, being Aboriginal was 'something at the core of your being but it is also in one's blood and one's bones. Yeah, also in the way in which you see the world' (P6).

The correlation between urban Aboriginal identity and a political stance is absent in the analysis of these participants' discussion of how they came to know they were Aboriginal. Of all these participants, only two directly mentioned politics as a critical part of the construction of their Aboriginal identity:

> I think the fact that you open your mouth and say you're Aboriginal is a political statement. I don't think you can escape that. (P13)

> I don't know, it's just politically, political sort of views and political stands that I think my identity has shaped. (P11)

There were, however, those participants who talked of the effects of historical policies and the legacy of these on their families and/or generally on wider social relations, and Aboriginal community dynamics did evidence the political positioning of being Aboriginal. These issues are discussed in more detail in later chapters.

CHAPTER 15

THE CONTINUING CONTEST OVER THE DEFINITION OF ABORIGINAL IDENTITY

> Yeah, you grow up your whole life knowing you're Aboriginal but without that piece of paper are you Aboriginal? (P10)

> I don't want one and I don't need one so it doesn't matter to me. I think it is wrong, in any case, having to prove who you are to other people and then they can still say no. (P25)

> The truth is if you are Aboriginal nobody can say you can't be. (P19)

A number of participants, whether they agreed or disagreed with the requirement of a Confirmation of Aboriginality, talked about the Confirmation process as an instrument of the Australian state. What was interesting, however, was not what participants said but what was *not* said about this. Across the handful of participants who spoke directly to this relationship with the Australian government, it is possible to discern their understandings of the Confirmation process: as a government mechanism that continued administrative control and regulation of Aboriginal people; as a government requirement that had little to do with how Aboriginal people understand and/or confirm who is or who is not Aboriginal; and as a government mechanism that was about the distribution of scarce resources.

CONFIRMATION OF ABORIGINALITY AND THE NATION-STATE

In the course of my interviews, a number of older participants invoked the language of 'dog tags', a term with longstanding colonial connotations. Breast plates (known colloquially as dog tags) were given to Aboriginal leaders in the colonial past by governments as a form of 'official' recognition of status but came to be reviled symbols of patronising oppression. Exemption Certificates were often viewed in the same way. For example,

> I think it's a dog tag in reverse like, you know. It's not about Aboriginal people protecting Aboriginal turf, it's about white people setting up programs and putting things in place and identifying us in ways in which they want to identify us. (P13)

The next statement suggests the requirement is an illegitimate imposition of the State and that Aboriginal people do not need such a process to determine who is Aboriginal or not, because we have our own way of demonstrating we are Aboriginal:

> I think the white man has made us follow his path in needing this type of proof because in our way, we know we are Aboriginal and we can tell people who we are. (P18)

Nevertheless, this participant understood that it was Aboriginal organisations making the determinations:

> I know that Aboriginal organisations ask people to provide who they are sometimes so that pretenders don't use the service and the community gets the services because funding isn't much and there's not enough to go around. (P18)

Here we see the issue of resource distribution emerge to rationalise the relation between Confirmation, the nation-state and Aboriginal organisations. And so, while recognising the problematic ties to historical antecedents, participants quickly draw in and struggle with the problem of 'pretenders' and fraudulent claims on scarce resources. For example, one participant who agreed with the need for Confirmation and who had a Confirmation document, nevertheless used it sparingly. He stated: 'I think in a way it's a dog tag. I think it's a necessary evil in this day and age' (P11). Further, he highlights what he underlines as his mixed feelings:

> I think, I've got mixed feelings about it…You're getting back to them days where you need your path to be Aboriginal or your path to go off to mission but I think in this day and age there are some people who will abuse the system and who

> aren't Aboriginal. So I think it's a necessary evil to protect the services and the funding to make sure it's going to our Indigenous communities. (P11)

Another participant disputed this view that the Confirmation process was needed to prevent people from taking advantage of benefits or that it worked to prevent this:

> I guess some would think that…I think a lot of people believe people take advantage of it but I really think that outside of the Aboriginal community, I am sure there are one or two or the odd person who does, but in general I don't think people who aren't Aboriginal think about…pretend[ing] to be Aboriginal. It is something you couldn't rule out…I guess you can't really prove they are not; but having the community believe that they are doesn't necessarily prove they are either. (P1)

This participant calls into question the difficulty with arriving at any absolute 'proof' that access to benefits motivates 'imposters' and that this works both ways. Those who are recognised and accepted may turn out not to be Aboriginal but with their claims unable to be 'disproved'. Those not accepted or whose identity status is questioned may well be Aboriginal but unable to 'prove' it.

Although these participants clearly identified the relation between Confirmation of Aboriginality and the requirements of the nation-state to regulate access to funds and services, very few articulated the tensions between the national position and local community levels. The national–local tensions are arguably at the crux of local Aboriginal community identity politics, and yet escape capture in the popular and everyday critical lenses for exploring the issue. Here I quote at length a participant who did speak about this tension when discussing the Confirmation of Aboriginality process. However, once again, the difficulties of articulating the issues are evident:

> On a national level, I think because it's been so inundated by mainstream conceptions, it doesn't recognise the differences within Aboriginal communities and Aboriginal identity. Identity is shaped by culture; it's shaped by all these external things which can be location specific. On a national level there is a broad thing of Aboriginal or Indigenous Australian,

> but I think 'where is that commonality between Aboriginal people and Aboriginal identity?' Things are always going to be different and what shapes identity is always going to be different from community to community and also from person to person on how they see their life. I think there is a common unity of being Aboriginal but also there's the external things that shape your identity. (P11)

This participant draws attention to the national collective, local community and personal aspects of Aboriginal identities as well as the tensions across these. However, something interesting was not talked about or brought into this and other analyses of relations with the nation-state. Firstly, there was no expressed view that the struggles over 'who is' and 'what counts' are fundamentally framed by the consultative arrangements with the nation-state organised under the principles of self-determination. In this frame, 'who' has the right to speak as an Aboriginal person rests on being 'unquestionably' accepted as Aboriginal. Much of the gate-keeping of Aboriginal identities and bodies is arguably a struggle to privilege some community representations of what it means to be Aboriginal over others.

Nor was there a clear view expressed by any participant, or even discernible more broadly, that relations with governments and the questions around 'who is' and 'what counts' as Aboriginal were fundamentally framed by resource issues. This closes off the possibility that if access to resources and services was not dependent on Aboriginality then the identity issues might be discussed differently. There was also no questioning of the scarce resources which shaped the need for Aboriginal people to regulate each other on behalf of the State in order to guard and distribute resources. What also appear to escape analysis are the grating and paradoxical ties between Aboriginal community organisations as symbols of self-determination and Aboriginal community organisations as de facto government administrators of 'who is' and 'what counts' as being Aboriginal. These are, however, the parameters of our freedom to determine our own affairs.

But perhaps what was most interesting was the absence of talk about the act of dispossession and disenfranchisement that is common to all Aboriginal Australians but has affected many of us differently. While this more fundamental political narrative remains submerged as the basis of a shared heritage, competition for scarce resources relies on narrower sets of assumptions about what constitutes the legitimate narrative of Aboriginal colonial/historical experience and what meanings constitute the possibilities for claiming to be Aboriginal. It is understandable that participants did not talk about the wider implications of these relations, because to do so requires a form of meta-analysis to construct a larger picture over time and place. In the everyday, more piecemeal popular analyses emerge from more limited spaces for making sense. However, in light of the absence of a wider analysis of the implications for Aboriginal organisations doing the administrative work of the nation-state, it is perhaps not surprising that most of the participants' reasoning and logic about Confirmation of Aboriginality was turned inwards to the assumed 'truths' of what it means to be Aboriginal. Nor was it surprising that reasoning and logic turned inwards onto the demands it made on Aboriginal individuals.

Given the history of Aboriginal administration in Australia, Aboriginal people policing identity boundaries is perhaps more tolerable than governments doing so. However, this relies on an implicit denial of our complicity with the ongoing regulatory regimes of the all-encompassing nation-state which still 'rules and divides' us. It also relies on an unproblematic acceptance of community organisations as the instruments of Aboriginal self-determination rather than as identity police and judges. It also relies on a denial of the facet that we now do to each other what was historically done to divide us. As one participant pondered, it's 'a government process…that has its merits also but can equally divide communities' (P4).

From here, participant statements begin to reveal how easy it is to be caught in a web that implicates us in our own predicament.

THE DEFINITIONAL CRITERIA OF ABORIGINALITY

A personal disagreement with the Confirmation of Aboriginality as an official form of proof, even if vehement, did not necessarily mean any disagreement with the official definitional criteria which constituted the evidence of Aboriginality: Aboriginal descent, self-identification and acceptance by the community in which one lives. And yet the definitional criteria only came into being as a response to the colonial legacy of dividing and differentiating Aboriginal people from one another for government administrative and regulatory purposes. As mentioned in Part One, the official definition emerged in the 1980s, and the responsibility of determining whether Aboriginal individuals met the criteria was given to Aboriginal community organisations. This was a well-intentioned design to remove non-Aboriginal people from imposing their meanings and constructs of what it means to be Aboriginal, even though the legal judgments about 'who is' and 'what counts' evidence the continuing role of wider jurisdictions on the matter. However, this design also assumes local Aboriginal community organisations 'know' or can determine who is Aboriginal and who is not in more fair or just ways than past administrators.

In the context of intergenerational disruptions to Aboriginal families due to past government policies, and the difficulties these produce for 'proving' Aboriginality, the assumption of community acceptance based on knowing and recognising an individual as Aboriginal becomes problematic. Nevertheless, the criteria of community acceptance, grounded in this notion of knowing or recognising someone as Aboriginal, came through in participant data as almost beyond question.

In the data can be discerned the real difficulties that participants have in upholding a positive, consolidated, and collectively coherent and recognisable Aboriginal identity on the one hand, and understanding and accommodating the diverse legacy of past policy on other Aboriginal people and families on the other. The meanings of Aboriginality as expressed in the definitional criteria become the 'regime' for its truth and are applied to all, irrespective of their family's historical experience, and how the legacy of that plays out in their everyday lives today. There is, in some participants' analysis of the issues around Confirmation, evidence of how individual Aboriginal identities and bodies are sandwiched between the larger constructed meanings of the definitional criteria and the interpretations of them at the local Aboriginal community level. There is also a suggestion in some of the data that such interpretations are filtered via the historical lens of the longest established members of the local Aboriginal community and of community politics. For example, one participant defined what Aboriginal people mean when they speak of the Aboriginal community: 'Usually they are referring to the largest and most dominant family group in the community' (P3). Another participant, talking about community acceptance for those without acceptable narratives supported this understanding:

> Unless they are from a very well known family, whose kinship groups are very powerful, and they have been brought up very close to their, in their kinship groups, and in their

> large community, then, sure, they're probably less likely to cop it. But if you're an Indigenous person who's light-skinned, who moved to an area with an Indigenous [local] community, they're very likely to not be accepted. (P21)

Another alluded to the political nature of challenges to individuals' identity via the Confirmation process: 'I don't think people should be challenged who are obviously Aboriginal, who have their family connection just because of community politics' (P11). Of course, who is 'obviously' Aboriginal is at issue.

One participant whose family had always identified as Aboriginal but who did not actively participate in the community related her sense of the community politics: 'We were kind of intimidated, we were intimidated about being judged by blackfellas and …we did try a little bit but I think we kinda knew we weren't gonna get very far' (P5).

This unease with community politics allows concerns about the problematic concept of 'community acceptance', as a workable or even valid definitional criterion, to be shifted to a concern about the processes involved in confirming Aboriginality.

The following two participants are examples of straightforward acceptance of the criteria. One who had not known about the definitional criteria commented when they were explained to her, 'I think that's fantastic' (P9). Another participant who had always known she was Aboriginal but did not know the definitional criteria expressed a similar view:

> I think it's kind of good in a way because for those who want to be recognised as Aboriginal, to express Aboriginality is a great thing and to know that they are accepted into the community as being part of the Aboriginal community is a great thing. (P3)

However, some fuzzy logic was in evidence in the way some participants stepped through the issues. For example, one participant who was against the Confirmation process and expressed resistance asserted: 'I am not going to get one ever and feel strongly about it that it is a dog tag and I won't be made get one' (P20). However, this participant then immediately qualified his statement: 'I think community should recognise you and that is good enough' (P20). However, when I suggested that the Confirmation process is a process for confirmation of community recognition, he replied that 'there are not too many people around here with the knowledge of being Aboriginal, so who is going to do that?' When I explained that it was the role of community organisations and the board of directors specifically, he countered: 'That is just funny when you know who is on the Board and I am not going to be judged by them and who says they are Aboriginal?' (P20) The question of what then constitutes 'community acceptance' and who is to judge, and how meaningful any judgment can be, could not be engaged further with this participant, who took the interview onto a different point. Thus his political stance against the nation-state did call into question the politics of Aboriginal identity at the community level but did not extend to his own analysis of the issues at stake.

The previous chapters confirm that community acceptance pivots on 'being known', and how an individual ensures that they 'are known' can be achieved in a range of ways, some of which are much easier for some than others depending on the individual's situation. So here the Confirmation process is brought into question rather than the criteria, which is rendered as not part of the problem but a non-negotiable 'truth' of Aboriginality. This participant had come from another community and his acceptance into the community had depended on 'Elders here who knew my family background, so I had no trouble being accepted' (P20). He nevertheless said how 'it can take a long time for people to be accepted' (P20).

In view of this, it wasn't surprising that some participants used the language of 'luck' in relation to the Confirmation process and the importance of 'being known'. One participant who had moved from another community talked of how confronting it was to be suddenly asked to produce verification. She came to the realisation of the 'taken-for-granted' aspects of 'the safe sanctuary of being known [in her own community] and who I was and that sort of thing' (P22). And yet the benefits of having a 'piece of paper' were acknowledged: 'It sure did [help] because if I was questioned I could say, "Well my community knows who I am and they have signed this paper to let you know who I am"' (P22). In a case like this, the documents of Confirmation work like identity papers or a passport in a foreign land. They are like the Exemption Certificates of past eras, but in reverse.

However, more than this acknowledgement of the benefits, this participant reinforced the pragmatism of accepting the request for official Confirmation while holding an ambivalent view of it:

> I don't think we should [require Confirmation] but in saying that, I am glad I had mine. My brother has had trouble with his identity and he doesn't have a Confirmation and he has found it harder than me [in the new community]. It is important to build your networks in the community so people know you and can say, yes, I know her she is involved in the community. (P22)

Thus for this participant the criteria of community recognition was problematic, but she still conceded that it

> is paramount but I can see how it could work against someone too…All it takes is someone to say you are not Aboriginal and if they are someone of influence, then the situation could become quite difficult. (P22)

The situation that two siblings might have different outcomes implicates the process but does it also implicate the criteria? This remains uncertain and unexplored, and yet such situations are not uncommon.

Another participant who had sought Confirmation at one point also considered herself 'lucky' (P4) because her father was involved in Aboriginal Land Councils and her Aboriginality could be confirmed via him. She also knew her family connections and history and this helped her to be recognised. She expressed ambivalence towards the need for Confirmation nevertheless: 'I kinda don't feel that I need to justify [my identity] through a Confirmation' (P4). However, she had been through the process of official Confirmation, had observed it, and expressed some reservations about the process where some organisations had robust conditions for distributing Confirmation of Aboriginality forms and other organisations did not:

> …and you can have issues come up there where people might question Confirmation of Aboriginality and because of that, that then, to me, puts a whole big cloud of questioning over, what is — if people are going to question them — what is the value in us having them…[if] they can be provided to people who are non-Aboriginal, um, then that then I suppose puts a mark on every other person that has one of those Confirmations. (P4)

Thus it was the inconsistency of the process of Confirmation that was at issue, not the criteria.

The criterion of community acceptance was also non-negotiable by some participants who supported the need for Confirmation of Aboriginality documents, even when they didn't see the need to have it themselves. Like others, one participant explained how she had no need for official Confirmation documents because '[e]veryone up and down the coast knows me and nobody questions me' (P23). Asked about what the process could mean for people who hadn't grown up in the local community, she reflected: 'They can ask their own community for the papers if they need them'. Probed further about those Aboriginal people who hadn't lived anywhere else but had not been part of the community, she argued: 'I think you should be part of the community. I have always been part of the community that is why I am known. So they should be part of the community' (P23). And then asked about those people who were just finding out they were Aboriginal, this participant confirmed the importance of the journey taken by many:

> They just have to explain that, then look into their background and find out the information they need — who are their family — so they can work out where they belong. Some people say they are Aboriginal but they don't know what that means or they just think they are or want to be. That is why community is important, so that those people can be part of the community, if they are Aboriginal. (P23)

This stance was not unusual and applied as well to the difficulties that individuals might have in establishing the 'of Aboriginal descent' criterion. Once again, the issues of community recognition and acceptance came to the fore — as did insensitivities to the different subjectivities of individuals with different family histories and narratives of colonial or more recent experience. One participant who was unequivocal about the role of the nation-state in defining Aboriginality extended her disdain to the legal definition of Aboriginality: 'Yeah, the legal definition, the government definition of who we are and what we are' (P14). Nevertheless, she had little dispute with the criteria of the definition and did not think they were particularly difficult,

> You know what? Aboriginal communities know who's related to who. And if a person comes into a community with an

understanding that he or she has links or genealogical links to that community, people should be able to place that person because they have a history. (P14)

But when questioned about people who didn't have a history that could be narrated, she responded: 'Well they should. They should have a history and if they don't have a history then the first person's talking to the wrong people' (P14) When asked about people who had been disconnected over generations, she talked of people having to talk to people in the region about the names of forebears to see if someone could link the name to the community: 'I think the community should be able to validate any newcomer who hasn't [recognised links]. I don't think that, well [the community] should do, shouldn't it? Doesn't that fit into that definition?'

So here, an Aboriginal person who does not believe in the process believes that nevertheless the community should have to recognise a person for that person to be accepted as Aboriginal. While my analysis has to allow for the 'interview effect' of being put on the spot, this participant's use of circular logic allows disdain for the definition on political grounds but nevertheless upholds the 'truth' of the criteria of Aboriginality by appealing to the 'government's' definition. She also assumes that all Aboriginal people, no matter what their historical circumstances, can find and establish genealogical links through people who are still alive today. Given the historical experience of colonisation and administration, a question arises as to how we Aboriginal people understand the diversity of circumstances and experiences beyond the various relatively small and long-established local communities. The difficulty of separating discursive entanglements is in evidence here. A wider perspective than the local community interest is also not in evidence.

Some participants also expressed the view that the proof of descent criterion was essential. When asked about how people would do that, one participant replied:

> You should provide the family jungle...but also show where you're from... it's pretty much a straightforward thing. It's just when you come from outa town it may be necessary that you go back to your community and you may encounter some problems there. (P11)

Another participant who thought the requirement of proof was a whitefella process and who was sympathetic to those who could not provide proof, nevertheless emphasised the importance of learning about culture and history and how this enabled him to get his Confirmation:

> We went back to our people's land and delved into our culture to learn about who we are and I did lots of research so I made the effort to find out and know about our culture and identity. (P18)

Following the logic of his own experience, he thought that other people 'need to go to their community and build up relationships and learn their culture then come to the [Aboriginal Organisation] and say, "this is who I am"' (P18). Thus many who did not agree with the process agreed with the criteria as measures of Aboriginality.

The importance of community involvement and recognition was, from the stance of these participants, an essential standard for judging exclusion/inclusion into the Aboriginal community. Even the criterion of self-identification was considered to be best demonstrated by 'being community active, being involved' (P11).

These are the imperatives of being Aboriginal. Within some of these positions, there is some circular self-fulfilling logic which evidences the discursive construction and the discursive limits of being Aboriginal. Descent or heritage is not sufficient and not the same as 'being' Aboriginal. An individual cannot be accepted as Aboriginal without visibly being part of the community. Under these conditions, as understood by participants in this study, it is impossible to be recognised as Aboriginal and not be part of the community, even if your life, work and interests construct multiple identities and ways of being 'in the world'. The identity journeys and the processes of negotiation described by participants in previous chapters literally 'make sense' in this logic and become the 'essential' identity work of becoming, being and expressing what it means to be Aboriginal in Australia in the twenty-first century.

However, the 'hard work' that participants have described both for learning to be Aboriginal in order to be recognised and accepted, and to meet the proof criteria for official Confirmation, evidences the exclusive rather than inclusive tendencies at the limits of these boundaries. These boundaries are 'tested' by the Confirmation criteria of community acceptance but some participants' statements provide evidence of how risky it is to contest them. A pragmatic view of compliance with the accepted discourses of Aboriginality is able to be understood.

But what is also opened up for further contemplation is the lack of accommodation for those descendants of Aboriginal people who have been intergenerationally disconnected through the same administrative policies as those Aboriginal community members whose identities are placed beyond question. Inclusion requires an individual to conform and demonstrate their acceptance of the criteria of community acceptance. In some respects the process resembles the learning and commitment required for Christian religious confirmation. There is less understanding of the different Aboriginal subjectivities constructed through historical experiences. These can include having been designated Aboriginal or not Aboriginal under previous policies, having been removed under previous policies, having married 'interracially', and having lived away from 'country' or in a number of communities in order to survive.

QUESTIONING THE DEFINITIONAL CRITERIA OF ABORIGINALITY

Some participants, however, did express some concern about the definitional criteria, often but not always with reference to 'community acceptance'. The following participant, for example, makes a broad assessment of his concerns:

> In some ways yes [the definitional criteria are good], in some ways no. I think the criteria in its broader sense is a good thing. I'm only talking [about it] in the Confirmation thing. It's good, but, however, the criteria it's very broad and I think it's a national thing. You're Aboriginal, you identify, you're accepted by your community. I think they are the three fundamental basics of being an Aboriginal person living within the community and being recognised. However there is so much more from that piece of paper which makes you Aboriginal and which shapes you identity, so in a way it's a necessary evil, if someone can think up a better way! (P11).

However, for this participant the criteria seemed to be not comprehensive or specific enough to accommodate all Aboriginal people and he talked of the differences between urban and remote Aboriginal people and the need for different Confirmation criteria to accommodate all specificities of Aboriginal identity. That said, he suggests that for remote areas 'it's going to have to be organised specifically for each clan, community.' Here this participant is unclear about whether the suggestion is for more narrowly defined community criteria, or whether the national criteria are unworkable at the community level and whether other criteria could be applied in some situations but not others. This logic seems to suggest the need for finer definition of locally specific boundaries in order to determine 'who is' and 'what counts' as being Aboriginal in different communities. This reproduces the current problem of those Aboriginal people who have been dislocated, either intergenerationally or through moving around for the requirements of family, work and education

Another participant was more forthright in her views that the criteria were questionable because all the different specificities of being Aboriginal could not be accommodated. However, she stopped short of trying to solve the problem: '[T]here is a criteria but I don't think it works too well. I don't think it works at all' (P7).

Another participant also brought to light awareness of the difficulties imposed for some by the proof requirements. She illustrated how her work in the community has assisted her, demonstrating how she understands the significance of community recognition:

> Unfortunately in this country, there's a lot of politics around identity that not only get fed to us through external sources, whether it be government or the wider population. We also do it to ourselves and set it up so that …if you don't fit into the traditional owner category or if you don't fit into a historical connection category…like…I'm not a local person cause I haven't lived here all my life…my country is further south… so kind of where do you fit into being a community member. And that's where I kind of fit in through my work. (P4)

Nonetheless, participants generally talked about their issues with the criteria in the context of the difficulties of providing proof for Confirmation purposes. As with understandings of the relation between the Confirmation requirements and the nation-state, talk about these difficulties often, but not always, shifted the focus of the problems from the criteria to the processes of Confirmation.

DIFFICULTIES AND FLAWS IN THE CONFIRMATION PROCESS

The difficulties that participants mainly talked about were in relation to proving they met the definitional criteria and how this indicated flaws in the process. The difficulties of proof posed by the three definitional criteria mostly related to the criteria of descent and community acceptance. For some, these difficulties led them to not pursue Confirmation processes. One of the difficulties talked about by participants was the effects of moving around and what this means for local community acceptance:

> I would find that [criteria] a bit challenging and I think a lot of people move around nowadays. To be [recognised as] part of the community, how do you classify that? That you were born and bred and everyone knows you, or that you come in, because sometimes coming in and being in the community for two years, are you still identified? Where's the boundaries? (P7)

Another participant explained the flaws in the process for people who live and work in communities in which they have not grown up. One thought the required process borders on the absurd, but this example is not unusual when trying to be confirmed by Aboriginal organisations:

> But it's so hard because I couldn't get one from down [regional city] where I [had] spent seven years of my life. I had to call back home where I haven't grown up, only my mum's grown up. So then I had to be accepted in that community, they had to know me and so it's hard. Imagine if my mum didn't grow up there or we had no way. If we didn't know the people, how would I identify as Aboriginal basically? How do I define my Aboriginality if I don't know people in the community? (P10)

This participant did see the need for Confirmation in order to prove eligibility for benefits. But she also saw how hard it was to prove it, especially for some young people:

> So how do you get it then? So you're clearly Aboriginal, you identify as Aboriginal but couldn't get one but someone who can prove it can get a confirmation and get a job. How do you go about proving that you're Aboriginal? (P10)

Some participants talked about being glad they had not needed a Confirmation document because of the difficulties they would have proving it. This illustrates the arbitrariness of community acceptance and the tying of the Confirmation process to the access to 'benefits'. As one fair-skinned person argued: 'Like I said, if [my darker-skinned sister] couldn't get one, I wouldn't be able to and I am lucky I don't have or haven't needed one. I don't want anything so I don't think I need one' (P25). This participant talked of the stumbling block of the community acceptance criterion:

> I don't agree with that. I think it is your own private business if you say you are or not and you shouldn't have to say, 'Oh yes, I am Aboriginal' like and prove it. So no, I don't think I would bother. Who has the right to say if I am Aboriginal or not. No, I don't like that. (P25)

These difficulties could only be set aside by some participants by placing more emphasis on the personal meanings of being Aboriginal. In this way, they conceded the need for Confirmation of Aboriginality for official purposes but claimed that they did not need it for self-affirmation, thus drawing the line between private and public selves and domains. For example, one participant illustrated her position in relation to the discursive constraints, which of course were also enablers of her Aboriginal identity, discovered as an adult:

> The way I feel it doesn't change anything with me but I reckon something like that I would feel proud and I could probably see it in a frame sitting where my pictures are. I would probably have a nice brown frame with dots decorating it. Not because I needed it for Studies or anything like that. (P9)

Another participant questioned the meaning of the Confirmation process by relating that he had 'heard that a lot of people had paid for their identity' (P2). On further probing, he stated he didn't have a Confirmation document because he didn't need one as a Native Title claimant. However, he revealed how his uncle viewed them as unnecessary because 'if you see them [Aboriginal people] walking a hundred yards down the street you can see who is an Aboriginal person' (P2). This is a persistent assertion that 'legitimate' Aboriginals are easily recognised by physical traits and is mirrored by another participant that Aboriginal people know who is Aboriginal.

Nevertheless, this participant expressed sympathy for the difficulties some Aboriginal people would have proving they were Aboriginal, including his own uncle who had always been recognised as Aboriginal. So when asked about how a person would go about gaining community acceptance, he reflected:

> Well you would have to identify as one first. I don't know, just…don't' know. It would be hard if, it would be easier if you are with your local people but if your mob is from, I don't know, Western Australia, or out of town or you don't know…that would make it difficult. (P2)

Probed further about members of his own family who were not involved in local community matters, he elaborated further about the difficulties:

> I don't think they would know [how to prove their Aboriginality] because the culture isn't there, they don't know their roots. I know that there is a lot of people who are from the Stolen Generation, I don't know how they would go. I don't even know how an adopted person would go if…told they were Aboriginal by their adopted parents. I don't know how they would go proving it. My main thing on it is if you identify as Aboriginal and in your heart you're Aboriginal, you should be Aboriginal, it don't matter. (P2)

Here we see the complex layers and tensions that require a circular logic that returns the question of proof back to 'knowing' it in the personal sense or even in the unofficial sense of community acceptance in the case of his uncle. And yet, this is the sticking point, which leads to the need to 'prove' Aboriginality using the logic that not insisting on proof provides a space for the fakers, frauds and pretenders.

Indeed, three participants seriously discussed the value of DNA testing to determine and prove their Aboriginality:

> Well I mean if you've got genetic proof that would be really good…I think that the capacity of DNA testing to identify family connections is more advanced than we know because I have asked, because I was sure this would help me to connect with what tribe, I think I know where. (P6)

And another:

> I just reckon they should do a blood test, line us all up... They wouldn't have to do an invasive test. They could tell from our DNA, they could do a swab. (P4)

Another participant, who contemplated how an Aboriginal person who identified as Aboriginal 'in the heart' would provide proof of that, answered:

> DNA...I'm not a big one for the scientific DNA but you need to find out for funds and stuff...I suppose it's a hard thing really (P11).

These statements are evidence of the levels of frustration with the requirement for proof, and yet biological descent is already established as insufficient, both according to the definition and within the limits of the discourses of 'who is' and 'what counts' as Aboriginal today.

FUTURE CONCERNS ABOUT THE REQUIREMENT FOR CONFIRMATION OF ABORIGINALITY

There was some evidence to support the notion that it was becoming more difficult to be officially confirmed as Aboriginal. Some who described the relative ease they had getting their Aboriginality confirmed were talking of past conditions. For example,

> Uncle [local Elder] signed my papers when he was working at [Aboriginal organisation]. I have had this in my wallet for years so if anyone questions me I can say, here you go, look at this...Things have changed a bit now and it is hard to come by the paper work and I know people who come to the [Aboriginal organisation] and we don't give them there but they ask and they can't get one so it isn't easy for some people to get it. (P19)

One response to the persistent questions that arise in public and Aboriginal community domains around various individuals' claims to be Aboriginal is the trend to more consistent application of official requirement to produce documented proof. This is particularly the case in government departments and for the awarding of educational scholarships.

Concern about the possibility for future generations of Aboriginal people to be confirmed officially as Aboriginal was also expressed by some:

> There needs to be some way to work forward from this for the future. I think it [proof criteria of Aboriginality] was good as a preliminary idea to address certain things. However, I think there needs to be some more national debate rather than just DNA testing to develop something that's truly going to reflect Aboriginal identities and the communities. (P11)

Two participants' concerns directly addressed the intergenerational effects for those who cannot obtain Confirmation of Aboriginality. One addressed this generally:

> I wonder about some of the kids if the parents didn't get recognition in the community or didn't identify, so it will be harder in the future. (P19)

The other described her personal situation in more detail. This participant had undergone an 'identity journey' since her teenage years. Although she was estranged from her well-known Aboriginal family whose identity was based in a different Aboriginal country, she was connected to and involved in the local community and held an identified position. Her children had Aboriginal fathers. Here can be discerned her ambivalence towards the Confirmation of Aboriginality process rather than the requirement to have one, as she contemplates what might be at stake for her children in the future:

> I don't have one, not because I don't want one but I can't get one. I need one for the kids for their sports but can't bring myself to go to the cultural centre and ask someone who I don't know to confirm my identity for me. It is an intimidating thing to have someone judge whether they accept you as Aboriginal or in some cases not. I am not emotionally ready for that. I have heard of other people's experiences down here and how distressing it can be. (P21)

She goes on to say,

> I worry about the kids and what it will mean in the future if they have to rely on that process. I mean my kids go to a private school and they don't hang out at Aboriginal community events or anything like that. They are proud to be

> Aboriginal but I don't know if they have worked out what being Aboriginal is. And what if their choices today impact on that discussion in the future? (P21)

Here the implications of the problems of the Confirmation processes in this local Aboriginal community context are already seen as holding implications for future generations. This person of dual heritage has always identified as Aboriginal, has worked hard to be Aboriginal and fits all the criteria of the definition, but the emotional effects of the politics of local community Confirmation process signals to her she cannot get one. Further, with the benefits of higher education and a good job, she works hard to pass on those benefits to her own children by placing them in a school that extends their horizons beyond the immediate confines of the Aboriginal community. In the light of her own difficulties and experiences, her children's teenage choices are already risking their future claims to be Aboriginal, even though they proudly identify and have been socialised in an Aboriginal family that includes Aboriginal fathers and an extended Aboriginal family. She questions her own reluctance to obtain an official document so that she might get one for her children. In the future, will her children be recognised as Aboriginal? It is a pertinent question.

CHAPTER 16
LEARNING AND PERFORMING AN ABORIGINAL IDENTITY

> The act that one does, the act that one performs is, in a sense, an act that's been going on before one arrived on the scene.
> (Butler 1999, p. 272)

Those participants in my study who had discovered later in life they had Aboriginal heritage, as well as those who had always known they were Aboriginal but for whom it had little meaning while growing up, spoke about the gaps in their knowledge about what it means to be Aboriginal.

Common ways of exploring the meanings of being Aboriginal included finding out about wider kin relationships and country, finding out about the Aboriginal historical experience and legacy, and finding out about Aboriginal culture in general. This quest for knowledge was often personal but also served as a bridge or transition towards acceptance and recognition from the wider Aboriginal community.

Knowledge emerged as the actual 'content' of 'being' Aboriginal and a firmer basis for then being able to 'be' Aboriginal. The other basis for knowing what was involved in being Aboriginal was the formation of relationships with Aboriginal people through participation in community events, organisations and workplaces and through making friends with other Aboriginal people undergoing the process of learning 'who they are'. This provided more than knowledge; it provided networks and models of behaviour, which all helped to affirm a sense of belonging and of being Aboriginal.

LEARNING AND UN-LEARNING

What emerged from the analysis of many participants' accounts was the sense of a journey over time. This journey was given a recognisable pattern by a process that helped draw participants into the Aboriginal 'everyday' world. The process involved getting to know 'things' about Aboriginal worlds and getting to know Aboriginal people. The process of acquisition often included formal education in some sort of Indigenous course at TAFE or university or both; moving closer to or interacting more with other Aboriginal people; participation in community events, organisations and workplaces; and learning from community people in such venues. Participating in one of these options often facilitated a participant's access to wider Aboriginal knowledge networks.

This process was explained by one participant, who had been involved in the family Link-Up[13] process for many years and had observed how many newly identifying Aboriginal people

> ...get involved one way or another in some field of Aboriginal interest. A few do [the tough stuff] but a lot of people get into the Arts of one kind or another. So I think it's a way of validating that identity and finding that other Aboriginal family if you haven't found your own. Giving you a place in an Aboriginal space that you wouldn't have if you didn't do it because you still may not have found our own mob. You may have and they may not have wanted to know you or whatever. I've noticed over the many years...that that is nearly standard. For those who knew of their Aboriginality it can be somewhat different but for those who didn't know or weren't sure it's a steep learning curve and so people grab on to this ladder or something else. (P14)

One participant exemplified the learning process as a series of stages or levels, which for her began as a teenager:

> I began to search out what Aboriginality meant, because obviously I didn't get that from my mother who was non-Indigenous, so I had to go and search that out. So that meant I joined up the local Aboriginal Lands Council, I played softball for the local Aboriginal group, I went to Land Council

---

13 Link-Up is a service established by the government in response to the recommendations of the *Bringing Them Home* Report (WIlson 1997) to assist Aboriginal and Torres Strait Islander people who were separated from their families as a result of past government policies and practices to find their family.

> meetings, and became involved with the community. I started going out at very young age with another Indigenous guy and, that was all a process of me finding out and being part, being belonging. So I think it was a matter of learning through experience. (P21)

Going out with Aboriginal men was a conscious self-discovery strategy for this participant: 'In some ways it confirmed for me a sense of being Aboriginal and it was about learning to be with my own mob and what they meant' (P21). This participant also went on to study Indigenous Studies at university level and now has a career via an identified position. Studying both Aboriginal history and culture enabled her to

> feel more confident in knowing that Aboriginality is about diversity and complexity and [about] not knowing and not feeling confident. And I realised that that was quite normal, so it wasn't until…later as an adult that I began to feel a foundation and security of being and identifying as an Aboriginal person. (P21)

Other participants undertook TAFE and university courses to learn and understand more of what it means to be Aboriginal, and to be able to work to help the broader Aboriginal community. One participant who had not always known she was Aboriginal explained this orientation for learning:

> I decided to go to TAFE and do the Indigenous Health Course…I know how serious the medical side of things are for the Aboriginals, so thought that would be good idea to study in that area. (P26)

As part of this course, this participant helped out at a local Aboriginal program and 'met some of the local people and Elders and Aboriginal staff' (P26). In turn, this led her to consider applying for an identified position in the local health context; she was told she would probably get the job 'because not many Aboriginals have the qualifications I have with TAFE and uni'. But further to this, she reported, 'I have just signed up to do the Aboriginal Arts course at TAFE…and I am looking forward to learning more about the culture and painting' (P26).

For some, learning and knowledge focused more on this cultural aspect. For example, a recent identifier described his experience:

> I did go to TAFE and did the Art course and it was such an eye opener and I learnt so much about the culture…I met all these other people and artists and we went out and walked on Aboriginal land and I felt the inspiration of the Ancestors and we talked with Elders and I learnt lots. Yeah I learnt lots. (P24)

This led him to become more involved in community through volunteering at a local community organisation. He also took every opportunity to go out onto the land for community days to learn 'about the culture' (P24).

Another who grew up not knowing she was Aboriginal reported a similar learning process that began with enrolling in a TAFE Aboriginal arts course. She loved being with other Aboriginal students and learning about culture. After six months she was approached to teach Aboriginal studies, and commented on the pace of learning this involved and her approach to learning: 'I basically had to research all of this stuff by going to Elders, by reading all sorts of things. So I've really educated myself really, really quickly' (P17).

Making friends with other Aboriginal people while undertaking formal study was emphasised by some participants. One participant who had recently discovered she was Aboriginal related how

> [i]t is hard but I came to Uni and did Aboriginal Studies so I am learning about being Aboriginal…and try to be with the other students and make friends and see if they can teach me or if there are others like me which I think there are…it is like a neither here nor there space. You are not really Aboriginal enough to be Aboriginal but are trying to be… (P12)

However, although this participant had joined student games and attended the Aboriginal centre at her university, she felt her vulnerable 'neither here nor there' status and so had also distanced herself from her non-Aboriginal friends:

> I feel like I just fit in…and when I know more I will feel more confident to make more friends and from them learn more about being Aboriginal. I try and make more Aboriginal friends and I don't really hang much with non-Aboriginal people anymore… (P12)

This participant did not seem to note this as contingent on an either/or choice of Aboriginal or non-Aboriginal identity. Rather it seemed to be more closely associated with the reorientation of herself as part of the process to become Aboriginal: '[My boyfriend] was not happy that I was now Aboriginal and he doesn't understand what I am doing' (P12).

Formal studies were an important knowledge element because, as one participant put it, 'you can't just say to an Aboriginal person can you tell me what I need to know' (P12). Even for some who grew up knowing they were Aboriginal, formal study of Indigenous issues was still important learning:

> It did open me eyes to the negatives in health…and it was a big shock…we even learnt about past Aboriginal injustices and we learned how Aboriginals are more disadvantaged than other groups in Australia which was a shock. (P2)

However, some participants did not emphasise formal study but rather family and kin or other Aboriginal people as sources of historical and cultural knowledge. For example, for one participant who had always known she was Aboriginal, but who grew up not knowing the meaning of this, learning about culture and language was not seemingly any easier than for others who did not always know they were Aboriginal:

> Culturally I'm not too sure. I'm at a loss at the moment. I just find it really hard to find culture and I want to learn language. There's not many people from my tribe still alive today who know the language. I'm still trying to learn and all I can do now is basically just meet the family and get to know people and I think that's a strong way that I am learning my culture. (P10)

For this person, working in an identified position was an important way of being Aboriginal: 'I was more accepted within the community because I was working in an Aboriginal identified position…and I just became better known in the community' (P10). However, going back to her home country and learning about history was viewed as an important ongoing process:

> I'm really interested in finding out all that, so that's the way I feel I'm strengthening my identity is by tracing back history. I feel that's a strong way to identify you culture. (P10)

One participant who found out the family was Aboriginal when he was ten or eleven, related how 'moving to be on our country and speaking with the family and extended family' (P18) helped him to learn more about culture and Aboriginality. He also related how high school played a part in learning what it means to be Aboriginal:

> I just wanted to learn so much about my culture and everything…And I learnt much more…when we actually relocated…when we went to Echuca High School, they were quite strong because…all around them areas is quite strong Aboriginal communities, all related, and then we actually did a whole study…called Aboriginal Studies…and that helped me a lot. (P18)

Few participants appeared to directly question the constructions of Aboriginality within the corpus of Western knowledge *about* Aboriginal people, whether they learnt through formal studies, from the television or from libraries. However one participant commented it was 'scary' (P12) thinking about some of the knowledge that newly identifying people were receiving or acting on:

> If people believe mainstream stereotypes about what you're supposed to be, you can run into a lot of trouble. Because those stereotypes are stereotypes for reasons and if you start to believe them, you're believing your own people are this and that. (P12)

Little reference was made to these sorts of underlying tensions within the production of knowledge about Aboriginal people by newly identifying people. When participants did, it appeared to be through learning from the mistakes that offended other Aboriginal people, such as using the term 'part-Aboriginal'. For example, one participant discussed how he had to 'unlearn' some things as part of the process of learning to be Aboriginal. This participant had found out he was Aboriginal when he was seventeen and it took another decade before he really connected with his people:

> To my knowledge being Aboriginal was what I was taught at school as a whitefella. They lived in the bush a long time ago, wore loin cloths and speared roos and that was my understanding of being Aboriginal. So I was lost and just had no idea of who I was after that. (P8)

On the basis of his school knowledge, this participant used the derogatory terms 'Abo', 'half-caste' and 'part-Aboriginal': 'Like I had to unlearn what I had been taught about Indigenous culture, which I said was bugger all' (P8). In the meantime, he attended community events and talked to people in the community. He also related his sense of anxiety about becoming Aboriginal:

> I felt real nervous. I didn't want to seem to the people I was hanging around with like I was trying to prove I was Aboriginal. I didn't want to seem like I was doing that, I just wanted to find out who I was. (P8)

The absence of genealogical proof and not being able to say where he was from and who he was connected to weighed heavily on this participant until his family line was established. His confidence to assert his Aboriginality grew with this knowledge but the learning process goes on: 'I think it's going to be a journey for me that's not going to stop. I'm going to keep learning more and more' (P8). However, his learning about colonial history had helped him to resolve the pressure to deny his non-Aboriginal heritage:

> From my experience, it's acceptable to recognise your other heritage, that you are mixed heritage, but it's not acceptable to say I'm half-blood, half-caste. Yes, I am Aboriginal and English. (P8)

For another participant, learning about her Aboriginal culture reinforced an oppositional relationship which positioned the now positive Aboriginal culture in contrast to the negative non-Indigenous society:

> I have learnt the knowledge right down to the berries, plants, little things like that and how bonded everyone is, whereas in the non-Indigenous people are really out for themselves, you know what I mean? (P9)

Possessing the 'right kind' of knowledge provides a sense of security and confidence when asserting an Aboriginal identity. But as one participant pointed out, learning the meaning of being Aboriginal 'is not a recipe' (P6). Most of these participants referred to the significance of knowing the cultural, historical and contemporary 'facts' of being Aboriginal and emphasised, as well, the importance of getting to know Aboriginal people, of speaking to Aboriginal family or community Elders, and of making

Aboriginal friends. This was not only a way to access and learn culture, language, ways of behaving, or other knowledge. It also enabled a sense of acceptance and belonging via participation in Aboriginal events, organisations, workplaces, identified positions and other programs. One participant's comments tied all these aspects together:

> It can take a long time for people to be accepted…When I was going to TAFE to study my welfare that was my target, to do work in the Aboriginal areas. I went to Aboriginal services and did all my field practice with them to help me. And I have always participated in all Aboriginal culture events and everything like that, because I would never want to lose it, you know. And I wouldn't like to see anyone lose it because it is, it's very precious.
>
> If you don't work at it and be part of it you can get non-accepted and then it's hard to get it back. (P20)

Acquiring knowledge to reclaim something that had been lost in previous generations was an important part of the identity journey for all. Acquiring knowledge with which to position oneself as a member of the Aboriginal community and in the world of identified Aboriginal employment was an important part of the identity journey for many. Acquiring knowledge through which to differentiate oneself from non-Aboriginal society was also important for some, but by no means all, participants. But just having 'knowledge' per se did not ensure acceptance or public recognition of being Aboriginal.

PERFORMING ABORIGINALITY

Many participants who were not visibly or recognisably Aboriginal talked about how and why they overtly signalled to others that they were Aboriginal. It is in relation to these ways of expressing or performing their Aboriginal identities that the erratic and meandering framing of Aboriginal identities emerges at the surface of everyday life to be embodied by individuals in a demonstration of allegiance to the Aboriginal collective.

Participants expressed their identities in private and public spaces. Even those participants who did not place much emphasis on overt signalling of Aboriginality talked about why it was important for some. For example, one participant reflected:

> I think a lot of people are, have an identity crisis at one stage and will look in the mirror and say I don't look Aboriginal but I am Aboriginal, what can I do to be more Aboriginal. Do I have to walk around with my Koori flag T-shirt on? (P3)

Another participant who had long been involved in Link-Up reported how signalling Aboriginality was important for newly identifying people who

> feel like frauds when they first identify. They feel like they don't have the right to identify so in order to validate their own identity they adopt all the trappings of, whatever those trappings maybe. So stick a Land Rights sticker on the back of your car, whatever. (P14)

Wearing Aboriginal regalia and collecting Aboriginal paraphernalia was a common way of both publicly and privately expressing Aboriginality. One participant had tattooed the story of his family history on himself:

> I wanted our journey told in this tattoo and I wanted people to see the story but there aren't many Aboriginal tattoos. More people are getting them in this style like the Koori flag and animal designs in Aboriginal style with dots and x-ray images but mine is unique because it is our story. (P18)

The following are less extreme but typical examples from participant interviews:

> I usually wear or I make up my necklaces with my colours red, black and yellow…I've started to do a few Indigenous paintings, I've done a didgeridoo… (P8)

> I think they must think I am [Aboriginal] that is why I wear it. I mean non-Aboriginals wouldn't wear it…maybe some do but I like it because it lets people know 'yeah, I am an Aboriginal and I am proud of it and I'm involved in what it is in the picture designs'. (P26)

> Yeah I have lots of clothing and beads….I like making things in our colours and it feels good to wear this stuff so people know, 'hey I am Aboriginal and I don't care what you think'. (P17)

> If I've got something with the flag on it or if I even have a hat with Aboriginal art on it, you know, I will proudly wear them. (P2)
>
> I think when I was younger you would always have your little wrist band and things like that. (P11)

For Participant 11, as it was for other participants who also emphasised the wearing of Aboriginal jewellery, this was more a matter of pride rather than any need to signal Aboriginality. For example, Participant 19 stated how he

> like[s] wearing those [Aboriginal] shirts and I am proud to wear those logos with the Koori flag so people can see I am not ashamed of who I am. (P19)

However, he also stated that he didn't 'have to tell anybody who I am and that' (P19).

So, the line between the two positions of pride and the need to signal was not always clear and provides further evidence of the tensions in the everyday world. One participant, for example, mentioned he was proud to wear necklaces to signal he was Aboriginal but that in summer he goes 'really, really, really dark so it doesn't matter' (P9). However, although he stated that 'you are expected to be Aboriginal all the time and it can be hard' (P9) he also stated 'that you don't need to wear your beads — that doesn't say you are Aboriginal. It's in here [pointing to heart]' (P9).

One participant reflected thoughtfully on her Aboriginal clothing and paraphernalia — and at some length, in the light of her shock at recently being questioned about her Aboriginality.

> I did have a moment actually when I think about maybe I should start wearing some more stuff to identify, but yeah, I try not to. I haven't done that specifically, like I do when I'm going to an event like a rally or something but it's more, I think, about wearing it in terms of supporting a cause, not 'cause it makes me visibly Aboriginal. I'm trying to think of other ways I would express my Aboriginality by wearing things. I suppose I do things like buy music like Aboriginal music…and I do things at home like I've got paintings on the walls and I collect different keepsakes and artefacts…and display them. (P4)

Another participant expressed her Aboriginality in a range of ways, including through learning, work in the Aboriginal sector and participation in the community. However, even though very fair-skinned, she resisted the pressure to signal her Aboriginality through dress or paraphernalia. She noted how this might be publicly perceived by other Aboriginal people.

> I don't really conform like that. I like high end clothes and jewellery so I would probably get called 'uptown', and I like having coffee in a nice coffee shop and doing things like that. In my office I have some items from South Australia which are from community and I like them in the office but in my home, not so much. I am a minimalist so don't have much at all. (P21)

Other participants in this study talked about the tensions between disadvantage of the Aboriginal experience and the 'non-Aboriginal' 'class' differences visible in different lifestyle choices in the contemporary Aboriginal space. This tension is discussed in more detail in the next section along with an analysis of tensions between private and public expressions of Aboriginal identity.

For some participants, the way they talked and the language they used was an important signal of Aboriginality, a way of identifying other Aboriginal people, and a way of fitting in and finding a sense of belonging in what is often acknowledged as a journey. For example, one educated participant mentioned that

> I've changed the way I talk and everything…I don't know… have to be on the same level as people in the community so I don't look upper-class or I don't look like or I don't identify. (P10)

Another admitted that,

> yeah, you know I use the lingo and my language and show I am Aboriginal and I know my culture. (P18)

Another commented that,

> I think that [language] is a way to identify who is Aboriginal especially if it is not immediately visible. So you will be able to know if someone is Aboriginal if you listen to what they say, or the words they use… (P22)

Another talked about the language of 'having close relatives, kids calling them Aunty and Uncle, cousins and stuff like that, yeah' (P3).

Some participants considered overt signals such as dress and language as more important for those who were not recognisably Aboriginal. One participant discussed this at some length:

> Again, a lot of people who have lighter skin, that's another way they identify themselves with the bangles and Koori colours…
>
> Yep, provisionally and for, um, the way they speak and all that. That's another way they identify, they can only indentify. It is hard if you don't look Koori…
>
> People can tell I'm Koori, basically. I've been accepted straightaway in the community where a lot of other people have to fight to show they are Aboriginal and be accepted within the community. (P10)

For other participants the way to express and signal identity was through identified employment positions and community participation. As one participant put it:

> I don't do anything that says, 'hey look at me, I'm Aboriginal'. But I do associate with Koori people and my family and I do go to like the Survival Day concert… (P25)

Thus expressing an Aboriginal identity was for some participants more closely associated with being involved in community: 'not even doing community events but just being involved in community' (P8). For another it was about contributing in practical ways to the community and to the process of education to impart knowledge about Aboriginal people and mentoring students, both Aboriginal and non-Aboriginal. This participant considered this a much more substantial expression of Aboriginal identity: 'I've done the hard yards and a lot of fields that are probably regarded as the tough stuff' (P14).

Despite all these ways of performing Aboriginal identity, the importance of understanding the process of becoming Aboriginal as something negotiated over time through a lot of hard work was a constant reminder that there was no single way, 'no recipe' for learning to be Aboriginal and that learning to be Aboriginal was neither straightforward nor easy. Not looking or sounding Aboriginal might make it more difficult to be recognised as Aboriginal. However, signalling Aboriginality through superficial adornment or by 'acting Aboriginal' was not sufficient even though some felt it was necessary or a sign of pride. As one participant commented about another person:

> She just started coming here and hanging out. At first she didn't speak to anyone or join in. Now she is involved in everything and walking around in her Koori T-shirts and now she is Aboriginal…
>
> Well it isn't just that easy. It is hard work building relationships and networks and she just thinks she can join us. I didn't just get to be Aboriginal…
>
> I had to do the work, build up the relationships and stuff…
>
> Being Aboriginal is about building the relationships and networks. You just can't identify without them. (P5)

The way that participants talk about the 'signs' of being Aboriginal provides evidence of the discursive conditions and 'materiality' of the space, which individuals enter and in which they make and mark themselves as Aboriginal. This is the space, which is 'already ready', as D'Cruz (2001) puts it, but full of possibilities for testing its limits and reconstituting its boundaries.

CHAPTER 17
TENSIONS AT THE CULTURAL INTERFACE

> The Interface is…the space of ongoing historical continuities and discontinuities as people discard and take up different ways of understanding, being and acting in a complex and changing environment.
>
> (Nakata 2007, p. 208)

As much as many of the participants in my research accepted and worked at becoming or being Aboriginal within the debated meanings of Aboriginality, so did many of them question these discourses as limiting the meaning of being Aboriginal. There was evidence in the transcripts of the interviews of the push–pull of the discourses of Aboriginality. A push against them as they operated to exclude some subjectivities, and the pull of them for the newly identifying trying to enter into the world of Aboriginal meaning or those wanting to belong and work as a member of the collective community. At times it may seem as though some participants are basing their own and/ or Aboriginal identity more broadly on negative racial stereotypes of Aboriginal people. It is important not to just simply dismiss such expressions and understandings of Aboriginal identity but to adopt Nakata's approach. Nakata (2007, p. 195) suggests we seek to examine 'how particular knowledges achieve legitimacy and authority at the expense of other knowledge'. It is more important then, to question how negative racial stereotypes achieve legitimacy and authority in determining what it means to be Aboriginal.

AGENCY AND TENSIONS AT THE CULTURAL INTERFACE

In the many accounts of different participants' identity journeys, there was evidence of the tensions described in Nakata's notion of the Cultural

Interface as a complex space of converging discourses and contradictory, ambiguous and confused sets of meaning. In the way that many participants discussed their personal negotiations of the available meanings of Aboriginality, they revealed much about these tensions, which emerged between their own experiences and views and their knowledge of the accepted debates around Aboriginality, as revealed in earlier chapters. These conversations often mediated judgments about a person's Aboriginal identity in public spaces. Some major areas of tension emerged around the push–pull between being Aboriginal and being part of a wider Australian society. This was particularly the case for some who had 'grown up white', or those who identified as Aboriginal but who also recognised their other genetic and cultural heritages. But these tensions also included the tensions between being educated and Aboriginal, between Aboriginality as an expression of disadvantage and the interpretations of advantage or 'class' associated with different Aboriginal lifestyles, and around knowledge, language and Aboriginality.

Tensions that are evidence of living at the Interface where a range of discourses converge are messy and difficult to articulate and make sense of. Disadvantage as a signifier of Aboriginality, for example, becomes a matter of conflict, confusion or contest for an Aboriginal individual who is not disadvantaged. Language as a signifier becomes a matter for contest if an individual doesn't speak 'like an Aboriginal'. Education is implicated in both, and in the identification of 'class' as evidence of not 'really' being Aboriginal or not being 'proper' Aboriginal (P3).

The politics of the Aboriginal position implicates education as a tool of assimilation but this also constrains and limits the choices of Aboriginal people who consider themselves to be educated, middle-class, English-speaking but knowledgeable about the Aboriginal world, who are also members of Aboriginal families, workers in Aboriginal communities, and therefore still Aboriginal. Thus political discussions about Aboriginality and 'who counts' uphold the possibility for 'remaining' distinctly Aboriginal and differentiated in some way from other Australians. But they also inadvertently hold Aboriginal people to colonial positions of marginality and disadvantage. These tensions and contests are best brought to the surface through the statements of participants.

Some participants discussed the tensions of the Cultural Interface in terms of individual/collective identity and Indigenous/non-Indigenous society in relation to assimilation through education. Western education as a tool of assimilation forms an important argument in Indigenous analysis. For example, one participant emphasised a common community position:

> Education is important but you have to remember your culture and not start being like the white man, still be Aboriginal and remember how hard it is for the mob, not go get a fancy job and forget about the community. (P23)

An Aboriginal academic responded to these tensions by pulling away at the fabric of this discourse:

> Some would argue, yes, you become more assimilated if you come to universities and conform to white man's privileges, but I think that finding ourselves and our places within non-Indigenous societies, we draw on the strength of being a collectivist society, to redefine ourselves as Indigenous people....And I think the more we can empower ourselves about what the conflict is about being an Aboriginal person, because we're not hunters and gatherers, and don't want to be assimilated, then where does that leave us? And we need to find comfort in that, politically, socially, legally, within, you know, society. (P21)

Another participant also exposed the tensions between the notion of adaptation and assimilation that she grappled with as a higher education student:

> It gets to the point of are you assimilating and if you are assimilating does that mean you are losing your identity, losing your culture or are you adapting and keeping both. My sister said this to me heaps of times before, saying because I want a better lifestyle and I want better health, I am an upper class black. And I am like, what, just because you know I am black I have to go sit in a park and drink goon bags all day, like what do you think this is? And she is like, you know, you think you are too good for everyone else and I am like it doesn't make me less black, where did you get that idea from. (P3)

Evident in this account is the deployment of polarised positions that emerge from discourses of what it means to be Aboriginal as differentiated from white. These are discussed as either/or and antithetical.

In contrast, one participant discussed how she 'battled' (P4) with her two heritages at primary school as a result of learning Creation stories from both the Dreaming (on family camps) and from Christianity (for Catholic religious confirmation), and how she gained a better perspective later in life.

> But I supposed I really questioned both, I mean I always asked a lot of questions to try and figure it out, how, what it was that was being taught to me, what I was learning and how it would fit into what I learnt at home…and sometimes it's hard to grapple with two very, very different concepts and beliefs and yeah it was hard. I suppose we were lucky 'cause by moulding them together or by realising that it's two different aspects of our lives that we don't have to only be one or only be in the other… (P4)

This participant demonstrates the importance of questioning and thinking to navigate her way through the contradictions at the Cultural Interface and the possibility for embodying the multiple meanings in this lived position, without losing her sense of being Aboriginal. She also gave an example of negotiating the Interface in the course of her work with Aboriginal communities, which is evidence of the possibilities for being an educated professional and being Aboriginal. She talks about tailoring her language for specific audiences and using appropriately pitched language for community people:

> [T]hey are very knowledgeable…a meeting environment with them on one side of the table and you on another, trying to discuss or compromise, they have been doing that a lot longer than I have been writing stuff on a piece of paper, so I have to put that respect into place when I am going to speak to them. It is not really about dumbing it down but making sure what I am delivering to the audience is understandable…and equally back that I am able to understand what they are delivering… (P4)

Also discussed by this participant was the association of disadvantage with Aboriginality, which inferred being successful was not being Aboriginal:

> It doesn't just happen in my work life, it happens in my family life, in community life…I cop it a lot because I'm young and relatively successful and I don't necessarily make apologies for [it]…I've worked hard for it and I'm not going to let anybody take it from me…
>
> I know I'm working hard but it still does give you a twinge of self doubt…and a couple of other people have said it to me about my pay and I say, 'Well it's funny but interestingly enough I fought for so long so that these kind of positions in the community can be paid on par…with…the wider community' and it's interesting to find people within your own community with that question and I think, well, if you weren't paying me that much we'd be whingeing cause we would not being paid equivalent to other roles. (P4)

Nonetheless, this participant situated this 'jealousy' as something that emerged from history and perhaps from the welfare/handout experience that instilled an expectation of everyone being in it together and receiving the same.

Another participant navigated this tension somewhat differently by mediating her own behaviour according to community sensibilities. Because she identified with the community,

> I just want to be on the same level as them, so I don't show off. I try to be modest about what I do, about what I have succeeded in and everything and people started using me as an example in the community and I just don't feel comfortable with it because then I don't feel like I'm on the same level as a lot of other people. (P10)

The links between education and perceptions of class were also described by another participant as a barrier to acceptance within the community as Aboriginal:

> Yeah, there is even [a barrier] in my own family unit. My mum…really pushed for us children to have educations… But even in my own family being educated was seen as obviously a bit more upper-class, which I don't think we are. It's just that we had different opportunities. (P7)

Her mother had grown up on a river bank and mission and told anyone who gave her children 'flack' for being educated: 'Well you had a choice too' (P7). Thus, the choice of 'equal opportunity' which was fought for by Aboriginal people as part of the struggle for justice, can also be used against those who seemingly take 'advantage' of it.

One participant described some of the contradictions within the Indigenous community with respect to eschewing the success of some Aboriginal individuals. In this analysis, the competition within the Aboriginal community was situated within or as an extension of, perhaps, the tensions with the nation-state.

> With a lot of Aboriginal people there is always a lot of fighting for something, always fighting against non-Indigenous people to prove we can be successful and all this stuff and then within Indigenous communities we are always fighting to show who is the better family, who is more successful, who's a better community and all that stuff. Who's got more culture within their community, who's missing out and all that stuff. (P10)

Another participant polarised these tensions with the nation-state in terms of unproblematised conflicting values, through the acceptance of a universalised and essentialised Aboriginal characteristic:

> And even though we are in modern times now, I think there is still a conflict in…the way Aboriginals interact with white society. Aboriginal people share everything in their family, they share their income, they share what they have, and that doesn't really fit with the selfish white mentality of society. (P17)

A newly identifying participant who had grown up white, demonstrated his positioning within this discourse:

> I used to think about money and having nice things and be worried about what people think and keep everything for myself and my children. But now I know that is the white way, the way whites think, so I try hard to be in touch with my culture and share what I have, because that is the cultural way… (P24)

On the other hand, one participant questioned the narrative of disadvantage, which he thought was over-embraced as a universal condition of being Aboriginal:

> I studied about health...and the focus is usually how we are all disadvantaged. I think Aboriginal people have taken on this thought now that we are rather a large disadvantaged group of people. To a certain extent, yes I agree with that, and in some areas definitely worse than others. But I think they are really hanging on to it in a lot of situations, And don't want to move from it. So, this thought that we are very disadvantaged, we should have this, we should have that, I think it's time to move on from that. (P15)

Some participants spoke of tensions in cultural terms and in terms of the ongoing Aboriginal relationship to the nation-state. Speaking about the challenges for urban Aboriginal identities, one participant talked about how to embrace Aboriginality in the current world:

> Like how can I still be Indigenous, how can I still be cultural yet get by in this world that I'm forced to live in. Like I can't still go out hunting this all the time, I can't do this, I can't do that. Whitefella say I can't eat this food, I need a permit for that. (P8)

However, urban Aboriginality invoked internal cultural tensions when individuals grew up, lived, and worked away from their traditional country of origin: 'I spent my whole life growing up on Dharawal land so I actually see myself more as a Dharawal man' (P8). For this participant, one pathway through this conundrum was to embrace a broader Aboriginal identity: 'I think it's more important to be Indigenous than it is to be from that one area' (P8). However, another participant discussed these tensions in almost the opposite terms, even though he was attempting to uphold the individual and personal identity in the face of the political collective identity:

> I think there has been a trend to try and homogenise Aboriginal people and you can even look at the term 'Indigenous Australian' to look at homogenising and in a way the political correctness can take away people's self-identity. Like instead of saying 'what mob, you from?' they're saying 'oh well, I'm Indigenous Australian'...which I don't think adequately reflects the identity

of all people. It's a collective thing and it can be utilised in certain political struggles as a good unifying thing. However, to the mainstream Australian it can be misleading I think. (P11)

Some participants described tensions at the Interface in terms of the pressure of constantly negotiating and demonstrating the meanings of Aboriginality. As one recent identifier explained:

> I need to be with other Indigenous people to be part of the culture. It can be hard, 'cause I don't know and I get upset 'cause I don't know and trying to do the right thing. But when I am at home, I just relax and don't worry about being Aboriginal, you know?
>
> I just go home and forget all about it, ya know, just be like everyone else I guess. I know I am Aboriginal and I don't have to prove it to anyone else at home. I can just do my own thing. (P9)

Another also emphasised the private space as providing a refuge from having to be Aboriginal all the time:

> I guess at home, I am like anybody else and I suppose it is a bit of a relief to not have to be so constantly aware of being Aboriginal and being involved. I know I am but I don't always have to be demonstrating it if you know what I mean… In public, I work in an identified job, I support community initiatives, I mentor Indigenous students, so I guess I am more involved with being Aboriginal in the public space. I don't have many Aboriginal people come to my place, especially more grassroots people because they might judge the way I live and think I am more white in the way I live…
>
> I mean some grassroots type people don't hold a great deal of value in material possessions like a nice house in a nice street and think if you do live like that you are following white ways. I don't believe that and think it is OK to have nice things and be Aboriginal but you know what I mean, people get a bit funny about that. (P22)

Another, who had always known she was Aboriginal, explained how she felt unable to be herself, given the narrow choices and rules associated with the 'performance' of Aboriginality:

> We are still in limbo, don't know which world to fit in, which is, I face that too I guess. I don't know when I should start saying 'cuz' or bruz', yeah, I don't know when I should start acting Aboriginal…When I go back home I just feel comfortable. It's when I am not around Aboriginal people…I still feel comfortable being Aboriginal around my friends and all that. I still openly identify and they still accept me and all that. Yeah, but I still don't feel like I can be who I am. I still don't feel I can say what I want and call them whatever I want. There's just not that connection there. (P10)

Similarly, one participant who acknowledged her white heritage, related the pressures to conform that came from other Aboriginal people:

> Yeah, they are like, people do this or that or don't listen to that music or go there, and like when I travel you know, Aboriginal people don't do that. So people are looking at me thinking is she really Aboriginal, what is she saying to us, why is she saying that to us? (P25)

Another participant, however, although mindful of the particularities of different experiences of being Aboriginal, brought to the surface some of the tensions around 'living the life' and about 'selective' identification that emerge in the discourses of Aboriginality:

> What I mean about living the life is I honestly don't believe in selective identification, like you're either Aboriginal or you're not…It's about identification but I don't think you should selectively identify in certain situations because that's taking away from your own self identity and obviously there might be identity issues there if you're choosing to do that. (P11)

INTER-GENERATIONAL IDENTITY PROCESSES: ABORIGINAL CHILDREN'S IDENTITY

An unexpected area of discussion emerged around the importance of Aboriginal children learning and being socialised into ways of being Aboriginal. This was considered important for re-establishing a sense of continuity with Aboriginal family lines and culture, for cultural pride, and in the preparation of children to be able to navigate identity issues through teenage and adult years.

For some, the importance of children understanding and being proud of their heritage and learning to be Aboriginal was very strong. For others, it was important that children grew up knowing about their history and heritage, but as adults they are able to express their Aboriginal identity in ways of their own choosing. For most of the participants who discussed such issues, passing on knowledge — cultural and/or historical — was at the heart of raising children to be proud of their heritage and confident to call themselves Aboriginal.

One participant expressed the importance of cultural transmission for instilling pride:

> Passing on stories, histories, and stories our Elders have...Try to make them proud of who they are. I know the more stories and the more...culture I'm immersed in I feel even prouder being Indigenous and I try to pass that on to my kids all the time. And I can see it now, like my four-year-old, he gets now, out of the blue, picks a didj, starts playing it, starts clapping his boomerang on it and he's proud of who he is. My eleven-year-old is the same, so proud of who he is. He gets up in front of his school and plays his didj and he tells all his friends he's Indigenous. He's not worried at all and I think that it would be great if more of kids had that...I just think it's important to keep our culture alive. (P8)

Another talked about the need to instil knowledge and pride, when children were growing up in predominately white communities. One participant described the tensions not just between Aboriginal–white relations, but between cultural meanings derived from older traditions and practices and popular urban cultural meanings:

> Because he's grown up in [white community]...and of course all his friends are non-Aboriginal, so his social interactions, I think he's quite a coconut. But, in the same time...we taught [son] a lot about culture [when younger]...we were teaching about building a camp...fire, making spears...and things like that, where to find bush tucker, getting pippies, fishing, all that sort of stuff. So we taught him to be really proud of being

> an Aboriginal person, being proud of being able to survive on the land, and know about the land. So I hope, and I think it seems to be so far because he doesn't have a lot of trouble... And it's important because he's dark-skinned, so to be proud of what culture is. And maybe not necessarily learn about the distortion of culture now, but to go back to the essence of the culture, which is the thing to be proud of. (P17)

Another newly identifying family spoke about how crucial the school was for their children to learn their culture. This involved having to assert their new Aboriginal status to a hesitant school so the children could be considered eligible to attend cultural activities.

> They are really proud to be Aboriginal and have been learning all about the culture at school because they have a Aboriginal worker there and they do Aboriginal cultural activities...learn about the culture and play the didjeridoo and do dot paintings and they can join in and learn the dancing if they want but they haven't done that but they can. (P26)

Another family joined a local organisation for children — Koori Youth Network — to give 'the boys an opportunity to get in touch with, and to interact with other Aboriginal children within their region' (P18). This family had moved from a different region and wanted their children to belong in the new community. When his boys were young, teaching them culture, language and songs was important so they knew they were Aboriginal from the 'word go', as was seeking out Koori schools and day care centres.

It was also the case in other families that children who grew up or discovered they are Aboriginal along with their parents did not always choose to 'live it' in the sense of full community participation. One participant who had two adult children and a much younger child born at the time she first discovered she was Aboriginal talked about her efforts with her younger child which included such things as wearing beads, playing the didgeridoo, performing in a dance team, and doing art work, such as decorating photo frames with dot paintings (P10). However, her adult children, who had not grown up knowing they were Aboriginal, acknowledged their Aboriginality without living it.

There was also evidence of differences in the choices of adult children within a family. For example, one participant related how his son acknowledges his Aboriginality but doesn't pursue it and how his daughter accepts her Aboriginality and does pursue it:

> That's their choice, I never had a choice. I gave them their choice and that. Whatever they do with it, it's up to them. I'll guide them both, because I can only guide them, I can't walk their footsteps for them. Yeah, that's important, where I had to walk someone else's footsteps throughout life. (P19)

Parents appeared to support adult children's choices. Another participant, for example, explained adult choices in terms of the transition from childhood to adult autonomy:

> [Y]ou often socialise kids to be Aboriginal in family groups, and I think that half of it's done unconsciously, about life and living and surviving…and I think we need to, Aboriginal people obviously remind their children of our history, our history of colonisation and so kids often grow up quickly knowing about that social position…My kids are very politically aware, more so, very critical…You know if…my high school student is doing an assignment often I'll sort of try and use that as an opportunity to look at an Indigenous musician, but she sort of gets the shits with that, 'Just because I'm Aboriginal doesn't mean I have to do this' and she is right…as she gets it as an adult, because she's starting to ask those questions and trying to form an identity. But with my primary age child, it's just a matter of him learning about his heritage, and identity, through family mainly, and we choose to go. (P21)

Some participants who discovered at a later age they were Aboriginal and who had raised their children in white society took a broader social view. One, for example, continued to emphasise values he associated with white society: completion of school; higher education; responsibility and employment (P16). Another similarly emphasised 'good ethics, good morals, to care about people, to care about family' (P15) but disagreed with some aspects of what was understood to be the 'Koori way'. For these participants, cultural and historical aspects were not mentioned but the reconnection to family led to an emphasis on instilling the importance of caring for family.

CHAPTER 18

ABORIGINAL IDENTITY, COMMUNITY AND SOCIAL MEDIA

> [Social media helps me] to connect up with others across the country, I do get to feel more connected with my own sense of identity. It doesn't operate by itself as an affirmation of identity, but it's certainly an interesting space for talking about identity. (SQ16)

The research I undertook regarding the politics of identity did not specifically aim to focus on the topic of Aboriginal identity online. However, several participants spoke about how they expressed their Aboriginality on the social media site Facebook. The potential of social media to foster, enable and enhance Indigenous connectedness and affirm identity was an exciting development. The use of social media by Indigenous Australians has increased dramatically in recent years, with the popularity of social networking sites such as Facebook and Twitter becoming central features of social interaction (Carlson 2013).

After I completed my studies and graduated with a Doctor of Philosophy, I was fortunate enough to receive a grant to conduct a national research project exploring Aboriginal people's engagements on social media. The aim of the project was to provide a better understanding of how Aboriginal people make use of online social network sites. One of the methods used in this new project was an online, social media driven survey that asked a range of questions in relation to Aboriginal identity and community online. The project has its own Facebook page and to date has over 380 likes (see https://www.facebook.com/AboriginalIdentityOnline?ref=hl). This final chapter, therefore, draws on both the findings from my earlier research, as well as from the more recent online survey. Participants from the former study are identified with a 'P' and those from the online survey with 'SQ'.

FACEBOOK

Facebook is a popular, online social network site. Providing free access, it allows users to create their own profile, and to link to and view other profiles. Facebook has experienced exponential growth in recent years. At the time of writing, the number of monthly active Facebook users worldwide was 1.44 billion. The site has attained worldwide popularity and is a 'household name' in everyday popular culture. In Australia, over 9 million people use the site daily. Facebook is relatively easy to navigate. Once a user creates a profile, the site can be used to join groups or add friends, which are then displayed on their sites for others to view. Facebook is a communication tool, but it also functions to create and (re)present to others a public identity, and to attract similar profiles as part of a broader network or community. The core functionality of Facebook is that users have the ability to connect with others ('friends'), and form or belong to groups which are similar or have similar interests. Professor of Behavioural Change at the University of the West of England, Adam Joinson, noted that online social networks may provide users with 'social capital' (2008, p. 1028).

Social networking sites provide possibilities for new communities to be formed by people who may not have met in the material world (Lumby 2010). Membership with online communities is about a commonality of interests and a sense of 'shared consciousness'. This can be thought of in the way that theorist Benedict Anderson refers to something that exists in the daily imaginings of national subjects as an 'imagined community' (1983, p. 6). However, unlike imagined communities, Facebook is not a disembodied space or an imagined social sphere that has no real substance as a community. It is real in that it is composed of communities generated by real bodies that compose, interact, wrangle and communicate with one another. It is also real in terms of the actual connections it provides for interaction, correspondence, making links and participating in other forms of technology (e.g. texts, phone conversations) (Lumby 2010). Social network sites, while varying in nuanced ways, typically share three common fundamentals. They allow individuals to '(1) construct a public or semi-public profile within a bounded system, (2) articulate a list of other users with whom they share a connection and (3) view and traverse their list of connections and those made by others within the system' (Boyd & Ellison 2007, p. 211).

ABORIGINAL PEOPLE AND SOCIAL MEDIA

The rapid advances in mobile technologies, and the uptake of these by Indigenous youth in particular, can be seen in many communities (see Kral 2011). While this is not to suggest there is no digital divide, it does counter any assumptions that Aboriginal people may have little interest in the possibilities of technology and the online environment. In terms of technology, I found that the majority of Aboriginal survey respondents stated they mostly accessed social media on smart phones. The evidence that Aboriginal people are active and enthusiastic social media users is readily accessible. For example, any Facebook user is able to access and engage with a variety of public Aboriginal specific sites, and deposit for public viewing trails of announcements on who they are or what they want to express or make comment on (e.g. *The Australian Aboriginal and Torres Strait Islander Community, Aboriginal and proud of it, I'm proud to be Aborigine, SOSBlakAustralia, Blackfella Revolution* and many others). It is also apparent that such use is not limited to Aboriginal people living in urban settings. Across Australia, Aboriginal use of social media is approximately 20 per cent higher than the national average and in remote communities over 60 per cent of the population are active Facebook users (Callinan 2014).

Research Fellow at the Centre for Aboriginal Economic Policy Research, at the Australian National University, Inge Kral (2011, p.5) conducted research into how Aboriginal youth in remote Australia utilise digital technologies and new media. She reported popular use of Facebook as a platform to 'upload their multimedia productions, comment on each other's mobile phone "pics" and announce the immediacy of their activities with online chat'. Interestingly, Kral (2011, p. 5) reports 'they are also using these channels to air their thoughts and the cultural activities and concerns of their community'. Similarly, the publication, *Our Place: People working with technology in remote communities* (Nadarajah 2011, pp. 6–9) includes a story about the remote community Ti Tree in Central Australia. The story features April Campbell, an Anmatyerre woman who uses Facebook actively to keep in contact with friends and relatives, but also to post news and information about her projects. Aboriginal people from all over Australia are connecting with April via Facebook, and various language speakers interact and network with her online (2011, p. 7). This is but one example of social media providing a forum where Aboriginal people can maintain contact even when hindered by vast distances and time, increasing their sense of social connectivity (Carlson 2014).

EVERYDAY ACTIVITY

It has become apparent that the use of social media is an everyday, typical activity for many Aboriginal people (Carlson 2013). Even five years ago this was the case. In one episode of *Living Black* (a television show featuring stories of interest to Indigenous people), entitled 'Cyber Wars' (19 April 2010) which dealt with racism on Facebook, several Aboriginal people commented on their use of social media and in particular Facebook. Allan Clarke, one of the Aboriginal Facebook users featured, stated that, 'It's an intrinsic part of our daily routine…' (Clarke quoted in Carlson 2013, p. 147). My research verified this trend: when asked how often they use social networking sites, most survey respondents selected 'very often' for Facebook and said that the average time they spent on social media was 1–5 hours per day.

Aboriginal people are using social media in much the same way they would interact with their offline networks — only with more frequency. An article titled 'Not so Black and White' in the *Weekend Australian Magazine* detailed Aboriginal man Dallas Scott's experience of applying for a Confirmation of Aboriginality certificate and subsequently being denied (Overington 2012, p. 15). Scott then logged into Facebook and updated his status, posting 'Dallas Scott…is apparently not Aboriginal after all' (Overington 2012, p. 15). Scott turned to the online community to air his discontent and this led to further discussion with his online 'friends' about his status as Aboriginal.

Social media not only helps people stay in touch with existing contacts then, but also facilitates new alliances. While connections are usually with people who share common interests, social media opens up the possibilities of discovering and learning new information, sharing ideas and interacting with others.

IDENTIFYING AS ABORIGINAL ON SOCIAL MEDIA

Several participants in my doctoral research stated they identify as Aboriginal on social media. In the more recent online survey the majority of respondents stated they openly identify as Aboriginal or Torres Strait

Islander on social media. One of the older participants in the earlier study explains how he identifies himself as Aboriginal online:

> I make sure people know I believe in Biami the god of all Indigenous people and I am part of the [local university] Indigenous Centre page and lots of the students are friends with me. I use it to keep in touch and make new friends too. (P13)

Others explained how they visually expressed their Aboriginality through the photos they post, the 'gifts' they exchange, and the friends, events and other sites through which they network more widely. For example,

> I have lots of Aboriginal family and friends and we... post pics. I have other Koori stuff too. Like you send each other, like, gifts but not real gifts, like pics really but [they] are meant to be gifts. You can join other groups, Koori groups and be involved in the discussion and post stuff about what you are doing or who you are connected to. It is cool because you can hook up to mobs all over the country. (P10)

Similarly in the online survey respondents explained the ways in which they identify online as Aboriginal,

> In my description on Twitter and Instagram I specifically state that I am an Aboriginal woman. On Facebook the majority of my reposts are articles on Aboriginal issues. I am also in Aboriginal specific groups on Facebook. (SQ12)

> My Aboriginality is the focal point of my identity both in society and online. Specifically on Facebook, my photos and page/groups and friends all highlight my Aboriginality. (SQ12)

Asked if she thought identifying oneself as Aboriginal on Facebook was important, one participant in my doctoral study replied, 'I think so, just like it is offline always identifying is important and it is important for others to see you are' (P22). She went on to state that even if her profile picture didn't immediately identify her as Aboriginal, then her page made it possible to 'see I have a connection or that I am identifying as Aboriginal on there' (P22).

The online survey asked respondents whether social media helped them express their Aboriginal identity and the majority stated that it did. Many commented that social media helped connect them with other Aboriginal people:

> Helps me connect to a broader community, supports me in my identity and Indigenous issues, shares great & specific information. (SQ16)

> In helping to connect up with others across the country, I do get to feel more connected with my own sense of identity. It doesn't operate by itself as an affirmation of identity, but it's certainly an interesting space for talking about identity. (SQ16)

The survey also asked respondents if they had ever been challenged about their online claim to be Aboriginal. A significant number stated that they had. Several said non-Aboriginal people challenged them, typically because they didn't 'look' Aboriginal. For example, responses included, 'Non-Indigenous people based on the fact that I "don't look Aboriginal" to them' (SQ18) and 'identifying as Aboriginal I was questioned as to how I identify as Aboriginal given my white skin' (SQ18). Others went on to state that they had experienced challenges from other Aboriginal people:

> It was indirect and I was not easily identifiable. It was a person who has a 'personal problem with me' — the way I understand it this particular individual has a personal problem with themselves so while I was concerned for them because they felt the need to do it I was not adversely affected by it. I also think that because I have always known who I am and my family story going back many generations I am fortunate enough to have had access to that knowledge and that has given me a solid sense of who I am in my family, my extended families, my community and how I relate to Aboriginal and Torres Strait Islander people generally. (SQ18)

And,

> I have been mocked for identifying as Aboriginal on a number of occasions, ironically from other Aboriginal people. Generally a stereotypical 'what would you know', or your

nation has lost its culture type argument. Also subtle inferences with regard to me only being Aboriginal for what I can get out of it. Used to make me angry, but I figure if you're going to talk like that in the first place, you're already more Gubba than I could ever be. (SQ18)

Very aggressive Aboriginal man who described me as 'a white person pretending to be black' and other forms of lateral violence. (SQ18)

ONLINE ABORIGINAL COMMUNITY

Respondents to the online survey overwhelming stated that there was an identifiable online Aboriginal community. Many suggested that they participate in online activities just as they would offline with friends and family and extended kinship networks:

> Sharing photographs of family & talking about family tree & genealogy, speaking in a shared language, sharing views and passion for the rights of Aboriginal and Torres Strait Islander peoples, talking about our shared history together, learning about how different indigenous groups had similar and different experiences of colonisation, learning about how different groups overcame hardship, generally sharing knowledge and growing a sense of place for who Aboriginal and Torres Strait Islander peoples are in all their diversity — the communication via social media provides a space for understanding and appreciating our diversity & commonalities. (SQ26)

> Connecting with mob and maintaining relationships with mob who are geographically close. (SQ26)

> Interaction on Twitter across long distances is the best! Gives you a sense of being part of a deadly community not just in Oz, but the World! (SQ26)

When respondents were asked whether they used social media to connect with Aboriginal friends and family across distances, 92 per cent agreed that they had. Respondents also stated that they had met relatives on social media who they may not have otherwise met. A majority of respondents also stated that they maintained online relationships with relatives who they may not maintain relationships with offline. Significantly, respondents stated they had become friends with other Aboriginal people via social networking sites and that they have attended specific Aboriginal events that they had learnt about through such sites.

However, similarly to offline, identifying oneself as Aboriginal online did expose individuals to challenges similar to those commonly experienced in the Aboriginal community. For example, one respondent claimed that, 'Although I have witnessed others cop challenges online, I have also questioned other people's identity, who have claimed tribal relations' (SQ18). In my earlier research, one participant described how one exchange prompted her to find out more about 'who she is' and 'where she comes from' in order to authenticate her claims to be Aboriginal:

> I was asked who I am and where I am from on another page where everyone was posting stuff and I don't know a lot about my culture…And now I have asked mum about stuff, you know, the basic stuff really. So things you might get asked like we are from the [group] mob and, you know, the things you get asked. (P25)

This participant went on to admit that she had sometimes fabricated some aspects of the cultural knowledge she used to identify who she is: 'I invent some aspects or just go a bit further than the real situation' (P25). When probed further she explained that in the online environment 'sometimes it's easy to get carried away with what others might expect' and when asked questions about who she is it is easier to answer online cause you can think about the answer so you don't get all flustered and say the wrong thing' (P25). This participant was quite aware of the possible challenges to her identity in the online environment. She had not initially attached photos of herself because 'you don't know what people might think 'cause I don't look Koori. So they might think I am a faker but there are heaps of others who have fair skin as well' (P25). Survey respondents had similar experiences, with one stating that their Aboriginality was questioned online because 'Apparently I'm not black enough for some. It's their problem not mine' (SQ18).

Another participant in my doctoral study, who had only recently began to identify as Aboriginal, also spoke of how her Facebook profile and activity helped her to gain acceptance and recognition in the offline Aboriginal community. This participant had 'friended' Aboriginal people in other parts of the country, even though she was not yet widely 'known' in her local community. She admitted that she 'tended to add more Indigenous friends than the non-Indigenous friends from high school, who have invited me to by friends' (P12) even if she had not known the Aboriginal 'friends' at high school. Locally, she did invite Aboriginal students to 'friend' her and some had. This led to a feeling of affirmation that felt

> pretty good 'cause that means they see me as Aboriginal too and it makes it easier to speak with them in person when you see them and then they can introduce you to other people. And it is easy if an Aboriginal person introduced you to another Aboriginal person 'cause it kind of confirms that you must be Aboriginal or it is kind of accepted you are. (P12)

IDENTITY SURVEILLANCE

Community conflict, surveillance and exclusion have now extended to the online environment. Here I relate a personal incident to reveal the ubiquitous nature of the politics of identity and the consequences for those who inadvertently test the limits.

At a recent conference where I presented research on social network sites, an Indigenous woman asked if I would join a Facebook site dedicated to Aboriginal and Torres Strait Islander scholars. The site is ostensibly for selected Indigenous people to discuss Indigenous topics of interest. Membership demanded confirmation of my Aboriginality by two existing members.

I was accepted and then asked to pose a question for the group. In line with my research interests, I posted, 'Can community recognition of someone's Aboriginality come from an online community'? One respondent stated, 'Community Recognition is just that!!!' which I took to imply that the respondent believed there is only one form of 'community'.

I responded that my question had emerged in the course of my research and was not a personal assertion but intended as an idea for consideration and discussion. Responses immediately shifted from my posed question to vitriolic demands for my authentication and in particular for documented evidence of my Aboriginality. I responded that I did have a Confirmation of Aboriginality. I was then asked for further corroboration: was I a member of an Aboriginal Lands Council? I replied affirmatively. Another respondent claimed I was 'NOT Aboriginal' and made mention of knowing my workplace and where they could find me. Finally, I was informed I would be removed from the group as my identity was under question. This notification was followed by a further response to my post: '[a]nd for the record community recognition in cyberspace please, nothing can replace the real thing'.

Given this experience, one of the questions I was particularly keen to ask in the online survey was whether Aboriginal people felt that social network sites could provide evidence of community recognition for the purposes of applying for a Confirmation of Aboriginality certificate. The majority of respondents knew what a Confirmation of Aboriginality certificate was and many stated they already had such a document. In terms of whether the online Aboriginal community could provide evidence of community recognition, respondents stated:

> The same criteria used to identify offline would still apply — the individual identifies, they belong to a community that 'understands' that they are a member and they are Aboriginal and/or Torres Strait. You could create a function for certain sites and/or groups that are able to confirm identity but I don't see how the criteria could or should change. (SQ34)

> It might be useful as a tool to prove your contributions and engagement/participation with community — and in turn the community's acceptance of you. (SQ17)

> Yes, but not simply by looking at friend lists. Lots of people are friends with many Indigenous people from a particular community, yet are not Indigenous. Their online relationship with other Indigenous people would need to be confirmed using their comments, statuses and other online activity. (SQ6)

> With slight reservation I think that action online is as valid as community interaction. It is utilised as a contact before and prior to real life interactions which can be put forward on a community forum for confirmation. (SQ67)

> They could but I think we would have the same problems. (SQ44)

So, if the online environment offers any enhanced possibilities, it also offers the same constraints applied in the offline Aboriginal community.

For one participant, there was an element of conflict in deciding who to accept as Aboriginal friends online and a suggestion that online choices were sites of wider surveillance, with consequences offline that led to some self-surveillance and regulation:

> On Facebook, [people] can see who [you are friends with] and you can be judged by that. [Name deleted] asked me to friend him and I had to think about that 'cause…well he isn't someone I want to know but he is pretty big in terms of being Aboriginal, so I have to think about that and what would happen if I don't accept him. (P5)

This same participant spoke of how she refused to 'friend' a person on Facebook precisely because she thought the person was 'trying to hang out with Aboriginal people so she can be accepted' (P5). This participant considered that the individual in question was using Facebook as a way to make friends with larger numbers of Aboriginal people in her attempts 'to become Aboriginal [when] she has no proof that she is and [when] she has only just in the last few months become Aboriginal' (P5). Another participant who had heard of questions being asked of the identities of people who joined all the Koori groups reported that in the course of arguments about it, 'sometimes they get unfriended' and that this was cause for 'shame' (P10). The potential use of Facebook as a 'networked' Aboriginal community surveillance tool is evident in these comments — and lends weight to concerns raised by participants in my doctoral research, as discussed earlier.

Thus, there are possibilities for accelerating the development of wider Aboriginal networks through the accumulation of Aboriginal 'friends' as an important part of a 'key identity signature' (Fraser & Dutta 2008, p. 14), and as an accelerated pathway to wider community recognition and acceptance. Yet, although online sites offer opportunities for creative expression, representation and affirmation of Aboriginality (see Dodson 1994; Manago et al. 2008), they are also sites where demands for authentication arise. The possibilities for asking questions and challenging Aboriginal people online, and the technological capacity for cross-posting to other sites and discussions, amplify and accelerate established community techniques of surveillance and technologies of self-surveillance. Online Aboriginal identities, as participants in my survey have described, engender a level of performativity in the sense that Judith Butler applies this term, as 'that reiterative power of discourse to produce the phenomena that it regulates and constrains' (Butler 1993, p. 2).

The data from my earlier study and from the online survey are interesting from a number of perspectives. Firstly, they are a tiny slice of much wider online activity by Aboriginal people. However, as such, they suggest there is much scope for further inquiry around the meanings, construction, negotiation, expressions and confirmation of Aboriginal identity in Australia. Secondly, it is interesting to consider what Aboriginal activity in the online environment means for the future notion of the 'Aboriginal community', particularly in terms of how this might affect present understandings of 'local' and 'pan-Aboriginal' communities. Thirdly, these limited descriptions of practices of Aboriginal identity in online environments suggest more analysis is needed to augment and complicate social media and identity theory (e.g. Robins 2000; Manago et al. 2008; Joinson 2008). While this data confirm broader understandings of identity practices online, they also raises important differences significant to relatively small communities where anonymity and transcendence of real identities are more difficult to achieve.

CONCLUDING REMARKS

This book began with a personal narrative of my own Aboriginal identity journey and my observations of the official confirmation process for others. My family history of disconnection and my parents' consistent references to our Aboriginal heritage when I was young led me, as an adult, to search out more about my family history. My journey is one shared with many Aboriginal people who in the course of colonial history have become disconnected from their Aboriginal roots, knowledge and/or kin.

The data generated in my interviews with participants in my study provided evidence of the historically and discursively constituted space of contemporary Aboriginal identity production. There was a strong consensus among participants around what it means to be Aboriginal today and a wide acceptance that the official definitional criteria of Aboriginality were legitimate identifiers of Aboriginality. There was also a discernible pattern to the process of 'making sense' of the Aboriginal historical experience and learning what it means for 'becoming' and being Aboriginal today. Like for so many, this journey involves establishing or learning family lineage and connections as evidence of Aboriginal heritage and identifying oneself with that heritage. It involves learning what it means to 'be' Aboriginal by learning about Aboriginal culture as much as the political, social and economic history of Aboriginal people and the legacy of this in the contemporary everyday world. It also involves learning how 'to do' Aboriginality by expressing this knowledge in overt or covert ways, through visible or coded signs and practices, such as dress, ways of talking, and/or through work, recreational activities or other ways of showing political and cultural solidarity with the Aboriginal community.

Through the ways these participants spoke of their journeys, it was clear that discovering and learning to be Aboriginal was not always straightforward or easy. Making those family and lineage connections was not always possible. Finding proof of them for confirmation purposes was often difficult, even if there was no real question about a person's heritage. As in the past, looking or sounding recognisably Aboriginal helped in the absence of proof and, in the case of all participants, having some community connections or involvement helped to establish and 'grow' a recognisable presence and a personal history of being Aboriginal. Moreover, the 'hard work' of 'growing' a recognisably Aboriginal identity appeared to be an approved and accepted practice in the Aboriginal community, according to these participants. There is a pathway back into the community for those who have been disconnected.

However, what was also revealed was that it is difficult just to 'be' Aboriginal. It is not sufficient to just 'know' that you are Aboriginal and 'identify' as Aboriginal on the basis of having proof of Aboriginal descent. An individual must 'do' Aboriginality to be recognised and accepted as Aboriginal in the community in which they live if they want official confirmation, and/or if they do not want to be the subject of accusatory questions and distressful challenges. Those not prepared to do the hard work of growing a publicly visible community presence run the risk of being refused recognition and acceptance in the community, even if they are without question of Aboriginal descent. But even official recognition and acceptance in the Aboriginal community is not always sufficient and some participants talked of the need to continue to 'do' identity work. Tacit criteria to secure continued acceptance and recognition implied the need to 'live and breathe' the Aboriginal community, as if there were no legitimate life space beyond it for a bona fide Aboriginal person.

Those participants who divulged the difficulties involved in being recognised, accepted and/or confirmed provide some evidence of a community politics of identity that regulates 'who is' and 'what specifically counts' as Aboriginal in this local community. This community politics is engendered via the authority of Aboriginal community-controlled organisations as official verifiers of Aboriginal status. But it is also engendered through all those Aboriginal people who participate in the surveillance of others' identity. Some participants in this study related how they had questioned another person's claims to be Aboriginal — even those who had been questioned themselves. Yet all participants strongly believed that they themselves were Aboriginal even when there was 'weak' evidence of it, or if it was impossible for them to get official confirmation. And those whose family histories were secure but rooted in other Aboriginal communities could still have a difficult time 'breaking in' and 'proving' themselves to the particular local community where they now lived and worked.

What was also revealed was that it was difficult for some participants to be Aboriginal while embracing other identities. Many participants voluntarily identified themselves as either dual or mixed heritage, or claimed Aboriginal heritage by going back to Aboriginal forebears in generations before their parents. Several participants acknowledged that they had ostensibly grown up in white society rather than Aboriginal society. But it was significant that very few questioned why they were called upon to deny another heritage to be recognised as Aboriginal. Here the politics of identity emerge again to call individuals into an either/or choice. This sort of identity politics often insists — as a condition of acceptance into the Aboriginal community — that individuals demonstrate Aboriginality by not talking or acting or living or even thinking 'white'.

The Aboriginal response to the historical 'grading' of Aboriginality on the basis of blood quantum in past eras is understandably one that refuses the designation of 'part' Aboriginal as a contemporary category. However, as in times past, this introduces personal identity ambiguities and conflicts for some Aboriginal people. It asks individuals to deny their full sense of themselves, to overwrite or erase subjectivities that are significant parts of their personal and family histories. For some, it asks them to deny their forebears' experiences of being Aboriginal, which led to decisions in the past that now position participants 'outside' the boundaries of Aboriginal identity discourses. In some cases it asks individuals to deny one side of the family that has brought them into the world, in the same way that Aboriginal people were once forced to do by administrators. In the process, the descendants of some Aboriginal people are being punished for having a history not of their own making. In the process significant parts of the stories of Aboriginal Australia are often denied, overwritten and silenced.

The desire of many of the 'newly-identifying' or the 'arriving from elsewhere' to belong in or be recognised by the local Aboriginal community appeared to elicit ready acceptance and compliance with the local and pan-Aboriginal community discourses and practices that state who is and what counts as Aboriginal today. What has been coined as 'racial loyalty' (see Paradies 2006) places political solidarity and survival of (reconstructed and often highly generalised) culture ahead of personal freedom for more creative and complex expressions of what it now means to be Aboriginal. This evidences the positioning effects of these discourses, and I was surprised how quickly many participants returned to an acceptance of the legal definitional criteria as the unproblematic measures of valid Aboriginal identities. In narrating their journeys, participants provided evidence that they knew — or, if not, they had to learn — the meanings of being Aboriginal and what they had to do to demonstrate, express or embody these meanings to be recognised, accepted and confirmed as Aboriginal. For many participants, the desire to 'belong', itself a part of a wider Aboriginal discourse of belonging, overrode any disquiet about either the expectation to comply or the narrowly prescriptive generalised cultural meanings and Aboriginal political 'correctness' demanded in this process.

However, some of the data did reveal more oppressive conditions of Aboriginality and its effects on the wellbeing of individuals. Some participants, including those who did not question the prescribed meanings or demands, spoke of nervousness, anxiety, intimidation, feeling inadequate, not being ready to deal with the emotion of confirmation, the hard work, giving up and always having to carry papers just in case they were questioned. Some participants spoke of the relief of going home where they didn't have to continually watch that what they did was 'Aboriginal'. Such responses are reminiscent of the conditions of a police state, always watching oneself, constantly under surveillance by others. Instead, it is twenty-first century life in an Aboriginal community in a major regional city in an open democracy.

Some participants also spoke of feeling guilty or worried about living in a 'nice' street, bringing other Aboriginal people home to see how well they lived, sending their children to private school, being considered 'uptown' blacks because they liked frequenting cafés and restaurants, or because they travelled. They spoke of being careful not to draw attention to personal success in order to stay on the same level as others to be accepted by the community. This is evidence of the tacit acceptance of socio-economic disadvantage as not simply a measure of Aboriginality but as a sign of cultural authenticity. For me, there was something quite sad and disturbing in the difficulties faced by participants who spoke of the narrow lifestyle prescriptions associated with being Aboriginal in this particular community, which led them to be worried by their relative material comfort compared to others and which often invoked forms of self-surveillance.

Without overstating it, there is a suggestion here that community discourses on Aboriginal identity position personal and material success as evidence of turning white and a contraindicator of Aboriginality. Those who are successful have to be careful to demonstrate in other ways that they are 'still' Aboriginal. This reinforces particular cultural and political modes of being Aboriginal and provides evidence of the complexity of Aboriginal identity politics. On one level, some Aboriginal community members may see these lifestyle prescriptions as a form of cultural continuity built around Aboriginal principles and values of sharing and reciprocity. However, this logic assumes that accumulation of assets or careful management of money indicates an abandonment of Aboriginal principles of reciprocity and sharing, when these may simply be managed in different ways and perhaps for more productive or strategic ends. The community logic also assumes that the non-accumulation of material assets is evidence that all available resources have been shared wisely or strategically rather than squandered, extorted or mismanaged. The subtext is also a denial of Aboriginal people to freely choose the manner in which they live and interact in the wider society, itself a principle of political self-determination. And yet, this is a widespread and popular discourse across Aboriginal Australia.

Thus Aboriginal community logic can be built on intolerance and ignorance of other ways of being in the world, ways that do not necessarily erase Aboriginal values but transform them in line with contemporary conditions of survival. To ignore the wider world is to not engage with the discursive and material constraints that frame our possible futures both as a collective and as individuals within that collective. So, in this Aboriginal community discourse we see the limits of community knowledge of our discursive position. And yet only one participant stated that she refused to apologise for being successful; others expressed guilt and self-surveillance, or associated their lifestyle with their non-pursuit of official confirmation — a process that involves community judgment.

Hence, there is evidence of how Aboriginal identity discourses call Aboriginal people back to the definitional criteria in ways that strongly regulate who we can be, how we can be, and who we can become on the grounds of narrow sets of understanding what it has meant, now means or can mean to be Aboriginal in 'the world'. So there was in participants' data the evidence of how contemporary Aboriginal identity is still tightly circumscribed by the available discourses of Aboriginality. There was also evidence that Aboriginal people ourselves are using similar colonial methods — definitions, control and surveillance of the meanings of Aboriginality, and official confirmation documents — to position

Aboriginal people differentially in relation to each other, and in relation to opportunities and resources available within or beyond the Aboriginal community. In the process, we close off other possibilities for the way we carry through the meanings attached to older traditions into ever-changing contemporary spaces. In the process, we cause emotional distress to our own people; we become pre-occupied with regulating ourselves rather than with contesting and transforming the boundaries placed around who we can be and what it can mean to be Aboriginal people moving forward into the twenty-first century. Nevertheless, only one participant acknowledged that we do it to ourselves.

Those participants in my study who resisted or questioned the current discursive boundaries and constraints also provide evidence of the limits placed on all Aboriginal people to construct their own identity meanings outside of the legacy of colonial history and practice. Transgressing the historically constituted discursive boundaries of the meanings of Aboriginality currently means an individual orchestrates an ambiguous and questionable status as Aboriginal, which may lead to their exclusion from the Aboriginal community. Without community acceptance or recognition, 'being' Aboriginal becomes restricted to the personal or family domain. Some participants were sufficiently affirmed by knowing they were Aboriginal and were defiant in rejecting the need for community recognition or judgment or the need for official confirmation. These participants were willing to test the limits of discourses of Aboriginality and to remain outside of its constraints. But what does this say about the limits of the available discourses that cannot recognise or accept people who know and identify themselves as Aboriginal? Do those who question individuals at the borders of Aboriginal identity, and who regulate and police the currently restricted and 'bounded' meanings of Aboriginality, orchestrate the rejection and exclusion of their own people? This is the unsayable that delineates the outer limits of the current discourses.

As a reflective researcher, I noted the constrained nature of most participants' statements about the community politics of Aboriginal identity. Some younger, newly identifying participants are arguably not well positioned to read the community politics. However, the silences among other participants generally indicated either a reluctance to stray outside the acceptable discourses of Aboriginality, or the absence of the circulation of a deeper analysis of Aboriginal identity regulation practices in the Aboriginal community. This may be an effect of the interview process where I avoided direct critical questions and provided only a loose framework to encourage participants to talk about what was significant for them. But it may also be the case that the circulating historical analyses of our relations with the nation-state are both limited and partial and wielded to serve particular and powerful sets of political interests — both Aboriginal and government. Undermining these analyses may be viewed as undermining the political solidarity, which is understood as fundamental to relations with the nation-state.

While some participants talked about or against the role of government, about or against the officially imposed need for confirmation, and/or about the practices of community or their organisations, this was not sufficient to bring forth any serious questioning about the relations between some of the fundamentals that construct an exclusionary rather than an inclusionary politics of Aboriginal identity. This is understandable; it requires a larger reading of the historical antecedents of current definitions and practices of inclusion/exclusion of Aboriginal identities. But I suggest that my study indicates that this wider picture is a necessary one for us, the Aboriginal community, to understand how we are the complicit agents of oppressive practices that restrict the creative regeneration and production of Aboriginal identities, as so hopefully expressed by Mick Dodson in his Wentworth Lecture (1994).

Aboriginal identity, whether we think of it in individual, local community or pan-Aboriginal terms, is a product of our position within and our relationship to the nation-state. The current criteria of Aboriginality came into being at a particular historical moment, when Aboriginal (and non-Aboriginal) activism had reshaped relations between Aboriginal Australians and the nation-state. The identification with the Aboriginal political struggle underlined a positive pride in being Aboriginal and enabled a regeneration of cultural knowledge and ways of expressing a positive sense of Aboriginality after centuries of oppression and destruction. Government recognition that Aboriginal people had survived and that Aboriginal self-determination could be expressed through the incorporation of Aboriginal-controlled organisations also determined a regime for distributing augmented yet still limited government resources to all Aboriginal people. This regime was able to be implemented in places where there was a recognisable community of Aboriginal people or a recognised set of needs or interests to be serviced. The mechanisms of self-determination became synonymous with a mode of representing 'Aboriginal interests' and with the distribution of limited government resources, a distribution process that still relied on being able to determine who was and who was not Aboriginal.

In this sense, at the local level, Aboriginal community-controlled organisations became the instruments of the nation-state and now do the work of the former Aboriginal administrators and protectors. The requirement to distribute resources designated for Aboriginal people only continues the need to define who is Aboriginal for the purposes of access to these resources and services. But the interpretation of the definitional criteria, which is in the hands of a few Aboriginal people in localised Aboriginal community-controlled organisations, supports and organises the ongoing evolution of Aboriginal identity discourses around this function. The creative evolution of the meanings of being Aboriginal in 'the world' are held hostage to this new 'centre', which now determines that some Aboriginal histories and expressions of Aboriginal identity are peripheral and illegitimate. In the process, many Aboriginal identities remain ambiguous — personally embodied and legitimate outcomes of Aboriginal historical experience but officially denied a recognised place in the new Aboriginal order.

These Aboriginal administrative developments, put in place in the transition from policies of assimilation to policies of self-determination, have ensured that Aboriginal identity continues to be predominately a practice of the social regulation of Aboriginal people as it has always been. The parameters of what constitutes the Aboriginal community are framed by this established regime for managing community representation to governments and other agencies, and for managing the distribution of resources. In this role, the official meanings of being Aboriginal and the official analysis of what it is at stake for Aboriginal people are deeply embroiled in community politics. Fairness and justice depend on the integrity of an organisation's practices and of the individuals within them. As in the past, the current regime of practice continues to fracture and control our sense of ourselves, and force us to take up subjectivities that are not of our own design but must fit the priorities of others and their incomplete readings of the Aboriginal world. Arguably, these practices do not unify and strengthen the political collective but contribute to conflict, divide the community, and render community membership toxic and unhealthy for some Aboriginal people. For some of the participants in my study, seeking an official confirmation was akin to reporting to the school principal with the expectation of being expelled for poor work or some transgression of the rules.

It was significant, therefore, that both the concept of the 'Aboriginal community' and the legal definitional criteria of Aboriginality were not questioned more than they were by the participants in my study. The assumptions on which the constitution of 'the community' rest were not called into question and the legitimacy of 'community' to arbitrate complex matters relating to individual identity was raised only by a few. In addition, acceptance of the definitional criteria as the 'truth' of Aboriginality was largely unquestioned by most participants in my study. And yet both these fundamentals construct as many problems as they purport to solve and both are constructs forged by colonial and subsequent governments and deeply implicated in the reproduction of the colonial regulatory techniques, which confined and restricted the possibilities for Aboriginal people in the changing circumstances of colonisation.

Can these fundamental elements in the production, regulation and surveillance of Aboriginal identity continue to be considered adequate for the future? Under the current constituting parameters — and given our history — can a local 'community' be the authority of all things Aboriginal? Can a 'community' which derives not only its sense of community but also its authority from its particular history in a particular 'locality' claim to 'know' who is Aboriginal and who is not in the current era? Are we accepting the 'rulings' of a community which simply cannot know us all?

Given our history, how is anyone to judge, let alone 'categorically' determine who is now Aboriginal or not Aboriginal? Who can say what it now *means* to be Aboriginal in any categorical or defined sense? Is the criterion of community recognition and acceptance workable given the diversity of Aboriginal historical experience and both the rapidly increasing Aboriginal population and the increasing movement of Aboriginal people all over the country? If it is not workable, is it fair and is it legitimate? Can the current definition be considered adequate if it merely overcomes ambiguity around colour and heritage with tightly prescribed ways of behaving and expressing oneself as Aboriginal? Do these render some Aboriginal identities ambiguous when they fail to conform? Are we simply reinstating and refining a hierarchy of cultural signs and meanings in place of degrees of 'blood' to determine Aboriginality?

These are important and legitimate questions for those Aboriginal identities whose family and personal histories have been submerged and overlooked in favour of the meanings forged from collective mission, reserve and fringe histories. They make it difficult for those with Stolen Generation narratives now coming to light through the uncovering of documented historical removals. Other undocumented histories are contained in the many Aboriginal experiences, many other sets of constrained circumstances, which divided Aboriginal families, fragmented Aboriginal groups and constrained individual choices over generations. These histories emerge out of the same historical policies as the more favoured narratives but are now harder to retrieve and narrate. And these varied circumstances still prevail again and again in each generation, as Aboriginal people move around, and as the imperatives of contemporary life shape individual and family decisionmaking towards pragmatism in the face of economic realities.

In this sense the historical similarities are clear. Decisions by individuals to move away from Aboriginal families or kin or communities were and are still decisions made by Aboriginal people. And they are valid decisions. Aboriginal people are the agents of their own lives, and as such they variously make self-interested, self-preserving, forced or pragmatic choices. These choices position Aboriginal people endlessly at a perpetual fork on the identity road when an economic or family decision to determine the best path in the circumstances might also affect whether an individual was or is considered Aboriginal or not-Aboriginal in the past, present and in the future. The 'truth' regime on which community recognition and acceptance rests denies not only the legitimacy of the histories of some Aboriginal people but also the hard-fought-for conditions of freedom that should allow all people of Aboriginal descent to lead contemporary lives of their choosing and still carry through their own sense of being Aboriginal and of belonging to the larger narrative of what it means to have been and still be descendants of the original inhabitants of this country.

This book set out to explore the discursive conditions of contemporary Aboriginality. I did not set out to find any solutions but to add to the existing literature. What has been revealed is the complexity of our position and how we are now, perhaps inadvertently but still nevertheless, complicit in carrying through the practices of our old colonial administrators. Those participants who talked of their concerns for their children's identity acknowledge that what the current generations of Aboriginal people do affects future generations. My glimpses into the online environment suggest that social media will only intensify and amplify the current regimes of community and self-surveillance.

There is in this web evidence that there is no pinpoint where blame or responsibility can be placed for the current struggle in which we are all involved, beyond the injustice of colonisation. We all uphold Aboriginal community practices when we fail to question the constitutive parameters of community relations with the nation-state and the role of community authority over Aboriginal bodies. We all uphold community practice in the way we support the singular choices to be or not to be Aboriginal. We all uphold community practice in the way we support the imposition of what are essentially membership rules on something so important and fundamental to the human psyche and sense of wellbeing as a person's individual identity. And while we uphold these things in the name of collective solidarity we overlook the curtailment of individual freedom to be all of who we now are after over two hundred years of disruption and varied experiences. In the process, we continue to deny some Aboriginal people their particular history of being Aboriginal and what it now means to them.

In all this busyness and surveillance about who counts as Aboriginal today, we witness also the inculcation of our younger generations into a divisive politics that will surely guarantee many more years of squabbling over the morsels the governments keep throwing at our feet as we tear ourselves apart for a share, rather than return our younger generations to our former political agenda of addressing the legacy of dispossession and disenfranchisement of all Indigenous peoples in Australia.

Without attempting to resolve any of the issues raised through this study, I suggest there is room for Aboriginal people to reflect on and examine our own practices and our compliance with a de facto government regime that insists on applying definitional criteria for access to government resources as the complete 'truth' of what it also means to be Aboriginal in all aspects of our daily lives. There is also room for reflecting on and extending our analysis of the discursive constraints that shape the possibilities and the limits of what it means to be Aboriginal. In what other ways can we express ourselves and conduct a community discourse that is open to all Aboriginal experiences? What can we achieve in our relations with the wider nation-state if we are not so preoccupied in our own community with regulating and surveilling each other for a few crumbs thrown under the master's table?

REFERENCES

Anderson, B. 1983, *Imagined communities: reflections on the origins and spread of nationalism*, Verso, London.
Anderson, C. 1985, 'On the notion of Aboriginality: a discussion', *Mankind*, vol. 15, no. 1, pp. 41–3.
——, Keen, I., Rowse, T., Von Sturmer, J., Anderson, C., Maddock, K., Tatz, C. & Thiele, S. 1985, 'On the notion of Aboriginality: a discussion', *Mankind*, vol. 15, no. 1, pp. 41–55.
Anderson, I. 1994, 'Black bit, white bit', in Papaellinas, G. (ed.), *Republica*, Angus & Robertson, Sydney.
—— 1997, 'I, the "hybrid" Aborigine: film and representation', *Australian Aboriginal Studies*, no. 1, pp. 4–14.
Ang, I. 2000, 'Identity blues', in Gilroy, P., Grossberg, L. & McRobbie, A. (eds), *Without guarantees: in honour of Stuart Hall*, Verso, London.
Anonymous, 2006, 'Comments don't help', *The Koori Mail*, 6 December, p. 24.
Appiah, K. A. 1994, 'Identity, authenticity, survival: multicultural societies and social reproduction', in Gutmann, A. (ed.), *Multiculturalism: examining the politics of recognition*, Princeton University Press, Princeton, pp. 149–63.
Ashcroft, B., Griffiths, G. & Tiffins, H. 1989, *The empire writes back*, Routledge, London.
Attwood, B. & Markus, A. 1997, *The 1967 Referendum or when Aborigines didn't get the vote*, Australian Institute of Aboriginal and Torres Strait Islander Studies, Canberra.
—— 2004, *Thinking black: William Cooper and the Australian Aborigines' League*, Aboriginal Studies Press, Canberra.
—— 2007, *The 1967 Referendum: race, power and the Australian Constitution*, Aboriginal Studies Press, Canberra.
Australian Institute of Aboriginal and Torres Strait Islander Studies n.d., *Proof of Aboriginality or Torres Strait Islander Heritage, Fact Sheet 18*, viewed on 30 March 2005, <http://www.aiatsis.gov.au/lbry/fmly_hstry/fmly_hstry_aboriginality.htm>.
Australian Law Reform Commission 2003, '36. Kinship and identity', *Essentially yours: the protection of human genetic information in Australia* (ALRC 96 Report), viewed on 20 April 2011, <http://www.alrc.gov.au/publications/

essentially–yours–protection–human–genetic–information–australia–alrc–report–96/36–kins>.

Bartlett, B. 2006, 'Coming full circle', *The Koori Mail*, 6 December, p. 24.

Barth, F. (ed.) 1969, *Ethnic groups and boundaries: the social organisation of culture difference*, Oslo, Bergen.

Barthes, R. 1970, *Mythologies*, Seuil, Paris.

Barwick, D. 1961, 'Economic absorption without assimilation? The case of some Melbourne part-Aboriginal families', *Oceania*, vol. 33, no. 1, pp. 18–23.

Bayart, J. 2005, *The illusion of cultural identity*, Randall, S., Roitman, J., Schoch, C. & Derrick J. (trans.), C. Hurst & Co., London.

Beckett, J. 1958, 'A study of mixed-blood Aboriginal minority in the pastoral west of New South Wales', Masters thesis, Australian National University, Canberra.

—— 1965, 'Kinship, mobility and community among part-Aborigines in rural Australia', *International Journal of Comparative Sociology*, vol. 6, no. 1, pp. 7–23.

—— (ed.) 1988a, *Past and present, the construction of Aboriginality*, Aboriginal Studies Press, Canberra.

—— 1988b, 'Kinship, mobility and community in rural New South Wales', in Keen, I. (ed.), *Being black: Aboriginal cultures in Australia*, Aboriginal Studies Press, Canberra, pp. 117–36.

Behrendt, L. 1994, 'Aboriginal urban identity: preserving the spirit, protecting the traditional in non-traditional settings', *The Australian Feminist Law Journal*, vol. 4, pp. 55–61.

Bell, J. 1955/1956, 'The economic life of mixed-blood Aborigines on the South Coast of New South Wales', *Oceania*, vol. 26, pp. 181–99.

Berndt, C. H. 1961, 'The quest for identity: the case of the Australian Aborigine', *Oceania*, vol. 32, no. 1, pp. 16–33.

Berndt, R. M. 1977, 'Aboriginal identity: reality or mirage', in Berndt, R. M. (ed.), *Aborigines and change*, Australian Institute of Aboriginal Studies, Canberra. pp. 1–12.

—— (ed.) 1971, *A question of choice: an Australian Aboriginal Dilemma*, University of Western Australia Press, Perth.

Berndt, R. M. & Berndt, C. H. 1964, *The world of the First Australians*, Ure Smith, Sydney.

—— 1988, *The world of the first Australians, Aboriginal traditional life: past and present*, Repr. with additions, Aboriginal Studies Press, Canberra.

Berry, J. P. 1970, 'Marginality, stress and ethnic identification in an acculturated Aboriginal community', *Journal of Cross Cultural Psychology*, vol. 1, no. 3, pp. 239–52.

Bhabha, H. 1994, *The location of culture*, Routledge, New York.

Bianchi, G. N., Cawte, J. E. & Kiloh, L. G. 1970, 'Cultural identity and the mental health of Australian Aborigines', *Social Science and Medicine*, vol. 3, no. 3, pp. 371–87.

REFERENCES

Biddle, E. 1969, 'The assimilation of Aborigines in Brisbane, Australia 1965', Doctoral thesis, University of Missouri.

Birch, T. 1995, 'A Mabo blood test', *The Australian Journal of Anthropology*, vol. 6, nos. 1 & 2, pp. 32–42.

Blackmore, E. 2007, 'Speakin' out Blak: an examination of finding an "urban" Indigenous "voice" through contemporary Australian theatre', Doctoral thesis, University of Wollongong.

Bleakley, J. W. 1929, 'Bleakley Report', *Parliamentary Papers General*, vol. 2.

—— 1961, *The Aborigines of Australia*, Jacaranda Press, Brisbane,

Boladeras, J. 2002, 'It's easier to be black if you're black: issues of Aboriginality for fair-complexioned Nyungar people', Masters thesis, Curtin University of Technology.

Bolt, A. 2009, 'White is the new black', *Herald*, Sun April 15th, viewed on 22 May 2009, <http://blogs.news.com.au/heraldsun/andrewbolt/index.php/heraldsun/comments/column_white_is_the_new_black>.

Bolt, R. 2010, 'Urban Aboriginal identity construction in Australia: An Aboriginal perspective utilising multi-method qualitative analysis', Unpublished Doctoral thesis, University of Sydney.

Bond, C. 2007, '"When you're black, they look at you harder": narrating Aboriginality within public health', Doctoral thesis, University of Queensland.

Bourke, C., Bourke, E. & Edwards, B. (eds) 2006, *Aboriginal Australia: an introductory reader in Aboriginal studies*, University of Queensland Press, St Lucia.

Boyd, D. & Ellison, N. 2007, 'Social network sites: definition, history and scholarship', *Journal of Computer-Mediated Communication*, vol. 13, no. 1, pp. 210–30.

Brandl, M. 1970, 'Adaptation or disintegration? Changes in the Kulama initiation and increase ritual of Melville and Bathurst Islands, N. T. of Australia', *Anthropological Forum*, vol. 11, no. 4.

Brereton, J. L. 1962, 'An estimate of assimilation rate of mixed-blood Aborigines in New South Wales', *Oceania*, vol. 32, no. 3, pp. 187–90.

Briggs-Smith, N. 2006, 'Proof of Aboriginality', *The Koori Mail*, p. 24.

Broome, R. 2002, *Aboriginal Australians*, Allen & Unwin, Crows Nest, NSW.

—— 2015, *Fighting hard: the Victorian Aborigines Advancement League*, Aboriginal Studies Press, Canberra.

Brown, P. Y. 2006, 'Underpinning knowledge of Aboriginal lore', *The Koori Mail*, 12 September, p. 22.

Butler, J. 1990a, *Gender trouble: feminism and the subversion of identity*, Routledge, London.

—— 1990b, 'Performative acts and gender constitution: an essay in phenomenology and feminist theory', in Case, S. E. (ed.), *Performing feminisms: feminist critical theory & theatre*, Johns Hopkins University Press, Baltimore, pp. 270–82.

REFERENCES

—— 1993, *Bodies that matter: on the discursive limits of 'sex'*, Routledge, New York.

—— 1999, *Gender trouble: feminism and the subversion of identity*, Routledge, New York, (anniversary edition).

Callinan, T. 2014, 'Remote Indigenous Australians rely on Facebook to stay in touch', Special Broadcasting Service, viewed on 29 September 2014, <http://www.sbs.com.au/news/article/2014/08/26/remote–indigenous–australians–rely–facebook–stay–touch.

Carlson, B. 2013, 'The "new frontier": emergent Indigenous identities and social media', in Harris, M., Nakata, M. & Carlson. B. (eds), *The politics of identity: emerging indigeneity*, University of Technology Sydney E–Press, Sydney, pp. 147–68.

—— 2014, 'Well connected Indigenous kids keen to tap new ways to save lives', The Conversation, viewed on 20 September 2014, <https://theconversation.com/well–connected–indigenous–kids–keen–to–tap–new–ways–to–save–lives–30964>.

Cawte, J. P. 1973, 'A sick society', in Kerney, G. P., Lacey, P. R. & Davidson, G. R. (eds), *The Psychology of Aboriginal Australians*, Wiley & Sons, Sydney, pp. 365–79.

Chase, A. K. 1981, 'Empty vessels and loud noises: views about Aboriginality today', *Social Alternatives*, vol. 2, no. 2, pp. 23–7.

Clark, J. 2008, *Aborigines and activism: race, Aborigines and the coming of the sixties to Australia*, University of Western Australia Press, Crawley.

Connor, M. 2011, 'Andrew Bolt on trial', *Quadrant Online*, viewed on 17 May 2011, <http://www.quadrant.org.au/magazine/issue/2011/5/andrew–bolt–on–trial>.

Coombs, H. C. 1976, 'Decentralization trends among Aboriginal communities', *Search*, vol. 5, no. 4, pp. 135–43.

Coombs, H. C., Brandl, M. & Snowdon, W. 1983, 'A certain heritage: programs for and by Aboriginal families in Australia, CRES Monograph 9', *Centre for resource and environmental studies*, Australian National University, Canberra.

Copas, R. 2006, 'Validating Aboriginality', *The Koori Mail*, 11 October, p. 25.

Cowlishaw, G. 2004, *Blackfellas, whitefellas, and the hidden injuries of race*, Blackwell Publishers, London.

Davis, E. 1991, 'Ethnicity and diversity: politics and the Aboriginal community', Doctoral thesis, University of Adelaide.

Dawson, J. L. M. 1969, 'Exchange theory and comparison level changes among Australian Aborigines', *British Journal of Social and Clinical Psychology*, vol. 8, pp. 133–40.

D'Cruz, C. 2001, 'What matter who's speaking? Authenticity and identity in discourses of Aboriginality in Australia', *Jouvert: A Journal of Postcolonial Studies*, vol. 5, no. 3, viewed on 20 April 2011, <http://english.chass.ncsu.edu/jouvert/v5i3/cdcr.htm>.

REFERENCES

Deane, W. 1996, *Some signposts from Daguragu, The inaugural Lingiari Lecture*, Council for Aboriginal Reconciliation, Canberra.

de Certeau, M. 1988, *The practice of everyday life*, Rendall, S. (trans.), University of California, Berkeley, California.

Dillon, A. 2011, 'Identifying as Aboriginal can hurt', *The Australian*, 11 April, viewed on 27 April 2011, <p://www.theaustralian.com.au/news/opinion/identifying–as–aboriginal–can–hurt/story–e6frg6zo–1226036879026>.

Dixon, C. 1975, 'Chapter Seven', in Tatz, C. & McConnochie, K. (eds), *Black viewpoints: the Aboriginal experience*, Australian and New Zealand Book Co., Sydney, pp. 32–8.

Dodson, M. 1994, 'The end in the beginning: re(de)finding Aboriginality', The Wentworth Lecture, *Australian Aboriginal Studies*, vol. 1, pp. 2–13.

—— 2003, 'The end in the beginning: re(de)finding Aboriginality', in Grossman, M. (ed.), *Blacklines: contemporary critical writings by Indigenous Australians*, Melbourne University Press, Carlton, pp. 25–42.

Droste, M. 2000, 'A discussion paper on the issues of Aboriginal identity in contemporary Australia', *Aboriginal and Torres Strait Islander Health Worker Journal*, vol. 24, no. 6, Nov/Dec, pp. 11–13.

Eades, D. 1981, '"That's our way of talking": Aborigines in South East Queensland', *Social Alternatives*, vol. 2, no. 2, pp. 11–14.

Eckermann, A.-K. 1973, 'Contact: an ethnographic analysis of three Aboriginal communities including a comparative and cross-cultural examination of value orientation', Masters thesis, University of Queensland.

—— 1977a, 'Half-caste, out-cast: an ethnographic analysis of the processes underlying adaptation among Aboriginal people in rural town, south-west Queensland', Doctoral Thesis, University of Queensland.

—— 1977b, 'Group organisation and identity within an urban community', in Berndt, R. M. (ed.), *Aborigines and change: Australia in the 70's*, pp. 288–319.

Eckermann, A.-K., Dowd, T., Martin, M., Nixon, L., Gray, R. & Chong, E. (eds) 1998, *Binan Goonj: bridging cultures in Aboriginal health*, University of New England Press, Armidale.

Elkin, A. P. 1951, 'Reaction and interaction: food gathering people and European settlement in Australia', *American Anthropologist*, vol. 53, no. 2, April–June, pp. 164–86.

—— 1964, *The Australian Aborigines: how to understand them*, 4th ed, Angus & Robertson, Sydney.

Erikson, E. H. 1950, *Childhood and society*, WW Norton Inc., New York.

—— 1968, *Identity: youth and crisis*, WW Norton Inc., New York.

—— 1979, *Dimensions of a new identity: the Jefferson Lectures in the Humanities*, WW Norton Inc., New York.

REFERENCES

Fanon, F. 1963, *The wretched of the earth*, Farrington, C. (trans.), Grove Press, New York.

—— 1967, *Black skin, white masks*, Markham, C. (trans.), Grove Press, New York.

—— 1970, *A dying colonialism*, Grove Press, New York.

Ferguson, K. 1993, *The man question: visions of subjectivity in feminist theory*, University of California Press, Berkeley.

Fields, T. 1975, quoted in Tatz, C. & McConnochie, K. (eds), *Black viewpoints: the Aboriginal experience*, Australian and New Zealand Book Co., Brookvale, p. 105.

Fink, R. 1957/58, 'The caste barrier — an obstacle to the assimilation of part-Aborigines in North-West new South Wales', *Oceania*, vol. 28, no. 1, pp. 100–10.

—— 1960, 'The changing status and cultural identity of Western Australian Aborigines: a field study of Aborigines in the Murchison District, Western Australia, 1955–1957', Unpublished Doctoral thesis, Columbia University.

Fison, L. & Howitt, A. W. 1880, *Kamilaroi and Kurnai*, Robertson, Melbourne.

Flood, J. 2006, *The original Australians: story of the Aboriginal people*, Allen & Unwin, Crows Nest, NSW.

Foucault, M. 1979, *Discipline and punishment*, Vintage Press, New York.

—— 2004, *Archaeology of knowledge*, Routledge, Abingdon, UK.

Fraser, M. & Dutta, S. 2008, *Throwing sheep in the boardroom: how online social networking will transform your life, work and world*, John Wiley & Sons Ltd, West Sussex, UK.

Fredericks, B. 2004, 'Urban identity', *Eureka Street*, December, pp. 30–31.

Frith, N., Hausfeld, R. G. & Moodie, P. M. 1974, *The Coasttown project: action research in Aboriginal community health*, Australian Government Publishing Service, Canberra.

Gale, F. 1964, *A study of assimilation: part Aborigines in South Australia*, Libraries Board of South Australia, Adelaide.

—— 1972, *Urban Aborigines*, Australian National University Press, Canberra.

Gale, G. & Brookman, A. 1975, *Race relations in Australia: the Aborigines*, McGraw Hill, Sydney.

Ganter, R. 2008, 'Turning Aboriginal: Historical bents', *Borderlands e-journal*, vol. 7, no. 2, pp. 1–19.

Gardiner-Garden, J. 2002–2003, *Defining Aboriginality in Australia*, Department of Parliamentary Library, Canberra, viewed on 26 April 2008, <http://www.aph.gov.au/library/pubs/CIB/2002–03/03cib10.pdf>.

Gascoigne, J. 1994, *Joseph Banks and the English Enlightenment: useful knowledge and polite culture*, Cambridge University Press, Cambridge.

Gilbert, S. 1995, 'A postcolonial experience of Aboriginal identity', *Cultural Studies*, vol. 9, no. 1, pp. 145–9.

Godwell, D. 1997, 'Aboriginality and rugby league in Australia: an exploratory study of identity construction and professional sport', Masters thesis, University of Windsor, Ontario, Canada.

Goldsworthy, D. 1988, *Development studies in Australia: themes and issues*, Monash Development Studies Centre, Monash University, Melbourne.

Goodall, H. 1982, 'A history of Aboriginal communities in New South Wales, 1909–1939', Doctoral thesis, Department of History, University of Sydney.

Gorringe, S., Ross, J. & Fforde, C. 2011, '"Will the real Aborigine please stand up": strategies for breaking the stereotypes and changing the conversation', AIATSIS Research Discussion Paper, vol. 2011 28, Australian Institute of Aboriginal and Torres Strait Islander Studies, Canberra.

Gramsci, A. 1971, *Selections from the prison notebooks of Antonio Gramsci*, in Hoare, Q. & Smith, G. N. (eds & trans), Lawrence & Wishart, London.

Green, N. 2006, 'Proving identity', *The Koori Mail*, 11 October, p. 24.

Greenop, K. 2009a, *Place meaning, attachment and identity in contemporary Indigenous Inala, Queensland*, Aboriginal Environments Research Centre, School of Architecture, University of Queensland, St Lucia, Queensland, pp. 1–29.

—— 2009b, *Housing and identity in an urban Indigenous community: initial findings in Inala, Queensland*, Aboriginal Environments Research Centre, School of Architecture, University of Queensland, St Lucia, Queensland, pp. 1–19.

Griffiths, G. 1995, 'The myth of authenticity', in Ashcroft, B., Griffiths, G. & Tiffen, H. (eds), *The post–colonial studies reader*, Routledge, London and New York, pp. 237–41.

Grossman, M. & Cuthbert, D. 1998, 'Resisting aboriginalites', *Postcolonial Studies*, vol. 1, no. 1, pp. 109–24.

Guilliatt, R. 2002, 'A whiter shade of black?', *Good Weekend, Sydney Morning Herald*, 15 June, pp. 18–23.

Hall, S. 1990, 'Cultural identity and diaspora', in Rutherford, J. (ed.), *Identity: community, culture and difference*, Lawrence & Wishart, London.

—— 1996, 'Cultural identity and cinematic representation', in Baker, H., Diawara, M. & Lindeborg, R. (eds), *Black British cultural studies: a reader*, University of Chicago Press, London, pp. 210–22.

Hanson, P. 1996, 'Pauline Hanson's maiden speech in the House of Representatives', viewed on 21 May 2011, <http://australianpolitics.com/1996/09/10/pauline–hanson–maiden–speech.html>.

Hardy, B. 1976, *Lament for the Barkindji: the vanished tribes of the Darling River Region*, Rigby, Adelaide.

Harding, S. 2004, 'Introduction: standpoint theory as a site of political, philosophic and scientific debate', in Harding, S. (ed.), *The feminist standpoint theory reader: intellectual and political controversies*, Routledge, New York, pp. 1–16.

Hausfeld, R. G. 1977, 'Basic value orientation, change and stress in two Aboriginal communities', in Berndt, R. M. (ed.), *Aborigines and change: Australia in the 70's*, pp. 266–87.

Heiss, A. 2003, *Dhuuluu-Yala (to talk straight): publishing Indigenous literature*, Aboriginal Studies Press, Canberra.

—— 2007, 'Writing Aboriginality: authors on "being Aboriginal"', in Birns, N. & McNeer, R. (eds), *A companion to Australian literature since 1900*, Camden House, New York.

Hinton, M. 2006, 'Proving our identity', *The Koori Mail*, 8 November, p. 25.

Holland, W. 1996, 'Mis/taken identity', in Vasta, E. & Castles, S. (eds), *The teeth are smiling: the persistence of racism in multicultural Australia*, Allen & Unwin, St Leonards, NSW, pp. 97–111.

Horner, J. 2004, *Seeking racial justice: an insider's memoir of the movement for Aboriginal advancement, 1938–1978*, Aboriginal Studies Press, Canberra.

Howard, M. (ed.) 1978, *'Whitefella business': Aborigines in Australian politics*, Institute for the Study of Human Issues, Philadelphia.

Howitt, A. W. 1904, *The native tribes of south-east Australia*, Macmillan, London.

Huggins, J. 2003, 'Always was, always will be', in Grossman, M. (ed.), *Blacklines: contemporary critical writings by Indigenous Australians*, Melbourne University Press, Carlton, pp. 60–5.

Hunter, B. H. & Schwab, R. G. 2003, 'Practical reconciliation and continuing disadvantage in Indigenous education', *The drawing board: an Australian review of public affairs*, vol. 4, no. 2, pp. 83–98, viewed 21 May 2011, <http://www.australianreview.net/journal/v4/n2/hunter_schwab.pdf>.

Jacobs, J. 1988, 'The construction of identity', in Beckett, J. (ed.), *Past and present, the construction of Aboriginality*, Aboriginal Studies Press, Canberra, pp. 31–44.

Johnson, D. 1993, 'Ab/originality: playing and passing versus assimilation', *The Olive Pink Society Bulletin*, vol. 5, no. 2, pp. 19–22.

Johnston, S. 1997, 'The New South Wales Government policy towards Aborigines, 1880 to 1909', Master thesis, University of Sydney.

Joinson, A. 2008, 'Looking at, "looking up" or "keeping up with" people? Motives and uses of Facebook', *Proceedings: online social networks*, Florence, Italy, pp.

1027–36, 5–10 April 2008, viewed on 24 July 2009, <http://people.bath.ac.uk/aj266/pubs_pdf/1149–joinson.pdf>.

Jordan, D. 1983, 'Identity as a problem in the sociology of knowledge: the social construction of Aboriginal identity with special reference to the 'world' of education', Doctoral thesis, London University, London.

Kelly, L. 2010, 'Being Aboriginal: what does the community think about the definition?', *The Big Read — National Indigenous Times*, 10 June, p. 24.

Kickett, M. 1999, quoted in Oxenham, D., Cameron, J., Collard, K., Dudgeon, P., Garvey, D., Kickett, M., Kickett, T., Roberts, J. & Whiteway, J. 1999, *A dialogue on Indigenous identity: warts 'n' all*, Gunada Press, Perth, Western Australia.

Kolig, E. 1973, 'Tradition and emancipation: an Australian Aboriginal version of nativism', *Aboriginal Affairs Planning Authority*, vol. 1, no. 6, supplement, Western Australia.

Kral, I. 2011, 'Youth media as cultural practice: Remote Indigenous youth speaking out loud', *Australian Aboriginal Studies*, vol. 1, pp. 4–16.

Living Black, 2010, 'Cyber Wars', 19 April, Special Broadcasting Service.

Lacan, J. 1977, *The mirror stage as formative of the I as revealed in psychoanalytical experience*, Sheridan, A. (trans.), WW Norton Inc., New York.

Lamb, N. 2007, 'Aboriginalising racism — regional experiences of racism between Aboriginal groups', a paper presented at the *International conference on racism in the new world order: realities of colour, culture and identity conference*, University of the Sunshine Coast, Maroochydore, Queensland, pp. 177–83.

Lambert-Pennington, A. 2005, 'Being in Australia, belonging to the land: the cultural politics of urban Aboriginal identity', Doctoral thesis, Duke University, Durham, North Carolina.

Langton, M. 1981, 'Urbanizing Aborigines: the social scientists' great deception', *Social Alternatives*, August, vol. 2, no. 2, pp. 16–22.

—— 1994, 'Aboriginal art and film: the politics of representation', *Race and Class*, vol. 35, no. 4, pp. 89–106.

—— 2003, 'Aboriginal art and film: the politics of representation', in Grossman, M. (ed.), *Blacklines: contemporary critical writings by Indigenous Australians*, Melbourne University Press, Carlton, pp. 109–24.

—— 2005, 'Aboriginal art and film: the politics of representation', *Rouge*, 2005, viewed on 4 December 2005, <http://www.rouge.com.au/6/aboriginal.html>.

—— 2007, 'Trapped in the Aboriginal reality show', *Re-imagining Australia*, Griffith University Review, no. 19, Griffith University, Brisbane.

—— 2011, 'Aboriginal sophisticates betray bush sisters', *The Australian*, 15 April, viewed 17 May 2011, <http://www.theaustralian.com.au/national-affairs/

commentary/aboriginal-sophisticates-betray-bush-sisters/story-e6frgd0x-1226039349353>.

Lattas, A. 1993, 'Essentialism, memory and resistance: Aboriginality and the politics of authenticity', *Oceania*, vol. 63, no. 3, pp. 240–68.

Lumby, B. 2004, 'Aboriginal community and identity: an Aboriginal and sociological analysis', Unpublished Honours thesis, University of Wollongong.

Lumby, B. 2010, 'Cyber-Indigeneity: urban Indigenous identity on Facebook', *The Australian Journal of Indigenous Education*, vol. 39, supplement, pp. 68–75.

Macherey, P. 1990, 'The text says what it does not say', in Walder, D. (ed.), *Literature in the modern world: critical essays and documents*, Oxford University Press, Oxford, pp. 215–22.

Maddison, S. 2009, *Black politics: inside the complexity of Aboriginal political culture*, Allen & Unwin, Sydney.

Manago, A. M., Graham, M. B., Greenfield, P. M. & Salimkhan, G. 2008, 'Self–presentation and gender on Myspace', *Journal of Applied Development Psychology*, vol. 29, pp. 446–58.

Marcia, J. 1966, 'Development and validation of ego identity status', *Journal of personality and social psychology*, no. 3, pp. 551–8.

Martin, K. L. 2008, *Please knock before you enter: Aboriginal regulation of outsiders and the implications for researchers*, Post Pressed, Brisbane.

Maxley, J. 1991, 'Kooris adapting: an anthropological case study of the maintenance and reconstruction of the cultural identity of Aboriginal Australians in New South Wales, Australia', Doctoral thesis, The Ohio State University.

Maynard, J. 2007, *Fight for liberty and freedom: Fred Maynard and the Australian Aboriginal Progressive Association*, Aboriginal Studies Press, Canberra.

McCorquodale, J. C. 1986, 'The legal classification of race in Australia', *Aboriginal History*, vol. 10, no. 1, pp. 7–24.

—— 1997, 'Aboriginal identity: legislative, judicial and administrative definitions', *Australian Aboriginal Studies*, vol. 2, pp. 24–35.

McKeich, R. 1977, 'The structure of a part-Aboriginal world', in Berndt, R. (ed.), *Aborigines and change: Australia in the 70's*, Humanities Press, New Jersey.

Melohn, P. 2006, 'Lost…and accused of supplying fake documents', *The Koori Mail*, 13 September, p. 22.

Moodai Robinson, C. D. 1997, 'The effects of colonisation, cultural and psychological on my family', Masters Thesis, University of Western Sydney, School of Social Ecology.

Morgan, S. 1987, *My Place*, Fremantle Arts Centre Press, Fremantle, Western Australia.

Moreton-Robinson, A. 2003, 'I still call Australia home: Aboriginal belonging and place in a white postcolonizing society', in Ahmed, S., Castameda,

C., Fortier, A. & Sheller, M. (eds), *Uprootings/regroundings: questions of home and migration*, Berg Press, New York, pp. 23–40.

—— 2014, 'Towards an Australian Indigenous women's standpoint theory', *Australian Feminist Studies*, vol. 28, no. 78, pp. 331–47.

Morris, B. 1988, 'The politics of identity: from Aborigines to the first Australian', in Beckett, J. (ed.), *Past and present: the construction of Aboriginality*, Aboriginal Studies Press, Canberra, pp. 63–86.

Muecke, S. 1992, *Textual spaces: Aboriginality and cultural studies*, University of New South Wales Press, Kensington.

Nadarajah, H. 2011, 'Can you be my Facebook friend? Reaching out across language groups', *Our place: people working with technology in remote communities*, no. 39, pp. 6–9.

Nakata, M. 2003, 'Better', in Grossman, M. (ed.), *Blacklines: contemporary critical writings by Indigenous Australians*, Melbourne University Press, Carlton, Victoria.

—— 2007, *Disciplining the savages, savaging the disciplines*, Aboriginal Studies Press, Canberra.

NACCHO, also National Aboriginal Community Controlled Health Organisation, Definitions, as decided at the NACCHO Broome conference, December 1995, viewed on 9 December 2016, <http://www.naccho.org.au/aboriginal-health/definitions>.

National Aboriginal Education Committee 1986, 'Policy statement on tertiary education for Aborigines and Torres Strait Islanders/National Aboriginal Education Committee', Australian Government Publishing Service, Canberra.

Noble, F. 1996, 'Who do we think we are: people who are learning about their Aboriginality', Masters thesis, Griffith University.

Overington, C. 2012, 'Not so Black and White', *Weekend Australian Magazine*, 24–25 March, pp. 14-18.

Oxenham, D., Cameron, J., Collard, K., Dudgeon, P., Garvey, D., Kickett, M., Kickett, T., Roberts, J. & Whiteway, J. 1999, *A dialogue on Indigenous identity: warts 'n' all*, Gunada Press, Perth, Western Australia.

Paradies, Y. C. 2006, 'Beyond black and white: essentialism, hybridity and indigeneity', *Journal of Sociology*, vol. 42, no. 4, pp. 355–67.

Perkins, C. *The Australian*, 8 April 1968, p. 8.

Peters-Little, F. 2000, *The community game: Aboriginal self-definition at the local level*, Research discussion paper, Australian Institute of Aboriginal and Torres Strait Islander Studies, no. 10, Canberra, viewed on 13 July 2007, <http://www.aiatsis.gov.au/__data/assets/pdf_file/5579/DP10.pdf>.

—— 2001, 'The community game: Aboriginal self definition at the local level', in Morphy, F. & Sanders, W. (eds), *The Indigenous welfare economy and the CDEP scheme*, Centre for Aboriginal Economic Policy Research, The Australian National University, Canberra, pp. 187–92.

REFERENCES

Peterson, N. 1990, 'Studying man and man's nature': the history of the institutionalisation of Aboriginal anthropology', The Wentworth Lectures, viewed 20 November 2009, <http://www.aiatsis.gov.au/lbry/dig_prgm/wentworth/m0006639_a.rtf>

Phillips, G. 2009, Healing and identity, *AIATSIS Seminar Series*, 18 May, Canberra.

Pierson, J. 1977, 'Aboriginality in Adelaide: an urban context of Australian Aboriginal ethnicity', *Urban Anthropology*, vol. 6, no. 4, pp. 307–25.

Pohlhaus, G. 2002, 'Knowing communities: an investigation of Harding's standpoint epistemology', *Social epistemology*, vol. 16, no. 3, pp. 283–93.

Pollard, D. 1985, 'Welfare policy and Aborigines: towards an understanding of recent developments in New South Wales government policy in Aboriginal welfare', Doctoral thesis, University of Sydney, Sydney.

Read, P. 1998, 'Whose citizens? Whose country?', in Peterson, N. & Sanders, W. (eds), *Citizenship and Indigenous Australians: changing conceptions and possibilities*, Cambridge University Press, Cambridge, pp. 169–78.

Reay, M. 1944/1945, 'A half-caste Aboriginal community in North–Western New South Wales' *Oceania*, vol. 15, pp. 296–323.

—— 1951, 'Mixed-blood marriage in North-Western New South Wales: a survey of the marital conditions of 264 Aboriginal and mixed-blood women', *Oceania*, vol. 22, no. 2, pp. 116–20.

Reay, M. & Sitlington, G. 1948, 'Class and status in a mixed-blood community', *Oceania*, vol. 18, no. 3, pp. 179–207.

Reynolds, H. 1972, *Aborigines and settlers*, Cassell, North Melbourne.

Ricoeur, P. & Blarney, K. (eds) 1995, *Oneself as another*, Blamey, K. (trans.), University of Chicago Press, Chicago.

Rigney, L. I. 1997, 'Internationalization of an Indigenous anticolonial cultural critique of research methodologies: a guide to Indigenist research methodology and its principles', *Wicazo Sa Review*, pp. 109–21.

Rigsby, B. 1981, 'Land rights in Queensland', *Social Alternatives*, vol. 2, no. 2.

Robins, K. 2000, 'Cyberspace and the world we live in', in Bell, D. & Kennedy, B. (eds), *The cybercultures reader*, Routledge, London.

Rolls, M. 2001, 'The meaninglessness of Aboriginal cultures', *Balayi: Culture Law and Colonialism*, vol. 2, no. 1, pp. 7–20.

Roth, W. E. 1897, *Ethnological studies among the north-west-central Queensland Aborigines*, Government Printer, Brisbane.

Rowse, T. 1985, 'On the notion of Aboriginality: a discussion', *Oceania*, vol. 15, no. 1, pp. 45–6.

Rowley, C. D. 1971, *Outcasts in white Australia*, Australian National University Press, Canberra.

Said, E. 1993, *Culture and imperialism*, Vintage Books, New York.

Salih, S. 2002, 'On Judith Butler and Performativity', pp. 55–67, viewed on 12 March 2009, <http://www9.georgetown.edu/faculty/irvinem/theory/Salih–Butler–Performativity–Chapter_3.pdf>.

REFERENCES

Schwab, R. G. 1991, 'The "Blackfella Way" ideology and practice in an urban Aboriginal community', Doctoral thesis, Australian National University.

Smith, D. 1987, *The everyday world as problematic: a feminist sociology*, Northeastern University Press, Boston.

Smith, L. T. 2012 (2nd ed.), *Decolonizing methodologies: research and indigenous peoples*, Zed Books, London.

Spencer, B. 1914, *Native tribes of the Northern Territory of Australia*, Macmillan, London.

Spencer, B. & Gillen, F. J. 1899, *The native tribes of Central Australia*, Macmillan, London.

Spivak, G. 1988a, *In other worlds: essays in cultural politics*, Routledge, New York.

—— 1988b, 'Can the subaltern speak', in Nelson, C. & Grossberg, L. (eds), *Marxism and the interpretations of culture*, Macmillan Educational, London, pp. 123–39.

Stanner, W. E. H. 1979, *Whiteman got no Dreaming: essays 1938–73*, Australian National University Press, Canberra.

Sutton, P. 1981, 'Land rights and compensation in settled Australia', *Social Alternatives*, vol. 2, no. 2, pp. 6–10.

—— 2001, 'Kinds of rights in Country: recognising customary rights as incidents of Native Title', *Native Title Tribunal*, Perth, Western Australia.

Taffe, S. 2005, *Black and white together: FCAATSI, the Federal Council for the Advancement of Aborigines and Torres Strait Islanders, 1958–1973*, University of Queensland Press, St Lucia, Queensland.

Tajfel, H. & Turner, J. C. 1986, 'The social identity theory of inter-group behaviour', in Worchel, S. & Austin, L. W. (eds), *Psychology of intergroup relations*, Nelson–Hall, Chicago, pp. 7–24.

Tatz, C. 1977, 'Aborigines: political options and strategies', in Berndt, R. (ed.), *Aborigines and change: Australia in the 70's*, Humanities Press, New Jersey.

—— 1979, *Race Politics in Australia: Aborigines, politics and the law*, University of New England press, Armidale, NSW.

Tatz, C. & McConnochie, K. 1975, *Black viewpoints: the Aboriginal experience*, Australian and New Zealand Book Co., Sydney.

Taylor, C. 1989, *Sources of the self: the making of the modern identity*, Harvard University Press, Cambridge, Mass.

Thiele, S. J. 1982, *Yugul*, ANU Press, Canberra.

—— 1984, 'Anti-intellectualism and the Aboriginal problem: Colin Tatz and the self-determination approach', *Mankind*, vol. 14, no. 3, pp. 165–78.

Tonkinson, M. 1990, 'Is it in the blood? Australian Aboriginal identity', in Linekin, J. & Poyer, L. (eds), *Cultural identity and ethnicity in the Pacific*, University of Hawaii Press, USA.

Tuhiwai Smith, L. 2012, *Decolonizing methodologies: research and Indigenous peoples*, Zed Books, London.

Von Sturmer, J. 1973, 'Changing Aboriginal identity in Cape York', in Tugby, D. (ed.), *Aboriginal identity in contemporary Australian society*, Jacaranda Press, Brisbane.
—— 1985, 'On the notion of Aboriginality: a discussion', *Oceania*, vol. 15, no. 1, pp. 46–9.
Welsh, R. 2006, 'Confirmation of Aboriginality', *The Koori Mail*, 30 August, p. 26.
Wilson, S. R. 1997, *Bringing them home: National inquiry into the separation of Aboriginal and Torres Strait Islander children from their families*, Human Rights and Equal Opportunity Commission, Canberra.
Windschuttle, K. 2011, 'Chronicle', *Quadrant Online*, May, viewed on 17 May 2011 at, http://www.quadrant.org.au/magazine/issue/2011/5/keith-windschuttle.
Yamanouchi, Y. 2007, 'Searching for Aboriginal community in south western Sydney', Unpublished Doctoral Thesis, University of Sydney.
—— 2010, 'Kinship, organisations and "wannabes": Aboriginal identity negotiation in south-western Sydney', *Oceania*, vol. 80, pp. 216–28.

INDEX

Aboriginal and Torres Strait Islander Commission (ATSIC)
  abolition, 90
  establishment, 86
Aboriginal and Torres Strait Islanders' Affairs Act 1965 (Qld), 44
Aboriginal ethnicity, 61–3, 82–3, 98
  rejection of concept, 83
  see also Aboriginality
Aboriginal Family History Units, 91
Aboriginal Legal Service, 43, 161
Aboriginal Medical Service, 43
Aboriginal organisations, 42, 86
  community-controlled, 138, 143
  responsibility for Confirmation of Aboriginality, 132
  role in community acceptance of Aboriginality, 9, 207, 270–1
  tensions in, 150–2
Aboriginality
  Aboriginal determination of, 69–70, 124
  Aboriginal subjectivity, 171–3
  accidental discovery of, 199–202
  association with negative behaviours, 33–6
  authenticity, 119, 120–1, 128
  awareness of relatives, 196–9
  behaviours, 11
  belonging, 156
  biological vs cultural inheritance, 103–4
  blood memory, 146
  changing identity categories, 43–8
  changing meanings, 15, 69–84
  colonial constructions, 15, 19–21, 84
  community perceptions, 47
  criteria of, 70, 78
  cultural transmission, 245
  dominant discourses, 105–6
  education, 240–1, 249
  emergence of Aboriginal perspectives, 38
  as exclusive identity, 112–13
  experience when Aboriginality discovered, 196–205
  experience when heritage known, 183–95
  identity-privileged people, 145
  impact of location, 83
  inside views, 104–8
  learning, 226–38
  legal definitions of, 45–7
  legitimacy of concept, 69
  local history, 100
  multiple meanings, 104
  newly emerging, 107
  performance of, 166, 226–38, 233–8
  personal vs cultural identity, 98–100
  physical markers, 11
  political context, 100, 208
  private understanding of, 13
  public authentication, 6, 13
  quantifying, 53–68
  questioning, 10
  reconstructing identity, 70–3
  referral system, 54–5
  in relation to white society, 68, 72–3, 108–9
  research on, 37, 48–52
  right to choose as identity, 93–7, 108–12
  right to speak, 209
  self-belief in, 202–5
  signalling of, 13
  as singular construction, 19–20, 63–4, 125–6

INDEX

social practice, 6–7, 100
state determination of, 45
unlearning white perspectives, 231–2
see also blood quantum; Confirmation of Aboriginality; identity; inclusion and exclusion; pan-Aboriginality; politics of identity; plural identity; regulation of Aboriginal identity; social media
Aborigines in Australian Society project, 53–6
Aborigines Welfare Board, 31
absorption, 28
acculturation, 57, 68
activism, 37, 40
adaptation, 57, 68
  adaptive theoretical framework, 60–1
  local context, 58
affirmative action, 86
agency, 173–7
American Civil Rights movement, 40
Anderson, Ian, 120–3
Anderson, Kay, 79–80
Anderson, Michael, 73
anthropology, 29–30
  rescue, 30
  role in constructing Aboriginality, 76
assimilation, 15, 23, 26, 27–8, 30–3, 68, 79
  early resistance to, 34
Attorney-General (Cth) v State of Queensland, 92, 142
Attwood, Bain, 126
Australian Aborigines League, 51
Australian Institute of Aboriginal and Torres Strait Islander Studies (AIATSIS)
  acceptance of documentation, 136
  establishment, 30
  averment principle, 24

Barth, Fredrik, 167
Barthes, Roland, 167
Barwick, Diane, 24, 49–51
Beckett, Jeremy, 51–2, 82–4
Behrendt, Larissa, 95, 116–18, 119, 120

Bell, James, 33–4
belonging, 146–7
Berndt, Catherine, 38, 62, 84, 101
Berndt, Ronald, 62, 70–2, 84, 101, 120
bicentennial of white settlement, 15, 84, 85
Biddle, Ellen, 53–5
Blackmore, Ernie, 109–10
blood quantum, 21
  classification by, 22–6, 41, 134, 265
Boladeras, Jean, 107–8
Bolt, Andrew, 94–6, 152
Bolt, Reuben, 114–15
Bond, Chelsea, 110–12
Boney, 2
Bonner, Neville, 47
Boomali arts cooperative, 43
Brandl, M.M., 77–8, 101
Brereton, J.L., 55
Briggs-Smith, N., 157–8, 160
Bringing Them Home report, see National Inquiry into the Separation of Aboriginal and Torres Strait Islander Children from their Families
Butler, Judith, 175–7

Campbell, April, 253–4
census categories, 17
Chase, Athol, 73–4
child removal, 26, 27–8, 87–8, 91
citizenship rights, 38
Clarke, Allan, 254
class
  among Aboriginal people, 34–5
  colour and, 30–3
'coconut', 11, 111
Coe, Paul, 73
Cole, Bindi, 94
colonialism
  challenges to, 37–53
community councils, 43
community
  constructs of, 137–9, 211–12
  formation of identity, 112–15
  identity discourses, 266–8
  importance of geography, 67
  influence of individual identity, 66–8

politics of identity, 264
structure, 66–8
views of success, 266
see also Aboriginal organisations; Aboriginality; belonging
Conference of Commonwealth and State Aboriginal Authorities
1961 conference, 39
1965 conference, 39
Confirmation of Aboriginality, 7–10, 131–43, 178, 179
access to benefits, 142
arbitrariness, 11–12, 141
challenges to identity, 212
challenging the criteria, 91–3, 135–6, 143, 152, 218–19
community discourse on, 153–63
community politics, 137, 138–41, 162
community recognition, 7, 8, 9, 133, 134–5, 149
criteria, 7–8, 90–1, 131, 210–18
demand of nation-state, 162
descent criterion, 7, 8, 216–17
divisiveness of criteria, 91–2
DNA testing, 222–3
education, 133
employment, 133
future issues, 223–5
impact of relocation and dislocation, 136, 165
impact on urban Aboriginal people, 92, 219
implications, 133
inconsistency of process, 215
as instrument of nation-state, 206–10
intergenerational effects, 224–5
lack of documentation, 135–6
need for, 179–82, 221
online community as basis for, 260–2, 270
problems for organisations, 136–7
problems with process, 134–6, 220–3
process, 9, 15, 132
purpose, 131–2
role of Aboriginal organisations, 132, 136–7
self-identification of Aboriginality, 7, 17, 44

subjective assessment, 11–12
views about, 179–82
see also Aboriginality; Aboriginal organisations; factionalism; identity; inclusion and exclusion
continuity of tradition, 77–8
Coombs, Herbert C., 42, 77–8, 90, 101
Council for Aboriginal Affairs, 42
cultural artefacts, 114, 174–7
cultural hybridity, 126
Cultural Interface, 162, 170–3, 178, 183, 239–50
agency and tensions, 239–47
Cuthbert, Denise, 128

D'Cruz, C., 238
Davis, Edward, 100, 102–4
de Certeau, Michel, 173–5
Deane, Sir William, 47, 87–8
deficit mindset, 148
disadvantage as signifier of Aboriginality, 240, 242–3, 244–5
dislocation of Aboriginal people, 26–7
impact on community acceptance, 10
display of Aboriginality, 113–14, 233–8
cultural artefacts, 114, 174–7, 235–7
see also Aboriginality; identity
dispossession, 209
diversity of Aboriginal people, 77–8
Dixon, Chicka, 61
Dodson, Michael, 120–2, 123, 134, 269
dog tags, 142, 206
Donaldson, Robert, 26
Droste, Marjorie, 116–17
Drummond, Justice, 93
dual heritage, 110–11, 171, 186–8

Eades, Diana, 74–5
Eckermann, Anne-Katrin, 57–61, 67, 75, 140
economic assimilation, 33–4
education
Aboriginality and, 240
tertiary participation, 86
Elkin, AP, 30–3, 34, 39–41, 63
ethnic boundaries, 167

INDEX

ethnographies, 48–9
exemption certificates, 207, 213
extinction by regulation, 22–3

factionalism, 50, 139–41
Fanon, Frantz, 167
Fields, Ted, 102
Fink, Ruth, 34
folk beliefs, 59–60
Foucault, Michel, 18, 149–50, 151, 169, 177
French, Justice, 93
fringe-dwellers, 56
Frith, Nancy C., 58
'full-blood' Aboriginal, 4, 15, 20, 21

Gale, Fay, 53, 55–6
Ganter, Regina, 128–9
Gardiner-Gordon, John, 44, 47, 92–3, 96
Garland, Alf, 48
Gibbs v Capewell, 92, 93, 142
Gilbert, Stephanie, 116
Godwell, Darren, 177
Goodall, Heather, 63
Gramsci, Antonio, 167
Greenop, Kelly, 113–14
Grossman, Michele, 128

'half-caste', 4, 21
  see also 'part-Aboriginal'
Hall, Stuart, 123, 167–8
Hanson, Pauline, 5, 90
Hardy, Bobby, 63
Hasluck, Paul, 36
Hausfeld, R.G., 58
Hawke, Bob, 85, 86
Heiss, Anita, 144
Hinton, M., 156–7
Hinze, Russ, 47
Holland, Wendy, 117–18, 119, 125, 126
Howard, John, 85, 90
Huggins, Jackie, 126–8, 145
human rights, 35

identified Indigenous positions, 8, 163, 230–1
identity
  alternative ways of perceiving, 124–9
  authentic, 166
  community construction of, 112–15
  cultural aspects, 228–9, 232
  cultural constructions of, 81–4
  fixed vs fluid, 161–2, 166
  formation, 100
  inter-generational, 247–50
  as journey, 184–5, 226–8
  negotiating, 183–5
  online surveillance of, 259–62
  performance of, 166, 226–38, 233–8
  personal narratives, 116–20
  plural, 65, 104–5, 110–12
  politics, 7–10, 163–82, 264, 266–8
  as process of ethnogenesis, 82
  reassertion, 99
  self-representation, 120–4
  studies of, 15
  tensions around, 100–4
  theories of, 166–8
  variant selves, 172, 176–7
  see also Aboriginality; agency; belonging; diversity; pan-Aboriginality
inclusion and exclusion
  in colonial period, 25
  within Aboriginal communities, 12, 14
Indigenous standpoint theory, 168–71
intelligent parasitism, 33
Intervention, see Northern Territory Emergency Response

Jacobs, Jane, 81–2
Johnston, Darlene, 28
Johnston, Susan, 63
Joinson, Adam, 252
Jordan, Deirdre, 63–5

Kadachi Man, 2
Keating, Paul, 85
Kelly, Loretta, 161
Kolig, Erich, 72
Koori Mail, 153
Koori Radio, 43
Koori Youth Network, 249
Koori, Grandfather, 73

Kral, Inge, 253

La Perouse, 112
Lacan, Jacques, 167
Lamb, Natasha, 145–6
Lambert-Pennington, Amanda, 112–13, 115
land
   links to, 146–8
land claims
   identity and, 81–2
land councils, 43
Langton, Marcia, 31, 57, 65, 68, 75–7, 101, 118, 122, 124, 128, 177
language
   links to identity, 74–5
Lattas, Andrew, 120
Link-Up programs, 90, 227
Little Children are Sacred report, 88
Lockhart River, 74

Mabo judgment, 89
Macherey, Pierre, 162
Māori, 3, 4, 5
marriage between races, 32–3, 34
materiality of discursive practices, 80
Maxley, Julian, 100, 101–2
McConnochie, Keith, 102
McCorquodale, John, 20, 21, 25, 27, 44–8
McKeich, Robert, 48–9, 67
Merkel, Justice, 93, 143
missions, *see* reserves
Moodai Robinson, Cheryl Dorothy, 106–7
Moodie, P.M., 58
Moree study of inter-racial marriage, 32–3
Morgan, Sally, 106, 126–8

Nakata, Martin, 122, 123–4, 168–71, 183, 239
National Aboriginal and Islander Skills Development Association (NAISDA), 43
National Aboriginal Association of Community Health Organisations (NAACHO), 43
National Aboriginal Education Committee, 102

National Congress of Australia's First Peoples, 91
National Indigenous Times, 161
National Inquiry into the Separation of Aboriginal and Torres Strait Islander Children from their Families, 86–88
   Bringing Them Home report, 87–8, 90–1
Native Title Act 1993 (Cth), 89
Noble, Fiona, 105–6
Northern Territory Emergency Response (Intervention), 88–90
NSW Aboriginal Education Consultative Group (AECG), 43

Obama, Barack, 1
'octoroon', 21
Office of Aboriginal Affairs, 42
official criteria, *see* Confirmation of Aboriginality
Oxenham, Darlene, 127

pan-Aboriginality, 9, 69, 70–3, 98–100, 100–4, 124–6
   challenges to, 78–81
   as commonality, 76–7, 99, 103
   conditions of, 102
   emergence of 61–3, 99
   legitimacy, 102
   questioning of homogenous society, 63
Paradies, Yin, 122, 124–6
'part-Aboriginal' people, 15, 20, 22–6, 31, 69, 74
   degrees of Aboriginality, 27–8
   identity formation, 34–5
   impact of assimilation, 23
   positioning, 29–36
   regulation of, 25–6
   see also Aboriginality; identity
passing, 28, 33, 50, 55, 56–7, 108
   criteria for, 55
Perkins, Charles, 47
Peters-Little, Frances, 138, 139
Peterson, Nicolas, 29–30
Phillips, Gregory, 146
Pierson, James, 61–3
Pohlhaus, Gail, 169
politics of identity, *see* identity
Pollard, David, 66–7

practical reconciliation, 88
'problem areas', 48–9
problem discourse, 57
    pathologisation, 57
protection, 21, 26

'quadroon', 21
Racial Discrimination Act 1975, 133
racial loyalty, 115
racial theorising, 21
Read, Peter, 22–3, 27, 47
'real Aborigines', 68, 69, 73–7, 120–1
Reay, Marie, 31–3, 75
reconciliation, 86–90
    bridge walks, 88
    'sorry' discourse, 90
    see also practical reconciliation
reconnecting with Aboriginality, 108–12
Referendum of 1967, 37, 41–2, 80
regional affiliations, 99
    shared Aboriginality and, 99
regulation of Aboriginal identity, 22, 144–52
reserves, 54, 105–6
    forced connections between people, 140
revivalists, 73–7
Rolls, Mitchell, 119–20, 122–3
Rowley, Charles 24, 28
Rowse, Tim, 80
Royal Commission into Aboriginal Deaths in Custody, 86, 87
Rudd, Kevin, 89
Ruxton, Bruce, 47–8

Sax, Annette, 94
Schwab, Robert, 100–1
Scott-Young, Norman, 47
Scott, Dallas, 254
segregation, 26
self-determination, 22, 38, 41–2, 56–61, 77, 78–80, 135, 209
    policy, 42–3
    politics, 140–1
Shaw v Wolf, 92–3, 142
Sitlington, Grace, 32, 75
skin colour, 2, 25
Snowdon, W.E., 77–8, 101
social media
    Aboriginal people's use of, 251–62

connectivity, 254
Facebook, 252–3
identifying as Aboriginal on, 254–7
online Aboriginal community, 257–9
Social Science Research Council of Australia, 53, 56
specialness, 88–90
Spivak, Gayatri, 167
Stanner, W.E.H., 36, 89
Stolen Generations, 26, 86–8, 90, 97
success of individuals
    impact on identity, 67
surveillance, 27–8, 149–50
    by Aboriginal community, 142, 148, 149–50, 160, 273
    online identity surveillance, 259–62
    self-surveillance, 149–50
Sutton, Peter, 77

Tasmanian Aboriginal Centre, 92
Tatz, Colin, 47, 72–3, 78–9, 90, 102
Taylor, Charles, 167
them and us framework, 79
Thiele, Stephen, 78–9, 80, 101, 103
Tonkinson, Myrna, 17–18, 98–100, 102, 104, 140
Torres Strait Islander people, 123–4
    mixed heritage, 129
'touched by the tar brush', 1, 4
training organisations, 43
Tranby College, 43
tribal/detribalised dichotomy, 75

United Nations
    view of Australia's treatment of Indienous peoples, 35–6
urban Aboriginal people, 31, 49, 62–5, 110–12, 113–14
    cultural tensions, 245–7
    internal identity, 59, 205, 246
    patterns of social change, 49–52
    positioning of, 83
    right to choose Aboriginal identity, 94–7
    social mobility, 51
    social organisation, 62

variant selves, 172, 176–7

Von Sturmer, John, 70–2, 80

welfare assistance
  access to, 50, 269–70
Welsh, R. 153–5
white authority, 26
Whitlam, Gough, 42–3

Yamanouchi, Yuriko, 137–8